The Political Economy of Distributism

The Political Economy of Distributism

Property, Liberty, and the Common Good

Alexander William Salter

The Catholic University of America Press
Washington, D.C.

The paper used in this publication meets the minimum requirements of
American National Standards for Information Science—Permanence of Paper
for Printed Library Materials, ANSI Z39.48-1984.

∞

Cataloging-in-Publication Data is available from the Library of Congress
ISBN: 978-0-8132-3681-0
eISBN: 978-0-8132-3682-7

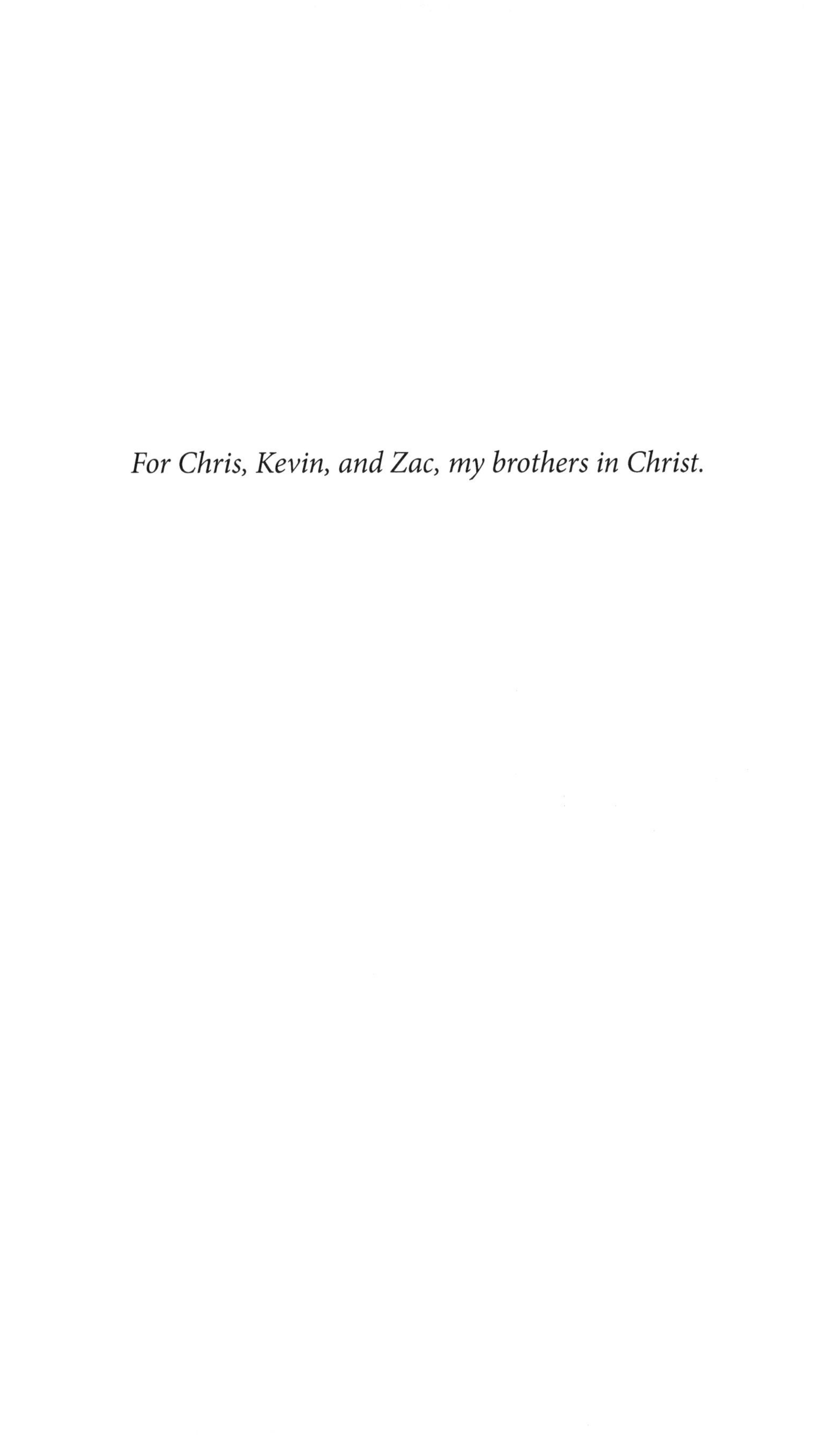

For Chris, Kevin, and Zac, my brothers in Christ.

Contents

Preface

Across the ideological spectrum, there is a growing consensus that political and economic institutions no longer serve the public interest. In politics, a movement chiefly but not solely on the right contends elites have captured the state and insulated government from democratic control. In economics, many believe increased inequality and dwindling employment opportunities have hollowed out the middle class. While both conservatives and progressives decry these outcomes, there is little agreement on why they happened or how to fix them.

I wrote this book to bring an important yet neglected perspective to bear on these questions. Distributism, a political-economic paradigm informed by Catholic social teaching, has an intriguing explanation for simultaneous erosions in political and economic order: a loss of economic security. A chief tenet of distributism is that capitalism concentrates productive property into fewer and fewer hands. As a result, citizens lose control over their own lives as well as the ability to check abuses of public authority. Economic security and political liberty are necessarily entwined, distributists maintain: one cannot exist without the other.

The chief distributist writers, Hilaire Belloc and G. K. Chesterton, noticed these troubling trends nearly a century ago, and their ideas deserve a new hearing. Using the tools of economics and the concepts of political economy, I analyze Belloc's and Chesterton's works, focusing on the enduring themes that can bolster contemporary scholarship on the institutional foundations of flourishing societies. I am not writing a history of distributist thought. Instead, I am engaged in an applied project at the intersection of politics, philosophy, and economics (PPE) that takes and builds upon the best distributism has to offer.

I advance a minor claim and a major claim. The minor claim is seemingly damning: the distributists were often poor economic reasoners. There is much they say about how economic systems work that is untenable. This is probably why, to the extent modern social science has noticed distributism, engagement with it has been cursory and dismissive. But these mistakes disguise a deeper and more enduring insight. My major claim (and original contribution) is that these errors *do not invalidate their most important argument*: societies cannot remain politically free unless they are economically secure and independent. This intriguing claim deserves careful study. We should pay attention to distributism when discussing how our economic and political institutions work, as well as how they *ought* to work.

I begin this book by surveying contemporary political and intellectual efforts to transform existing capitalism into "common-good capitalism." Distributist insights can and should play a role in adjudicating this dispute. Next, I survey the key teachings in Catholic social thought that inform the distributists' perspective on economic and political questions. Distributism was an explicit attempt to embody Catholic social teachings in political and economic institutions, and without this context, we cannot understand distributism. I then explore important works by Belloc and Chesterton, respectively. These are *The Servile State* and *An Essay on the Restoration of Property* (Belloc) and *What's Wrong with the World* and *The Outline of Sanity* (Chesterton). Finally, I link this material to contemporary scholarly debates in PPE, focusing on the literatures that explore the institutional foundations of prosperous societies. I also discuss how to rehabilitate distributism, using as my exemplar Wilhelm Röpke's writings on scientific economics in the service of humane political-economic ends.

I must briefly discuss two things before proceeding. First is how I use the term "freedom" (as well as "liberty") in this book. This matters because distributism's greatest claim to contemporary political-economic relevance is its understanding of freedom. Second is my own background, as well as my religious beliefs, because these differ significantly from the authors whose works I analyze.

Freedom is at the heart of distributism, but it is freedom of an unusual kind. As we will see in the second chapter, the distributist understanding of freedom derives from the Catholic Church's teachings on human nature. Distributist freedom has both positive and negative components, as I use the terms. By positive freedom, I mean freedom *to*. This means certain conditions and goals, as well as the resources to achieve them. By negative freedom, I mean freedom *from*. This means protection from coercive interference.

When applied to politics and economics, I have in mind the following understandings of freedom. Negative economic freedom means protection from force and fraud. Positive economic freedom means access to material conditions sufficient to prevent one party from dictating the terms of exchange to another. Likewise, negative political freedom means protection for widely respected rights, such as speech, assembly, and worship, from state infringement. Positive political freedom means the right of participation in the political process, of which the most obvious example is the democratic process.

Political philosophers use "positive freedom" and "negative freedom" in specific ways, and my own usage does not always map neatly onto theirs. For example, T. H. Green famously defended positive freedom, defined as liberation from our unreasoned habits or impulses.[1] Even more well-known is Isaiah Berlin's support for negative freedom, defined as absence of obstruction to our ends by other wills.[2] Gerald Gaus, in his *Political Concepts and Political Theories*, ably summarizes the difference. Negative freedom is infringed "when a possible course of action has been made ineligible by threats, even if it is still possible to perform the action. Not just force, but threats of force, limit freedom."[3] Positive freedom adds to this "internal obstacles" that prevent "the development of [a person's] capacities."[4]

Another complication is that most contemporary political philosophers are liberals. How they understand freedom and its social context reflects this. Although G. K. Chesterton and Hilaire Belloc, the two preeminent distributists whose works I analyze, both identified as liberals, distributism itself—as well as Catholic social teaching, from which distributism is derived—defies classification as either "liberal" or "illiberal." There are points of contact with current academic usage, but even the overlaps contain tensions. For example, St. Paul's lament in Romans 7:14–25 makes sense as a struggle against the self toward positive freedom.[5] But unless we keep in

1 T. H. Green, "Liberal Legislation and Freedom of Contract." This essay has been reprinted many times.

2 Isaiah Berlin, "Two Concepts of Liberty," in Isaiah Berlin, *Four Essays on Liberty* (Oxford: Oxford University Press, 1969).

3 Gerald Gaus, *Political Concepts and Political Theories* (Boulder: Westview Press, 2000), 97.

4 Gaus, *Political Concepts and Political Theories*, 97.

5 "For we know that the law is spiritual: but I am carnal, sold under sin. For that which I do I allow not: for what I would, that do I not; but what I hate, that do I. If then I do that which I would not, I consent unto the law that it is good. Now then it is no more I that do it, but sin that dwelleth in me. For I know that in me (that is, in my flesh,) dwelleth no good thing: for to will is present with me; but how to perform that which is good I find not. For the good that I would I do not: but the evil which I would not, that I do. Now if I do that I would not, it is no more I that do it, but sin that dwelleth in me. I find then a law, that, when I would do good, evil is present with me. For I delight in the law of God after the inward man: But I see another law in my members, warring against the law of my mind, and bringing me into captivity to the law of sin which is in my members. O wretched man that I am! who shall deliver me from the body of this death? I thank God through Jesus Christ our Lord. So then with the mind I myself serve the law of God; but with the flesh the law of sin" (Rom 7:14–25).

the foreground St. Paul's commitment to freedom *in Christ*, we do violence to his intended meaning.

Distributist authors often discuss freedom. The concept suffuses their works, and my definitions were chosen to match the ways they use these terms, at least as I interpret them. Undoubtedly, this will not be as precise as usage by contemporary political philosophers. Since this is a work of political economy rather than political philosophy, I think divergences from the standard academic lexicon is defensible and appropriate.

Finally, I should disclose my own religious, political, and economic beliefs. Whereas Belloc and Chesterton were Catholic and Röpke Protestant, I am Orthodox. I affirm the dogmas, doctrines, and teachings of the Orthodox Church without reservation. I do not think this is a barrier to analyzing distributism charitably. For example, I have no problem affirming the importance of the common good. Second, my politics and economics are decidedly (classical) liberal. I also accept the labels "conservative," "fusionist," and "libertarian," although I have reservations about each one. I bring this up because the reader should know I am much more optimistic about markets and capitalism than Belloc and Chesterton, and even Röpke. My disagreements with these authors are primarily about how markets actually work. I think many distributist claims are wrong, although I am often sympathetic to its social criticism. More importantly, I think distributism's "big picture" perspective on the interdependencies between political and economic freedom is right, which is why I wrote this book.

Acknowledgments

I am indebted to the Institute for Humane Studies (IHS) for sponsoring a manuscript workshop for early chapter drafts. The feedback I received was incredibly valuable. I owe special thanks to Adrienne DePrisco, Jeanne Hoffman, and Stewart Robertson at IHS for organizing the workshop. I am deeply grateful to the workshop participants for taking the time to help me improve my arguments: Caleb Bernacchio, Abby Blanco, Anne Bradley, Jim Caton, Chris Fleming, Zac Gochenour, Clara Jace, Jason Jewell, Steve Miller, Catherine Pakaluk, Ennio Piano, Bob Subrick, and Kevin Vallier.

Kevin Augustyn, Joseph Capizzi, Samuel Gregg, Stephen Higgins, Mary Hirschfeld, and Eileen Norcross helped organize a panel discussion, cosponsored by the Mercatus Center and the Institute for Human Ecology, about common-good capitalism. This helped me put the finishing touches on the manuscript. My thanks to all of them.

I received able research assistance from Michael Makovi, Gonzalo Macera, Gor Mkrtchian, and Wilson Whitener. I thank them all.

Administrative staff at my home institutions played an important role in helping me finish this project. At the Free Market Institute, I thank Chuck Long and Amanda Smith. At the Rawls College of Business, I thank Kellie Estes and Sandy Martinez.

Thanks also to John Martino at the Catholic University of America Press. I appreciate his support for this project from beginning to end.

Finally, I thank Fr. Peter DeFonce, my parish priest, for spiritual guidance, and Kenneth Gardener, my catechism instructor and friend, for always being willing to discuss religion, politics, and economics.

Chapter 1

Introduction: Distributism and Common-Good Capitalism

IN SEARCH OF COMMON-GOOD CAPITALISM

On November 5, 2019, Senator Marco Rubio gave a speech at The Catholic University of America's Busch School of Business. The theme of the address was "common-good capitalism." Drawing on Catholic social teaching, especially Pope Leo XIII's encyclical *Rerum Novarum*, Rubio echoed an increasingly common perception: Despite "years of robust economic growth, we still have millions of people unable to find dignified work and feeling forgotten, ignored, and left behind."[1] Castigating the excesses of both laissez-faire capitalism and authoritarian socialism, Rubio emphasized the need for a humanization of economic relationships "because after all, our nation does not exist to serve the interests of the market. The market exists to serve our nation and our people."[2]

"Free enterprise made America the most prosperous nation in history," Rubio recognized, "but that prosperity wasn't just about business making a profit; it was also about the creation and availability of dignified work."[3] The financialization of the American economy that took place over recent decades had dire consequences: "The right to return money to shareholders became a right above all others. And the obligation to invest for the benefit of our workers and our country became an afterthought."[4] Beginning with his campaign for the Republican presidential nomination in 2016, Rubio was persuaded that America's economic order

1 Marco Rubio. "Catholic Social Doctrine and the Dignity of Work." speech at Catholic University of America, November 2019, 3, https://www.rubio.senate.gov/public/_cache/files/6d09ae19-8df3-4755-b301-795154a68c59/C58480B07D02452574C5DB8D603803EF.final—-cua-speech-11.5.19.pdf. The quotations in this chapter are taken from the text of his prepared remarks.

2 Rubio, "Catholic Social Doctrine," 11.

3 Rubio, "Catholic Social Doctrine," 3.

4 Rubio, "Catholic Social Doctrine," 4.

"is bad because it is inflicting tremendous damage on our families, our communities, and our society."[5]

But the way forward is not socialism. The United States is culturally and historically hostile toward top-down planning: "The idea that government can impose a balance between the obligations and rights of the private sector and working Americans has never worked," he continued.[6] Granting the state the power it would need to implement socialism, or even extreme forms of social democracy, would destroy Americans' cherished freedoms, "because a government that guarantees you a basic income is also one that controls where you work and how much you make. A government that promises you free health care is also one that controls who your doctor is and what care you'll receive. . . . And a government that seeks to control all our societal needs is one that tells churches what they can preach and tells community members how we can interact."[7]

The solution is not to abolish free enterprise but to moralize it. "What we need to do," Rubio believes, "is restore common-good capitalism—a system of free enterprise in which workers fulfil their obligations to work and enjoy the benefits of their work, and where businesses enjoy their right to make a profit and reinvest enough of those profits to create dignified work for Americans."[8] Rubio discussed several policy proposals in his speech, but they all had one thing in common—the centrality of human dignity in commerce, politics, and civil society: "Common-good capitalism is about a vibrant and growing free market. . . . And the most impactful benefit the market can provide our people, our society, and the nation at large is the creation and availability of dignified work."[9]

Rubio's speech is just one example of a widespread revival of interest in rethinking our political-economic system. Following Donald Trump's unexpected rise to the presidency, many thinkers on the American right triumphantly proclaimed the death of prevailing conservative pieties. Months before Rubio's speech, the influential journal of religion and culture *First Things* publicly repudiated "warmed-over Reaganism," referring to the post–Cold War order as a "soulless society of individual affluence" whose

5 Rubio, "Catholic Social Doctrine," 8.

6 Rubio, "Catholic Social Doctrine," 8.

7 Rubio, "Catholic Social Doctrine," 9.

8 Rubio, "Catholic Social Doctrine," 9.

9 Rubio, "Catholic Social Doctrine," 11.

defenders were all too eager to "compromise on human dignity." The manifesto was signed by more than a dozen high-profile academics and public intellectuals.[10]

Although Trump is no longer in office, the tides that propelled his controversial administration are unlikely to ebb. Something has changed with the way millions of Americans, from all walks of life, think about politics and economics. Especially pronounced is the newfound suspicion of markets and capitalism, which until quite recently were thought to uphold human dignity, not trample it. Many important questions now confront students of society. What is "common-good capitalism?" Is it a uniquely Catholic proposal? Does it offer an escape from the "dead consensus"? What does the science of economics have to say about it? What political-economic institutions does it require?

NEW PATHS, OLD PATHS: THE QUEST FOR THE GOOD SOCIETY

The conversation surrounding common-good capitalism is part of a larger quest to discover the foundations of the "good society." Scholars and public intellectuals involved in this quest, especially those who prioritize the common good, tend to be of a conservative-traditionalist persuasion. Especially in recent years, the association between (American) conservatism and free enterprise has weakened. Searchers for common-good capitalism must believe that capitalism, if left to itself, will *not* advance the common good. Many new conservatives argue we need creative institutional reform oriented toward the common good to save capitalism from itself.

Contributors to this conversation often draw, explicitly or implicitly, on Catholic social teaching. Many social-philosophical concepts are difficult to define precisely yet are vital for social criticism. The common good is such a concept. One of the strengths of Catholic social teaching is that it concretizes the common good. The content and context of various papal encyclicals provide much-needed clarity, and the *Catechism of the Catholic Church* contains an important overview.

Common-good capitalism is not an ad hoc reform proposal. It must be viewed against the larger backdrop of decades-long conversations in which the interlocutors are concerned with social and political renewal. Focusing

10 "Against the Dead Consensus," *First Things*, March 3, 2019. https://www.firstthings.com/web-exclusives/2019/03/against-the-dead-consensus.

excessively on the *capitalism* part of common-good capitalism, without appreciating the larger context, can inadvertently lead to a kind of material determinism that is wholly at odds with permanent human truths. It is certainly an outrage if families lack bread, but unless we remember that "man does not live by bread alone," the search for the root cause of social injustice will turn up empty.

Ideas matter. How we understand concepts like property, inequality, and duty affect basic questions of social order. Seeking common-good capitalism first means seeking the common good itself. Whatever the content of their beliefs, American conservatives recognize the primacy of ideas. In one of the first significant works of the postwar conservative intellectual revival, Richard Weaver forcefully argued ideas were ultimately at the root of powerful social forces.[11] Weaver himself was not Catholic, but his apology for the High Middle Ages demonstrates his sympathy for the Catholic intellectual tradition. That his work was well received by young conservative intellectuals of the time, who were disproportionately Catholic and would shape American thought for decades to come, shows that the road paved by Catholic social teaching is wide enough to accommodate many kinds of travelers.[12]

Weaver famously argued that the doom of the West began with Occam's nominalist philosophy: rejecting transcendentals meant rejecting a crucial feature of reality itself. Perhaps this degree of conceptual determinism is objectionable in the same way as is economic determinism. Regardless, Weaver certainly took ideas seriously, and the model he presented of ideas as the prime mover in the affairs of men remains popular and compelling.

Patrick Deneen, a political theorist at Notre Dame, takes idea-centric social criticism seriously. In 2018, Deneen caused a stir among academics and public intellectuals with the publication of his book *Why Liberalism Failed*.[13] What Weaver did for the West, Deneen did for the United States. The sclerosis of our public institutions, the breakdown of community, and the stratification of social classes by a winner-take-all economy are all the result of liberalism, as a philosophy. These malignancies were baked into the American experiment from the beginning. Deneen's verdict, early in the introductory chapter, is stark:

11 Richard Weaver, *Ideas Have Consequences* (Chicago: University of Chicago Press, 1948).

12 George Nash, *The Conservative Intellectual Movement in America since 1945* (Wilmington, Del.: ISI Books, [1976] 2006), chaps. 2–3.

13 Patrick Deneen, *Why Liberalism Failed* (New Haven, Conn.: Yale University Press), 2018.

> Liberalism has failed—not because it fell short, but because it was true to itself. It has failed because it has succeeded. As liberalism has "become more fully itself," as its inner logic has become more evident and its self-contradictions manifest, it has generated pathologies that are at once deformations of its claims yet realizations of liberal ideology. A political philosophy that was launched to foster greater equity, defend a pluralist tapestry of different cultures and beliefs, protect human dignity, and, of course, expand liberty, in practice generates titanic inequality, enforces uniformity and homogeneity, fosters material and spiritual degradation, and undermines freedom.[14]

Many have pushed back against Deneen's thesis. It remains provocative nonetheless. The debates stimulated by Deneen's broadside on American individualism—not merely our politics, but the anthropological assumptions he believes animate both private and public institutions—will continue for many years. This is an important example of common-good thinking, since it is central to Deneen's argument that liberalism has no room for any conception of the common good that transcends the sum of subjectively evaluated private goods. Deneen himself is a conservative Catholic with strong communitarian leanings. His work, and the controversy it generated, is not intelligible without recourse to Catholic social teaching.

But Deneen is not the biggest skeptic of American liberalism among Catholic thinkers. As far as he goes, others go much farther. Adrian Vermeule, a professor of constitutional law at Harvard, is one high-profile example, and he is the de facto leader of a small but vociferous group of Catholic scholars who contend that basic American constitutional provisions, such as the separation of church and state, must be reexamined. In a much-discussed essay at the *Atlantic*, Vermeule castigates conservative legal scholars for their hidebound allegiance to originalism as a constitutional hermeneutic.[15] Originalism "has now outlived its utility, and has become an obstacle to the development of a robust, substantively conservative approach to constitutional law and interpretation," Vermeule contends.[16] In its place, he offers "common-good constitutionalism," which boldly asserts "government helps direct persons, associations, and society

14 Deneen, *Why Liberalism Failed*, 3.

15 Adrian Vermeulle, "Beyond Originalism," *The Atlantic*, March 31, 2020, https://www.theatlantic.com/ideas/archive/2020/03/common-good-constitutionalism/609037/.

16 Vermeulle, "Beyond Originalism."

generally toward the common good, and that strong rule in the interest of attaining the common good is entirely legitimate."[17] While Vermeule's common-good constitutionalism is not intended to be a constitutional philosophy for a specifically Catholic polity, the influence of Catholic social teaching on its core tenets is obvious:

> This approach should take as its starting point substantive moral principles that conduce to the common good, principles that officials (including, but by no means limited to, judges) should read into the majestic generalities and ambiguities of the written constitution. These principles include respect for the authority of rule and of rulers; respect for the hierarchies needed for society to function; solidarity within and among families, social groups, and workers' unions, trade associations, and professions; appropriate subsidiarity, or respect for the legitimate roles of public bodies and associations at all levels of government and society; and a candid willingness to "legislate morality"—indeed, a recognition that all legislation is necessarily founded on some substantive conception of morality, and that the promotion of morality is a core and legitimate function of authority. Such principles promote the common good and make for a just and well-ordered society.[18]

For jurists informed by Enlightenment liberalism, this raises several red flags! But that is the point. For Vermeule, the common good is non-negotiable. Any viable interpretive framework for the Constitution must confidently embrace the ancient conception of statecraft as soulcraft.

These examples make clear that common-good thinking is not simply an adjutant to debates over how to regulate liberal market economies. The goal is to rethink the boundary between markets and governments, as well as persons and community. We fail to treat common-good capitalism with the seriousness it deserves when we talk about it as just another form of regulated capitalism. The tricky element is that the *means* may be similar—for example, public policy implemented by administrative bureaucracies—but the *ends* are quite different. In fact, they are so different that we evaluate these ends using a different moral vocabulary. We typically judge economic outcomes in terms of efficiency and distribution. What common-good capitalism requires, however, is shifting the evaluative standards to the rights

17 Vermeulle, "Beyond Originalism."

18 Vermeulle, "Beyond Originalism."

and duties that flow from human dignity. Not all participants in this new discussion are Catholic, but the preeminence of concepts informed by Catholic social teaching means contributors must be familiar with this tradition.

WHAT ABOUT THE "THIRD WAY"?

Attempts to find a middle ground between socialism and laissez-faire are not new. The search for a "third way" is almost as old as industrialization. It is tempting to interpret common-good capitalism as a branch of middle-ground thinking. However, the similarities are superficial and the differences substantial.

Consider the settlement embraced by most Western democracies: the combination of the welfare state and the administrative state. To justify the social order to various stakeholders, governments regulate and redistribute. But this did not legitimize the economy in the eyes of those who depend on it for their livelihoods. Instead, it created an impenetrable web of ineffective and unaccountable bureaucracies, combined with enervating welfare programs. Technocratic regulations and transfer payments are thin gruel for those concerned with deeply entrenched social injustices. The result is a crisis of political legitimacy. As a result, conservative intellectuals are questioning, and in some cases outright repudiating, the post–Cold War consensus.

Because Catholic social teaching endorses "reasonable regulation" in economic affairs, it may appear that the Church's social doctrines fit neatly with third-way thinking.[19] After all, Catholic social teaching rejects pure socialism and pure capitalism. The former the Church regards as a "totalitarian and atheistic" ideology; the latter she regards as the reification of "the law of the marketplace" above the moral law. By process of elimination, the middle ground must be safest. This conclusion, however, reflects a frustratingly narrow scope of institutional imagination.

Whatever common-good capitalism is, it is not some middle ground between two equally unacceptable social systems. Neither hot nor cold, the regulative-redistributive state is unsatisfyingly lukewarm: Focused as it is on material comfort and social pacification, bureaucratized capitalism is oriented toward solving second-order problems, when the first-order problem is respecting human dignity. We must broaden our horizons to find institutional arrangements that can meet common-good capitalism's standards.

19 Catholic Church, *Catechism of the Catholic Church*, 2425. I explore these themes in greater depth in the next chapter, https://www.vatican.va/archive/ENG0015/_INDEX.HTM.

This book focuses on one imaginative alternative: *distributism*. Also called *distributivism*, it is a broad political-economic philosophy associated with early twentieth-century Catholic writers Hilaire Belloc and G. K. Chesterton and is explicitly based on Catholic social teaching, especially the principles set forth by Pope Leo XIII in his encyclical *Rerum Novarum*. John Médaille, a contemporary distributist author, writes that distributism's "key tenet is that ownership of the means of production should be as widespread as possible rather than being concentrated in the hands of a few owners (Capitalism) or in the hands of state bureaucrats (Socialism)."[20] Classical distributism, by which I mean the works of Belloc and Chesterton, regards freedom as a necessary component of human dignity, but this kind of freedom differs greatly from liberal or libertarian freedom. Rooted in Catholic social teaching, this kind of freedom refers to man's *personal* nature, his being-in-community, with major implications for the scale and scope of institutions at all levels. It is a composite of both positive and negative liberties, always with an eye toward the (Christian) anthropological components of dignity.

The differences between distributism and stale third-way thinking, while most obvious in terms of theological principles, are also stark in the case of comparative institutional analysis. Consider the following summary in a popular essay on distributism by Joseph Pearce:

> Unlike the socialists, the distributists were not advocating the redistribution of 'wealth' *per se*, though they believed that this would be one of the results of distributism. Instead, and the difference is crucial, they were advocating the redistribution of the means of production to as many people as possible. Belloc and the distributists drew the vital connection between the freedom of labour and its relationship with the other factors of production—i.e., land, capital, and the entrepreneurial spirit. The more that labour is divorced from the other factors of production the more it is enslaved to the will of powers beyond its control. In an ideal world every man would own the land on which, and the tools with which, he worked. In an ideal world he would control his own destiny by having control over the means to his livelihood. For Belloc, this was the most important economic freedom, the freedom beside which all other economic freedoms

20 John Médaille, "An Introduction to Distributism," *Distributist Review*, January 11, 2021, https://distributistreview.com/archive/an-introduction-to-distributism. Médaille classifies distributism as an "economic theory," which I dispute. See the discussion of the science of economics vs. the art of political economy in chapter 4.

> are relatively trivial. If a man has this freedom he will not so easily succumb to encroachments upon his other freedoms.[21]

As Pearce suggests, freedom is central to distributism, but it is freedom of a special kind. There are dimensions to the distributist conception of freedom that are simply beyond contemporary debates. Neglecting these dimensions is part of the reason why milquetoast welfarism has failed.

Distributist authors ground their economic and political analyses in an understanding of personhood and community rooted in Catholic social doctrine, but adherents of other religious traditions (or no religious tradition) can also appreciate the wisdom in distributism. Principles such as subsidiarity, social justice, and the common good permeate distributist writings. Since some of these terms, especially social justice, have been perverted by politics, we must take care to define our basic concepts correctly. Once this is done, distributism can be the subject of rich conversation by thinkers of diverse backgrounds. One of this book's claims is that distributism *should* command our attention. It is interesting, challenging, and can inform many of today's discussions on common-good capitalism, and the nature of the good society more generally.

This book revisits the classic texts of distributist thought. I focus on two works each by Hilaire Belloc and G. K. Chesterton showing how the principles derive from Catholic social teaching and critiquing the proposals for social-institutional reform. Belloc's works, *The Servile State* and *An Essay on the Restoration of Property*, are analytical and precise. Chesterton's works, *What's Wrong with the World* and *The Outline of Sanity*, are artistic and fanciful. These complementary books give us a powerful framework for thinking about dignity-centered institutional change. Those who find common-good capitalism exciting should find distributism exciting, too.

DISTRIBUTISM AND POLITICAL ECONOMY

John Neville Keynes, the father of John Maynard Keynes, usefully distinguished between the science of economics and the art of political economy.[22] Expanding on his classification, we may say that the science of economics consists of the formal properties of purposive human

21 Joseph Pearce, "What Is Distributism?" *Imaginative Conservative*, June 12, 2014, https://theimaginativeconservative.org/2014/06/what-is-distributism.html.

22 John Neville Keynes, *The Scope and Method of Political Economy* (London: Macmillan, 1904).

action.[23] It is descriptive, rather than prescriptive. Rational choice, along with its application to market phenomena (price theory), comprise the core toolkit of scientific economics.[24]

Political economy depends on economics, but its scope is broader, and unlike economics narrowly conceived, it does not shy away from prescription. James Buchanan, the 1986 Nobel laureate in economics, described political economy as "the study of what makes for a 'good society.'"[25] For a competent political economist, mastery of economics was necessary but not sufficient: "Political economists stress the technical economic principles that one must understand in order to assess alternative arrangements for promoting peaceful cooperation and productive specialization among free men. Yet political economists go further and frankly try to bring out into the open the philosophical issues that necessarily underlie all discussions of the appropriate functions of government and all proposed economic policy measures."[26]

According to this classification, distributism is a school of political economy, but not a school of economics. Few economists have discussed distributism, let alone noticed it. To the extent they have, their attitude has been one of bewilderment and contempt. In a sense, this attitude is understandable. Belloc and Chesterton make numerous *economic* errors in their writings. The strength of economic science is evaluating the appropriateness of selected means to attain given ends. Distributist authors often make policy proposals that will not achieve their stated goals, and sometimes, distributist proposals will even yield results that are more nearly the opposite of these goals. Means-ends consistency is important, and since it is the economist's specialty, economic scientists can be impatient with reforms that fail this test.

23 See Peter T. Leeson, "Economics Is Not Statistics (and Vice Versa)," *Journal of Institutional Economics* 16, no. 4 (2020): 423–25. The explanations and citations on p. 424 are especially helpful.

24 "Traditional price theory consists primarily in analysis of the pricing process under a free enterprise economy—under a system characterized by private property, free contract, and free exchange. . . . The central conception of price theory is that of an equilibrium adjustment with respect to relative prices and relative production." Henry Simons, *The Simons' Syllabus*, ed. Gordon Tullock (Fairfax, Va.: Center for the Study of Public Choice, 1983). For an historical perspective on the development of price theory, see Peter Boettke and Rosolino Candela, "Price Theory as a Prophylactic against Popular Fallacies," *Journal of Institutional Economics* 13, no. 3 (2017): 725–52.

25 James M. Buchanan, "The Thomas Jefferson Center for Studies in Political Economy," *University of Virginia Newsletter* 35, no. 2 (1958): 5.

26 Buchanan, "The Thomas Jefferson Center for Studies in Political Economy."

But this cannot be the last word on distributism. As it turns out, distributism's scientific errors do not destroy its artistic potential as political economy. Perspective matters: What is blurry and jumbled up-close can become clear and harmonious from a distance. Although its economics is sometimes unscientific, distributist political economy offers many overlooked and exciting insights. In our article separating the wheat from the chaff of distributism, Eugene Callahan and I write:

> Distributists' emphasis on private and widespread property ownership as a political-economic foundation of a "good society" highlights the importance of institutional foundations for markets. The assumption behind all distributist proposals, whether they are feasible or not, is that political and economic outcomes are a function of the underlying rules that constitute these social realms. Certain rules predictably result in cooperation and prosperity, while others predictably result in predation and poverty. Concern for simultaneously private and widespread ownership of private property, and in particular the factors of production, stems from the sound intuition that power must be dispersed in order for it to be wielded safely by anybody. The live and valuable thread of distributist thought recognizes that the background conditions for both markets and politics—conceptually but not in actuality separable realms of human action and potential cooperation—must be sound in order for the nexus of exchange relationships humans forge with each other to create mutually harmonious living.[27]

Callahan and I highlight the overlap between distributism and comparative institutional analysis. Understanding how the "rules of the game" channel individual behavior into social outcomes is an essential part of political economy.[28] But just as it is wrong to reduce distributism to its economic errors, we cannot say that comparative institutional analysis exhausts distributism's analytic potential. Distributism is also an ethical project, because political economy is also an ethical project. Distributism's moral content matters just as much as its narrow discussions of, say, wage rates or the distribution of land.

27 Eugene Callahan and Alexander William Salter, "Dead Ends and Living Currents: Distributism as a Progressive Research Program," *Christian Libertarian Review* 1 (2018): 118–39 (citations omitted).

28 See, for example, Douglass C. North, *Institutions, Institutional Change, and Economic Performance* (Cambridge: Cambridge University Press, 1990).

Scholars increasingly appreciate the complementarities between Catholic social teaching and institutional political economy. For example, Eileen Norcross and Paul Dragos Aligica recently argued that for scholars interested in "culture, ideas, and religious beliefs in the analysis of economic behavior, the economic and social theorizing developed by these scholars advances a framework that has significant affinities with CST's [Catholic social teaching's] foundational critique of economic concepts and theories and with its normative position regarding the nature and functioning of social and economic systems."[29] Their article suggests many avenues for cross-fertilization.

Importantly, Norcross and Aligica carefully distinguish science from art in the application of Catholic social teaching. We must not, they say,

> confuse CST with a corpus of economic theory or with a blueprint for an economic system design. The literature on the linkages between CST and economics identifies many areas of overlap between certain aspects of economic theory and practice and the teachings of the Catholic Church's social doctrine. However, the chief feature of CST is that it questions and challenges some of the main assumptions and philosophical foundations of standard modern economic theory. By implication, it questions also the design of policies and systemic features that are shaped or legitimized by the theory. Its most salient feature in relationship to economic theory is that it articulates a foundational challenge to it *but not as a theoretical competitor*. To the extent that one wants to make valid comparisons and associations (by comparing apples to apples), the comparison must be between two foundational visions, not between two theories.[30]

This brings us back to common-good capitalism. As a paradigm informed by Catholic social teaching, common-good capitalism operates on a different level than economic science. Applied political economy is "not . . . a theoretical competitor" to scientific economics. Nor is common-good capitalism (just) a proposal for political reform. Common-good capitalism shows immense promise as *research program*, constituted by an invitation to inquiry in the best traditions of political economy. And distributism, as one way of thinking about common-good capitalism, attains these lofty heights, too.

29 Eileen Norcross and Paul Dragos Aligica, "Catholic Social Thought and New Institutional Economics: An Assessment of Their Affinities and Areas of Potential Convergence," *American Journal of Economics and Sociology* 79, no. 4 (2020): 1241–69, at 1241.

30 Norcross and Aligica, "Catholic Social Thought," 1244, emphasis added.

ROADMAP

The scholarly, public-intellectual, and political work required to make common-good capitalism a reality will take many persons many years. My goal is comparatively modest: to help build a strong foundation for the necessary discussions to come. The book's concluding section, *From Property, Liberty*, captures the essential insight of distributist political economy: that property is a necessary precondition for humanistic liberty. In this spirit, I hope the book stimulates a discussion between economists interested in social philosophy and social philosophers interested in economics. Again, distributism is more comprehensive than its claims about land, labor, and capital, as the art of political economy is more comprehensive than the science of economics. But getting the economics right is important groundwork for any political economy that aspires to viability and robustness. The edifice of common-good capitalism needs a secure cornerstone. Working toward a synthesis of distributist insights with good economics can help us understand how to revitalize the good society.

I close this introductory chapter by outlining the substance of the book. Chapter 2 provides the necessary context for distributism by surveying Catholic social teaching. To understand distributism, we must engage the church's doctrine on economics and politics, expressed in papal encyclicals such as *Rerum Novarum* and *Quadragesimo Anno* and now contained in the *Catechism of the Catholic Church*. This chapter briefly discusses the historical developments that resulted in the church updating and clarifying her teachings.

Chapters 3 through 6 are each devoted to a specific book by Belloc or Chesterton. Belloc's *The Servile State* (chapter 3) and *An Essay on the Restoration of Property* (chapter 4) are the most important works for understanding the mechanisms of distributist political economy. Chesterton's *What's Wrong with the World* (chapter 5) and *The Outline of Sanity* (chapter 6) are the most important works for understanding the imagination of distributist political economy. In analyzing these works, I advance a major and a minor claim. The minor claim is that much in these works is not viable, evaluated as economic science. The major claim is that, despite these shortcomings, the lessons provided by these works concerning the economic foundations of human dignity should be taken seriously.

Chapter 7 brings distributist insights to the contemporary literature on comparative institutional analysis and political economy. Distributism teaches that political liberty requires economic liberty. Such liberty, however, must be understood according to Catholic social teaching: It is not merely the rights of property and contract but also the right to live a dignified life. This includes the means to secure human dignity; economic liberty means little without economic security. I bring this perspective to several ongoing scholarly discussions: the scale and scope of the state; the interrelationships among economic freedom, political freedom, and inequality; and conceptions of economic justice. I show that each of these conversations can be clarified and improved by engagement with distributism.

Chapters 8 and 9 focus on a specific thinker: Wilhelm Röpke, a German economist whose approach to political economy explicitly built on distributist insights. Economists today rarely read Röpke. Thankfully, this is changing. The growth in Röpke scholarship provides an opportunity to revisit his unique brand of humane economics. Although not Catholic, Röpke was deeply influenced by Catholic social teaching. He was also a first-rate price theorist, evaluated scientifically. His synthesis of means-ends reasoning and Christian social vision provides the blueprint for carrying forward the quest for common-good capitalism.

Chapter 10 concludes by revisiting the relationship between the science of economics and the art of political economy. Distributism can be a progressive research program in the service of common-good capitalism, but this requires respecting the proper spheres of science and art, to enjoy the comparative advantage of each. The chapter also discusses distributism's teachings about the nature of democracy and self-governance, as well as specific policy proposals.

To paraphrase Buchanan, the enduring lessons of political economy occupy the space "between predictive science and moral philosophy."[31] Economic science divorced from humanistic concerns makes for anemic political economy. In contrast, distributist political economy can offer a fruitful synthesis of scientific analysis and ethical vision. Getting the balance right is the first step on the long and uncertain, but nevertheless worthwhile, road to common-good capitalism.

31 James M. Buchanan, *Economics: Between Predictive Science and Moral Philosophy* (College Station: Texas A&M University Press, 1987).

Chapter 2

The Context for Distributism: Catholic Social Thought on Economic and Political Order

Classical distributism, by which I mean the writings of Belloc and Chesterton, is explicitly rooted in Catholic social teaching. This does not mean distributism is designed to appeal solely to Catholics, or to have validity only for members of the Catholic Church. Instead, it means distributism's earliest architects self-consciously built on the foundation of Catholicism's teachings on politics and economics. Catholic social teaching provides the context for distributism: it is the impetus behind distributism's development, as well as the key for properly interpreting it. We cannot understand distributism without being familiar with Catholic social teaching.

My purpose in this brief chapter is to survey key aspects of Catholic thought on matters of politics and economics. I restrict myself to the canonical teachings, as expressed in important papal encyclicals and the *Catechism of the Catholic Church*. As we will see, the themes developed in these writings will play a prominent role in Belloc's and Chesterton's works on politics and economics.

THE CHURCH AND MODERNITY

In some ways, the label "Catholic social teaching" is misleading. The Catholic Church has always applied its moral teachings to social issues. But with the economic and political upheavals in the West following the Industrial Revolution, the church recognized the need to provide more specific guidance. The resulting papal encyclicals, whose principles are now expressed in the church's *Compendium of Social Doctrine*,[1] addressed important social

1 Pontifical Council for Justice and Peace, "Compendium of the Social Doctrine of the Church," 2004, http://www.vatican.va/roman_curia/pontifical_councils/justpeace/documents/rc_pc_justpeace_doc_20060526_compendio-dott-soc_en.html#At%20the%20dawn%20of%20the%20Third%20Millennium.

questions of the day, including the duties of labor and capital and the proper scope of political institutions. While each encyclical contributes something new and valuable, the first two—Pope Leo XIII's *Rerum Novarum*[2] and Pope Pius XI's *Quadragesimo Anno*[3]—are the foundational documents upon which the church's teachings rest concerning the moral dimension of economic and political modernity.

These encyclicals were motivated by the revolution in the production and distribution of wealth caused by industrialization.[4] The transformation of agricultural economies into industrial economies throughout the West entailed rapid economic growth. Income per capita, which was stagnant for more than a millennium after the fall of the Roman Empire, began increasing rapidly, first in the Netherlands, then in England, and finally in the rest of Europe soon after. The British case is most telling: Income increased by at least 0.3 percent per year from 1700 to 1760 and then by 1.98 percent between 1830 and 1870. In the span of less than a century and a half, British living standards more than doubled. They nearly doubled again by 1914.[5]

Major changes in economic organization accompanied rising incomes. Large industrial concerns, which could more effectively capture economies of scale, replaced smaller agricultural and craft enterprises.[6] Contrary to the popular narrative, this was not an era of "robber barons" cartelizing industry and causing mass impoverishment.[7] First, productivity growth in

2 Leo XIII, *Rerum Novarum*, 1891, http://w2.vatican.va/content/leo-xiii/en/encyclicals/documents/hf_l-xiii_enc_15051891_rerum-novarum.html.

3 Pius XI, *Quadragesimo Anno*, 1931, http://w2.vatican.va/content/pius-xi/en/encyclicals/documents/hf_p-xi_enc_19310515_quadragesimo-anno.html.

4 "The social doctrine of the Church developed in the nineteenth century when the Gospel encountered modern industrial society with its new structures for the production of consumer goods, its new concept of society, the state and authority, and its new forms of labor and ownership. the [sic] development of the doctrine of the Church on economic and social matters attests the permanent value of the Church's teaching at the same time as it attests the true meaning of her Tradition, always living and active." Catholic Church, *Catechism*, 2421.

5 Joel Mokyr, *The Enlightened Economy: Britain and the Industrial Revolution* (London: Penguin, 2011), 256.

6 See notably Stephen Broadberry et al., *British Economic Growth, 1270–1870* (Cambridge: Cambridge University Press, 2015).

7 Numerous scholars have pushed back against the "robber barons" narrative. These researchers distinguish entrepreneurs who got rich by providing goods and services that consumers wanted from entrepreneurs who lobbied legislatures for special privileges (e.g., subsidies, tariffs, legal monopolies). See B. W. Folsom, *The Myth of the Robber Barons: A New Look at the Rise of Big Business in America* (Herndon, Va.: Young America's Foundation, 1991); Werner Troesken, "Exclusive Dealing and the Whiskey Trust, 1890–1895," *Journal of Economic History* 58, no. 3 (1998):

new industries lifted workers' wages.[8] Second, improved production meant falling costs for consumption goods for rich and poor alike. The result was increased real wages, especially for those at the bottom of the income distribution.[9] New employment opportunities in urban centers absorbed much of the labor force that was released from traditional modes of production. Many voluntarily left the countryside in pursuit of wage employment in cities, which was becoming increasingly remunerative compared to work in rural areas.[10]

While critics of the Industrial Revolution often make absurd claims, we must avoid the opposite error of romanticizing this era. Industrialization greatly increased living standards, but it also had some troubling social consequences. The conspicuousness of new capitalist fortunes caused many to overlook the enrichment of laborers, focusing instead on inequality.[11] For workers, mass wage employment was occasionally accompanied by large-scale unemployment, as the developing capitalist economic system was subject to unpredictable recessions. Factory employment often meant long hours, uncomfortable conditions, and physical danger. These unpleasantries were undoubtedly accounted for in workers' wages,[12] but the moral and aesthetic concerns with society-wide "creative destruction," which transformed the average citizen from a poor yet propertied yeoman to a wealthier but less secure laborer, remained an important public issue. Modern political movements, such as Progressivism, arose to combat these ills. Unfortunately, the cure often proved worse than the disease.

755–78; Charles D. DeLorme, W. Scott Frame, and David R. Kamerschen, "Empirical Evidence on a Special-Interest-Group Perspective to Antitrust," *Public Choice* 92, no. 3–4 (1997): 317–35; Thomas J. DiLorenzo, "The Origins of Antitrust: An Interest-Group Perspective," *International Review of Law and Economics* 5, no. 1 (1985): 73–90; Vincent Geloso, "Collusion and Combines in Canada, 1880–1890," *Scandinavian Economic History Review* 68, no. 1 (2020): 66–84.

8 Peter Lindert and Jeffrey Williamson, "English Workers' Living Standards during the Industrial Revolution: A New Look," *Economic History Review* 36, no. 1 (1983): 1–25.

9 Vincent Geloso and Peter Lindert, "Relative Costs of Living, for Richer and Poorer, 1688–1914," *Cliometrica* 14, no. 3 (2020): 417–42; Philip Hoffman et al., "Real Inequality in Europe since 1500," *Journal of Economic History* 62, no. 2 (2002): 322–55.

10 Jeffrey Williamson, *Coping with City Growth during the British Industrial Revolution* (Cambridge: Cambridge University Press, 1990).

11 But important kinds of inequality, such as mortality inequality, fell during this period. Sam Peltzman, "Mortality Inequality," *Journal of Economic Perspectives* 23, no. 4 (2009): 175–90.

12 Workers also captured nonpecuniary benefits, such as increased leisure time. Michael Huberman and Chris Minns, "The Times They Are Not Changin': Days and Hours of Work in Old and New Worlds, 1870–2000," *Explorations in Economic History* 44, no. 4 (2007): 538–67.

Rerum Novarum was the first papal encyclical to confront the changed social landscape. Addressing capital-labor relations specifically, Pope Leo counsels that employees and employers each have rights and duties commensurate with social justice and advancing the common good. Workers must faithfully execute the tasks to which they have contractually agreed and refrain from individual and collective acts of violence against their employers. Employers must pay workers a wage consistent with human dignity. More generally, the encyclical strongly affirmed the church's commitment to the right of private property but also cautioned that this right was not absolute. The state must regulate ownership and its attendant privileges in the interests of the common good. At the level of economic and political systems, the church does not mandate any specific political form or regime, but it strongly condemns both the coerced collectivism of socialism and the unbridled individualism of industrial capitalism.

Quadragesimo Anno, issued forty years after *Rerum Novarum*, elaborates on many of the earlier encyclical's themes while also breaking new ground. Whereas Leo's encyclical dealt primarily with capital-labor relations, Pius brought moral evaluation of the entire political-economic order to the forefront. Perhaps this document's most important contribution is the principle of subsidiarity: the duty of higher-order communities, such as national governments, not to interfere with the operation of lower-order communities, such as families and local governments, without just cause. In addition, Pius reaffirmed the importance of private property and condemned the totalitarian regimes developing in Europe at the time. He also called for cooperation between social classes as a way to ameliorate conflict without infringing on associational freedom.

The church's contemporary teaching on the moral aspects of economics and politics expresses the principles elucidated in these encyclicals. The teachings have been explicitly incorporated into the *Catechism of the Catholic Church*, which summarizes doctrine and lays out the beliefs of the faithful. The following exposition of church teaching on political economy draws upon the relevant tenets from the *Catechism*. I intend the survey to be representative, not exhaustive. From this survey, we will acquire a clear picture of the church's universal principles, which must be applied anew to present challenges.

AUTHORITY, ORDER, AND THE COMMON GOOD

Man is social by nature. He becomes most fully himself when living in community: "The human person needs to live in society. Society is not for him an extraneous addition but a requirement of his nature. Through the exchange with others, mutual service and dialogue with his brethren, man develops his potential; he thus responds to his vocation."[13] Importantly, society is not merely an aggregate of individuals. Social groups at various levels, from the family to the state, are real, and are not reducible to the sum of their members: "A society is a group of persons bound together organically by a principle of unity that goes beyond each one of them. As an assembly that is at once visible and spiritual, a society endures through time: it gathers up the past and prepares for the future."[14]

A healthy civilization contains multiple overlapping societies. These communities should help persons to develop their potential and orient them to their true good: "Certain societies, such as the family and the state, correspond more directly to the nature of man; they are necessary to him. To promote the participation of the greatest number in the life of a society, the creation of voluntary associations and institutions must be encouraged. . . . This 'socialization' also expresses the natural tendency for human beings to associate with one another for the sake of attaining objectives that exceed individual capacities. It develops the qualities of the person, especially the sense of initiative and responsibility, and helps guarantee his rights."[15]

Human communities bestow gifts on their members. These gifts appear gratuitous to any one person, but the communities that provide them require cultivation. Thus, the rights and duties of persons exist at a deeper level than explicit consent: "By means of society, each man is established as an 'heir' and receives certain 'talents' that enrich his identity and whose fruits he must develop. He rightly owes loyalty to the communities of which he is part and respect to those in authority who have charge of the common good."[16] Loyalty to communities also requires loyalty to the authorities—those who give orders and receive obedience[17]—duly constituted to sustain

13 Catholic Church, *Catechism*, 1879.

14 Catholic Church, *Catechism*, 1880.

15 Catholic Church, *Catechism*, 1882.

16 Catholic Church, *Catechism*, 1880.

17 Catholic Church, *Catechism*, 1897.

those communities and advance their interests: "Human society can be neither well-ordered nor prosperous unless it has some people invested with legitimate authority to preserve its institutions and to devote themselves as far as is necessary to work and care for the good of all."[18] Obviously, the church herself is such an authority. As the continuing presence of Christ in the Holy Spirit, the church has a unique mission to uphold the natural and revealed moral law. Other sources of authority, with their own proper spheres, are the family and the state.

No authority is self-justifying. Its rights depend on it upholding some good that the authority cannot define nor alter: "Authority does not derive its moral legitimacy from itself. It must not behave in a despotic manner, but must act for the common good as a 'moral force based on freedom and a sense of responsibility.'"[19] Thus, authority is justified only if it promotes the common good, and "by common good is to be understood 'the sum total of social conditions which allow people, either as groups or as individuals, to reach their fulfillment more fully and more easily.' The common good concerns the life of all. It calls for prudence from each, and even more from those who exercise the office of authority."[20] Every human community possesses a common good. A community's common good is the essential factor that constitutes the community qua community.[21]

The common good has three elements. First, it requires authorities to respect the fundamental rights all persons possess because they bear the *imago Dei*, the image of God, which is the source of intrinsic dignity.[22] Second, the common good requires authorities to steward the community, preserving its interests by arbitrating disputes among members, giving each member of the group his or her due, and reconciling each to the good of all.[23] Third, the common good requires authorities to maintain peace and order in society, both within and between communities.[24]

Closely linked with authority and the common good is social justice. Those who esteem the church's principles of communitarian personalism

18 Catholic Church, *Catechism*, 1897.

19 Catholic Church, *Catechism*, 1902.

20 Catholic Church, *Catechism*, 1906.

21 Catholic Church, *Catechism*, 1910.

22 Catholic Church, *Catechism*, 1907.

23 Catholic Church, *Catechism*, 1908.

24 Catholic Church, *Catechism*, 1909.

sometimes scorn the idea of social justice, but this is due to the perversion of the concept from decades of misuse. Social justice must not be severed from its theistic and ecclesiastic roots. "Society ensures social justice when it provides the conditions that allow associations or individuals to obtain what is their due, according to their nature and their vocation."[25] An important tenet of social justice is the promotion of solidarity, which can be thought of as "social charity."[26] Solidarity is a social expression of human rights, and it also helps reduce social conflict: "Socio-economic problems can be resolved only with the help of all the forms of solidarity: solidarity of the poor among themselves, between rich and poor, of workers among themselves, between employers and employees in a business, solidarity among nations and peoples."[27] First and foremost, respecting rights and pacifying social tension require giving people their due. Thus, social justice is not a repudiation but an extension of the fundamental precept of justice dating back to classical antiquity. Therefore, social justice cannot ignore "the distribution of goods and remuneration for work."[28] Social justice is the link between the church's teaching on authority, order, and the common good and her teaching on the proper organization of economic and political life.

THE BOUNTY OF CREATION: ORDER IN ECONOMY

The cornerstone of the church's economic teaching is the universal destination of goods. The earth and its bounty were created by God for the whole of humanity. Each of us has a right to enjoy the fruits of creation. However, the universal destination of goods does not preclude private property.[29] In fact, the church has always affirmed that "the appropriation of property is legitimate for guaranteeing the freedom and dignity of persons and for helping each of them to meet his basic needs and the needs of those in his charge. It should allow for a natural solidarity to develop between men."[30] Ownership is both permitted and encouraged, but the rights of ownership are circumscribed by the natural and revealed moral law: "Goods of production—material or immaterial—such as land, factories, practical or

25 Catholic Church, *Catechism*, 1928.

26 Catholic Church, *Catechism*, 1939.

27 Catholic Church, *Catechism*, 1941.

28 Catholic Church, *Catechism*, 1940.

29 Catholic Church, *Catechism*, 2401.

30 Catholic Church, *Catechism*, 2402.

artistic skills, oblige their possessors to employ them in ways that will benefit the greatest number. Those who hold goods for use and consumption should use them with moderation, reserving the better part for guests, for the sick and the poor."[31] Economic rights are properly under the purview of political authorities, whose duty it is to regulate these rights in the interests of social justice and the common good.[32]

The church is insistent that economic issues cannot be isolated from moral issues. The production and distribution of goods is a moral enterprise whose goal is human flourishing, which for Christians means beatification. Economic rights, including rights of property, are properly subordinated to this end. For example, the church forbids theft, meaning the use of property against the reasonable will of the owner. However, "there is no theft if . . . refusal [of the use of property] is contrary to reason and the universal destination of goods. This is the case in obvious and urgent necessity when the only way to provide for immediate, essential needs (food, shelter, clothing . . .) is to put at one's disposal and use the property of others."[33] Property rights are similarly restricted in the interests of the common good by declaring the following illicit: paying unjust wages, profiting from another's hardship or ignorance, attempting to manipulate the market, corrupting the judgment of those who make legal decisions, evading taxes, and spending wastefully.[34]

As part of its teachings on private property, the church recognizes the importance of respecting contracts: "Promises must be kept and contracts strictly observed to the extent that the commitments made in them are morally just. A significant part of economic and social life depends on the honoring of contracts between physical or moral persons—commercial contracts of purchase or sale, rental or labor contracts. All contracts must be agreed to and executed in good faith."[35] As with other property rights, contractual rights are viewed primarily through the lens of justice: "Contracts are subject to commutative justice which regulates exchanges between persons and between institutions in accordance with a strict respect for their rights. Commutative justice obliges strictly; it requires safeguarding property rights, paying debts, and fulfilling obli-

31 Catholic Church, *Catechism*, 2405.

32 Catholic Church, *Catechism*, 2406.

33 Catholic Church, *Catechism*, 2408.

34 Catholic Church, *Catechism*, 2409.

35 Catholic Church, *Catechism*, 2410.

gations freely contracted. Without commutative justice, no other form of justice is possible."[36]

Property rights and contractual rights are human rights, but the content of "human rights" derives from what persons owe and are owed as bearers of God's image. Property rights or contractual arrangements that infringe on human dignity are not permissible. Forbidden are "acts or enterprises that for any reason—selfish or ideological, commercial, or totalitarian—lead to the enslavement of human beings, to their being bought, sold and exchanged like merchandise, in disregard for their personal dignity. It is a sin against the dignity of persons and their fundamental rights to reduce them by violence to their productive value or to a source of profit."[37] Likewise, economic rights that disrespect the integrity of creation are illegitimate. Man is a steward of the earth, not its master: "Animals, like plants and inanimate beings, are by nature destined for the common good of past, present, and future humanity. Use of the mineral, vegetable, and animal resources of the universe cannot be divorced from respect for moral imperatives. Man's dominion over inanimate and other living beings granted by the Creator is not absolute; it is limited by concern for the quality of life of his neighbor, including generations to come; it requires a religious respect for the integrity of creation."[38]

The church's circumscription of property rights has several implications for economic activity more generally: "The development of economic activity and growth in production are meant to provide for the needs of human beings. Economic life is not meant solely to multiply goods produced and increase profit or power; it is ordered first of all to the service of persons, of the whole man, and of the entire human community. Economic activity, conducted according to its own proper methods, is to be exercised within the limits of the moral order, in keeping with social justice so as to correspond to God's plan for man."[39] This informs a unique perspective on the rights and duties of labor. Man has a duty to work—as St. Paul wrote, "The one who is unwilling to work shall not eat"[40]—but labor is neither curse

36 Catholic Church, *Catechism*, 2411. On the several classifications of justice, the church adds the following: "One distinguishes commutative justice from legal justice which concerns what the citizen owes in fairness to the community, and from distributive justice which regulates what the community owes its citizens in proportion to their contributions and needs."

37 Catholic Church, *Catechism*, 2414.

38 Catholic Church, *Catechism*, 2415.

39 Catholic Church, *Catechism*, 2426.

40 2 Thes 3:10 NIV.

nor drudgery. Through labor, man cooperates with God in the continual unfolding of creation.[41] Work is not merely a duty; it is also a right: "Everyone has the right of economic initiative; everyone should make legitimate use of his talents to contribute to the abundance that will benefit all and to harvest the just fruits of his labor."[42] The spiritual dimension of work is at least as important as the economic. *Ora et labora*—prayer and work—have always been linked in the church's tradition.

Owning and operating a business is also a legitimate form of work. Just as employees have rights and duties, so do employers. While employers "have an obligation to consider the good of persons and not only the increase of profits," the church recognizes that profits are both essential and proper in economic life: "Profits are necessary. . . . They make possible the investments that ensure the future of a business and they guarantee employment."[43] The rights of profit are tempered by the duty to pay just wages: "A just wage is the legitimate fruit of work. To refuse or withhold it can be a grave injustice. In determining fair pay, both the needs and the contributions of each person must be taken into account. 'Remuneration for work should guarantee man the opportunity to provide a dignified livelihood for himself and his family on the material, social, cultural and spiritual level, taking into account the role and the productivity of each, the state of the business, and the common good.' Agreement between the parties is not sufficient to justify morally the amount to be received in wages."[44]

Another important principle of the church is concern for the poor. Efforts to ameliorate poverty are an ancient tradition of God's people dating back to the Old Testament welfare laws: the jubilee for the forgiveness of debts, the ban on usury, the wages of day laborers, and the right to glean fields and vines.[45] But the church is not concerned only for reducing material poverty. The preferential option for the poor "extends not only to material poverty but also to the many forms of cultural and religious poverty."[46] These other forms of oppression that afflict the poor are just as concerning: "'In its various forms—material deprivation, unjust oppression, physical

41 Catholic Church, *Catechism*, 2427.

42 Catholic Church, *Catechism*, 2429.

43 Catholic Church, *Catechism*, 2432.

44 Catholic Church, *Catechism*, 2434.

45 Catholic Church, *Catechism*, 2449.

46 Catholic Church, *Catechism*, 2444.

and psychological illness and death—human misery is the obvious sign of the inherited condition of frailty and need for salvation in which man finds himself as a consequence of original sin. This misery elicited the compassion of Christ the Savior, who willingly took it upon himself and identified himself with the least of his brethren."[47] Providing for the poor is not only an act of mercy. It is an act of justice. As St. John Chrysostom argued, "Not to enable the poor to share in our goods is to steal from them and deprive them of life. The goods we possess are not ours, but theirs."[48] Love for the poor also requires an appropriate attitude toward created goods on the part of those who would give. One cannot love the poor while immoderately partaking of wealth in one's personal life.[49]

THE RESPONSIBILITIES OF AUTHORITY: ORDER IN POLITY

How wealth is produced and distributed depends on the institutions that govern economic life. Production and distribution are not autonomous but under the direction of various authorities, including political authority:

> Economic activity, especially the activity of a market economy, cannot be conducted in an institutional, juridical, or political vacuum. On the contrary, it presupposes sure guarantees of individual freedom and private property, as well as a stable currency and efficient public services. Hence the principal task of the state is to guarantee this security, so that those who work and produce can enjoy the fruits of their labors and thus feel encouraged to work efficiently and honestly.... Another task of the state is that of overseeing and directing the exercise of human rights in the economic sector.[50]

Moral order in the economy requires moral order in the polity.

But this is easier said than done. The church acknowledges that those in authority often succumb to the trappings of power. This has been especially dangerous since the rise of the centralized state. With the relative weakening of other sources of authority, additional duties to maintain the common good have fallen to the state, but excessive intervention, a perpetual

47 Catholic Church, *Catechism*, 2448.

48 Catholic Church, *Catechism*, 2446.

49 Cf. Jas 5:1–6; Mt 6:24; Catholic Church, *Catechism*, 2445.

50 Catholic Church, *Catechism*, 2431.

temptation by those who wield government power, can infringe on human dignity. In response, "the teaching of the Church has elaborated the principle of subsidiarity, according to which 'a community of a higher order should not interfere in the internal life of a community of a lower order, depriving the latter of its functions, but rather should support it in case of need and help to co-ordinate its activity with the activities of the rest of society, always with a view to the common good.'"[51] When families and civic organizations can solve social problems, government ought not to interfere. If a public-sector response is necessary, it ought to occur at the most feasible local level. National government should intervene only if lower-order communities are inadequate to the task, and if it can implement a solution that respects human dignity and upholds the common good.

Subsidiarity also limits the range of permissible political orders: "The principle of subsidiarity is opposed to all forms of collectivism. It sets limits for state intervention."[52] Totalitarian states, with their forced socialization and regimentation, are irreconcilable with the church's teachings on authority and the common good: "The Church has rejected the totalitarian and atheistic ideologies associated in modem times with 'communism' or 'socialism.'"[53] In addition, the church disapproves of regimes that outsource the moral order to the market: "She has likewise refused to accept, in the practice of 'capitalism,' individualism and the absolute primacy of the law of the marketplace over human labor."[54] The church tolerates neither tyranny nor passivity from political authorities: "Regulating the economy solely by centralized planning perverts the basis of social bonds; regulating it solely by the law of the marketplace fails social justice. . . . Reasonable regulation of the marketplace and economic initiatives, in keeping with a just hierarchy of values and a view to the common good, is to be commended."[55] But beyond this, the church pronounces no doctrine. Mandating a specific sociopolitical order is outside the church's purview: "If authority belongs to the order established by God, 'the choice of the political regime and the appointment of rulers are left to the free decision of the citizens.' The diversity of political regimes is morally acceptable, provided they serve the legiti-

51 Catholic Church, *Catechism*, 1883.

52 Catholic Church, *Catechism*, 1885.

53 Catholic Church, *Catechism*, 2425.

54 Catholic Church, *Catechism*, 2425.

55 Catholic Church, *Catechism*, 2425.

mate good of the communities that adopt them. Regimes whose nature is contrary to the natural law, to the public order, and to the fundamental rights of persons cannot achieve the common good of the nations on which they have been imposed."[56]

CONCLUSION

"The Church receives from the Gospel the full revelation of the truth about man. When she fulfills her mission of proclaiming the Gospel, she bears witness to man, in the name of Christ, to his dignity and his vocation to the communion of persons. She teaches him the demands of justice and peace in conformity with divine wisdom."[57] The church's possession of the truth entitles her to make moral judgments about economic and political life. Whatever the physical and social sciences discover about human behavior as it pertains to these spheres, the church retains its right to teach and guide. This does not obviate the need for political authority, however: "In the moral order she bears a mission distinct from that of political authorities: the Church is concerned with the temporal aspects of the common good because they are ordered to the sovereign Good, our ultimate end. She strives to inspire right attitudes with respect to earthly goods and in socio-economic relationships."[58] The church's social teaching "proposes principles for reflection; it provides criteria for judgment; it gives guidelines for action."[59] These doctrines are not ideologies. The church commands neither a specific economic system for the production and distribution of goods, nor a political system for governing nations. In her capacity as teacher and guide, the church actively promotes solidarity between society's classes and interests, for the betterment of each and all.[60] In these roles, the church serves as the protector of human dignity, on guard against economic or political forces that, if left unchecked, reduce human persons to means, instead of honoring them as ends in themselves.

The themes we have encountered in this chapter fill Belloc's and Chesterton's writings. Economically, they are especially concerned with the social dimension of property rights. As we will see, they argue economic solidarity

56 Catholic Church, *Catechism*, 1901.

57 Catholic Church, *Catechism*, 2419.

58 Catholic Church, *Catechism*, 2420.

59 Catholic Church, *Catechism*, 2423.

60 Catholic Church, *Catechism*, 2425.

requires not the attenuation of private property but its expansion: Ownership of productive assets should be widely available and diffused throughout society. Politically, subsidiarity and intermediary institutions play a crucial role. For obvious reasons, Belloc and (especially) Chesterton are particularly concerned with the institution of the family and, in conjunction with widespread property ownership, how healthy families contribute to free societies. Freedom, in its Christian sense, is a necessary component of personal and social flourishing. Therefore, it is central to distributism.

Ultimately, Belloc and Chesterton want to discover economic and political arrangements that institutionalize respect for human dignity, in the sense that society's fundamental rules actively promote man's highest good. To achieve this good, economics and politics—property and freedom—must be brought into harmony. Distributism can be viewed as a set of principles for arranging political and economic institutions such that property and freedom mutually reinforce each other. By the end of this book, we will have a clear view of where this project succeeds and where it fails.

Chapter 3

Belloc's *The Servile State*

Hilaire Belloc was one of the twentieth century's prodigious men of letters. He was born in France in 1870 to a French father and an English mother. Growing up in England, Belloc attended Balliol College, Oxford, and obtained first-class honors in history. After becoming a naturalized British subject in 1902, he served in Parliament as a Liberal Party member from 1906 to 1910. For most of his life, he was an independent writer and scholar. A lifelong Catholic, Belloc's faith strongly influenced his public positions and writings.

Belloc's *The Servile State*, first published in 1912, is probably his best-known nonfiction work. Belloc offers an overview of European economic history, with special focus on the High Middle Ages, and contrasts this history with what he regards as the distasteful situation in modern England. *The Servile State* argues that the tensions within English capitalism, caused by the concentration of private property in the hands of the few, can only be resolved by either collectivization (socialism) or by reestablishing widespread ownership of private property, as existed prior to the Reformation. A polity characterized by dispersed ownership of productive property Belloc calls the *distributive state.*

Belloc's argument in *The Servile State* is a bulwark of distributist thought, but his work also had notable influences outside this relatively narrow circle. In his introduction to the Liberty Fund edition, the great sociologist and defender of ordered liberty Robert Nisbet said of *The Servile State* that "its effect on me was profound. It has proved to be among the few books . . . which have had influence on me so great as virtually to turn my mind around. Suffice it here to say that never again, after reading Belloc's work, did I imagine there could be genuine individual freedom apart from individual ownership of property."[1] F. A. Hayek, cowinner of the 1974 Nobel Prize in economics, was sufficiently impressed with the work that he used as the epigraph for one of his chapters in his *Road to Serfdom* a quotation

1 Hillaire Belloc, *The Servile State* (Indianapolis, Ind.: Liberty Fund, 1977), 14.

from Belloc: "The control of the production of wealth is the control of human life itself."[2]

It is important to note at the outset that Belloc is not conducting an ethical critique of English commercial society, despite the normative connotations in his chosen title. In his preface to the second edition, he writes, "I am concerned in this book to say how and why we *are* approaching it [the servile state]; not whether we *should* approach it."[3] That being said, there are clear prescriptive aspects of his analysis. This does not invalidate his descriptive project. Doctors are driven by the moral impulse to eradicate disease, but this does not impugn the status of medicine as a science. A similar distinction applies here.

Belloc's Catholicism, and in particular the influence of Catholic social teaching, shines through his arguments. For example, concerns from *Rerum Novarum* on the rights and duties of capital and labor show in Belloc's treatment of the consequences of increasingly concentrated property ownership. His perspective on the exploitation of workers under industrial capitalism and the relationship of property ownership and freedom should also be read in light of Leo XIII's encyclical. *The Servile State* is thus an exploration of the world capitalism created, motivated by the Roman pontiff's calls to grapple with its ethical consequences.

LABOR, SERVILE AND FREE

Like a good Thomist, Belloc begins with his thesis and supporting conceptual definitions. He contends that the existing political-economic system of England, which he refers to as industrial capitalism (frequently just capitalism), is tending toward conditions of "*the establishment of compulsory labor legally enforceable upon those who do not own the means of production for the advantage of those who do.*"[4] This is, he believes, the essential condition of the servile state. Belloc's work is intended as a positive, not normative, exposition of both the rise of industrial capitalism and its instabilities, which tends toward the reestablishment, at first de facto and eventually de jure, of servile labor.

Since *The Servile State* is an essay in political economy, Belloc takes care to define the economic and political terminology he will employ. His defi-

2 F. A. Hayek, *The Road to Serfdom*, ed. by Bruce Caldwell (Chicago: University of Chicago Press, 2007), 124.

3 Belloc, *Servile State*, 31–32.

4 Belloc, *Servile State*, 39.

nitions of concepts such as wealth, labor, capital, and land are standard from the neoclassical economics literature of the early twentieth century.[5] This suggests that Belloc, while not an economist, was at least reasonably well read in economics, and thus his arguments cannot be dismissed out of hand based on lack of familiarity with his subject. One definition that merits special mention is property: "*Property* is a term used for that arrangement in society whereby the control of land and of wealth made from land, including therefore all the means of production, is vested in some person or corporation."[6] Belloc classifies societies based on their distribution of property. His classification of capitalism, including early twentieth-century England's particular form of industrial capitalism, rests on two features: "(1) that the citizens thereof are politically free: i.e., can use or withhold at will their possession or their labor, but are also (2) divided into capitalist and proletarian in such proportions that the state as a whole is not characterized by the institution of ownership among free citizens, but by the restriction of ownership to a section markedly less than the whole, or even a small minority."[7] The servile state is one where proletarians—those without property—are forced by law to work for capitalists. This legal compulsion is so widespread "as to stamp the whole community with the mark of such labor."[8] The boundary between free and servile labor, which Belloc regards as synonymous with slavery, is the right to refuse to work. A free man "can refuse his labor and use that refusal as an instrument wherewith to *bargain*."[9] As we will see later, labor's de facto bargaining power is a crucial component of Belloc's argument.

The next section of the book is a historical overview of laboring conditions from classical antiquity through early modernity. Belloc argues that the default condition of labor in ancient times was servile. Whether in the civilized Greek polis or among the wandering Germanic tribesmen, slavery was so common as to be taken for granted. It was viewed as "the economic pivot upon which the production of wealth should turn, and [was] never doubted but that it was normal to all human society."[10] Free men, usually

5 Belloc, *Servile State*, 45–48.

6 Belloc, *Servile State*, 48.

7 Belloc, *Servile State*, 50.

8 Belloc, *Servile State*, 50.

9 Belloc, *Servile State*, 51.

10 Belloc, *Servile State*, 64.

owning property, had a voice in public affairs; slaves, usually dispossessed of property and under a compulsion to labor, did not. While servile status was frequently imposed on conquered peoples or prisoners of war, the most common source of servile labor was impoverished individuals selling themselves into slavery, in exchange for a guaranteed minimum of material sustenance. The children of slaves were also slaves.[11] Manumission was possible, but rare.

Belloc explains the gradual erosion of slavery in the Old World as the result of the Christianization of the social order. The rise of Christendom in Europe saw "the exceedingly gradual transformation of this servile state into something other: a society of owners."[12] The process took almost a millennium and was not consciously intended as a liberation project. Even with the spread of Christianity, "the vast revolution through which the European mind passed between the first and fourth centuries . . . included no attack upon the servile institution."[13] A crucial event was the transformation of the villa, the chief agricultural-economic unit of the late Roman Empire. Villas were great landed estates, typically owned by a single proprietor (*dominus*, lord) and worked mostly by slaves. Initially, the land and its servile labor were under the complete control of the lord. The slave did not enjoy economic resources beyond what the lord saw fit to bestow upon the slave, in the interests of keeping the latter minimally productive. With the breakdown in political order accompanying the decline and fall of the Western Roman Empire, however, the de facto bargaining condition of servile labor increased. The lord of a villa could no longer count on Roman political power to enforce his claims to land and slaves. As a result, it was no longer incentive-compatible for the lord to expropriate the fruits of slave labor to the same degree. Instead of rigid production demands, lords found it more profitable "to make sure of that slave's produce by asking him no more than certain customary dues. . . . The arrangement was made workable by leaving to the slave all the remaining produce of his own labor."[14]

The decline in de jure political authority also had implications for the de facto organization and possession of land within the villa. Now it was divided into three portions: the land which was under the lord's sole and

11 Belloc, *Servile State*, 66.

12 Belloc, *Servile State*, 70.

13 Belloc, *Servile State*, 71.

14 Belloc, *Servile State*, 74.

absolute proprietorship (*domain*), the occupied lands of slaves and descendants of slaves, and land that was common to both, over which lords and slaves exercised specific usufruct rights. The first category of land was still worked by slaves, usually for a specified period. "Upon the second portion, 'land in villenage,' . . . the slaves worked by rules and customs which they gradually came to elaborate for themselves."[15] On the third, slaves still supplied labor, but the produce was divided between lord and slave along customary lines.

"During the eighth, ninth, and tenth centuries this system crystallized and became so natural in men's eyes that the original servile character of the working folk upon the villa was forgotten."[16] The slave had become a serf. Although the Latin root of the latter word, *servus*, still denotes the servile condition, the rights and duties of the serf were quite different from the slaves of old. While serfs were, theoretically, bound to the soil to which they were born, in practice, "all that is required of him is that his family should till its quota of servile land, and the dues to the lord shall not fail from absence of labor."[17] Serfs, once they discharged this duty, could and did find other occupations, such as trades within medieval towns. Gradually serfdom declined, and a free peasantry rose in its place. Although the owners of these great estates still exercised lordship, the rights of laborers strengthened such that by the fourteenth or fifteenth century, they could not be evicted from the land they worked, their dues of produce were fixed by custom, and, while they could not alienate the land, they could reliably pass it down within their families.

Complementary in Belloc's narrative to the free peasantry was the rise of guilds, which governed professions and crafts in medieval cities. These cities were usually independent of the formal feudal hierarchy, possessing charters of liberties and immunities from a sovereign authority. By the High Middle Ages (thirteenth and fourteenth centuries), urban commerce had revived and was usually under the purview of guilds: "private owners of capital whose corporation was self-governing, and was designed to check competition between its members . . . most jealously did the guild safeguard the division of property, so that there should be formed within its ranks, no proletariat upon the one side, and no monopolizing capitalist upon the

15 Belloc, *Servile State*, 75.

16 Belloc, *Servile State*, 76.

17 Belloc, *Servile State*, 77.

other."[18] The burgher guilds complete the trifecta of Belloc's conception of medieval liberty: "the serf, secure in his position, and burdened only with regular dues, which were but a fraction of his produce; the freeholder, a man independent save for money dues, which were more of a tax than a rent; the guild, in which well-divided capital worked cooperatively for craft production, for transport and for commerce.... All, or most—the normal family—should own. And on ownership the freedom of the state should repose."[19]

Belloc devotes a large portion of his manuscript, ostensibly on the conditions of servile labor in modern England, to the balance of economic and political forces of the High Middle Ages. This period for Belloc is the standard of a society characterized by *well-divided property*. Belloc sees these institutions as preserving economic freedom by guaranteeing families they would possess sufficient land, capital, or both that they could not be forced by circumstance into the servile condition of labor before the rise of Christendom. In brief, "the Middle Ages had instinctively conceived and brought into existence the *distributive state*."[20] Furthermore, Belloc clearly sees this kind of economic freedom and political freedom as mutually reinforcing. While a defense of medieval Europe on the grounds of human freedom may seem strange, a compelling case can be made that the political rights we take for granted in liberal democracies have their roots in the concurrence requirements among medieval powers—crown, church, fief, burghers, and even the free peasantry—for making important political decisions. Political rights stemmed from economic rights, and in turn reinforced those economic rights. It is no coincidence that institutions of representative government, requiring consensus among the estates of the realm, arose in medieval Europe, and nowhere else.

CAPITALISM AND THE RETREAT OF PROPERTY

But the political and economic balance of the High Middle Ages did not persist. Particularly in England, Belloc contends, trends were set in motion during early modernity that resulted in the proletarianization of society. Belloc's perspective here is both perplexing and intriguing, and it runs contrary to the standard narrative of England as the spearhead of liberty and

18 Belloc, *Servile State*, 79.

19 Belloc, *Servile State*, 79–80.

20 Belloc, *Servile State*, 81, my emphasis.

property in the West. But what precisely was the cause of England's change of course back toward a servile state? "What turned an England economically free into the England which we know today, of which at least one-third is indigent, of which nineteenth-twentieths are dispossessed of capital and land, and of which the whole industry and national life is controlled upon its economic side by a few chance directors of millions, a few masters of unsocial and irresponsible monopolies?"[21] Belloc has no patience for the standard answer, which is the Industrial Revolution: "No such material cause determined the degradation from which we suffer.... The industrial system was a growth proceeding from capitalism, not its cause. Capitalism was here in England before the industrial system came into being.... It was not machinery that lost us our freedom; it was the loss of a free mind."[22] Remember Belloc's (admittedly idiosyncratic) definition of capitalism: an economic *and political* system in which the means of production are controlled by a small subset of the population.

Belloc holds that well-divided property began to give way to capitalist oligarchy beginning in the sixteenth century. The most important event was the confiscation of monastic and other church lands by Henry VIII. In preindustrial England, as elsewhere, land was the chief source of wealth. The expropriation of the church by the crown—with the assent of Parliament, it should be noted—caused an enormous transfer of wealth. Belloc estimates that prior to the Reformation, the church owned outright roughly 30 percent of England's land and received another 30 percent of customary tenancy dues. This great economic power "lay until 1535 in the hands of cathedral chapters, communities of monks and nuns, educational establishments conducted by the clergy," and other religious organizations within the church.[23] But the crown did not long benefit from seizing this wealth. It soon relinquished most seized property to the great magnates of the realm. Some was sold to pay for wars; some was granted to court favorites or in exchange for services. The English gentry's large country estates date to this period: "*After* the Reformation there began to arise all over England those great 'country houses' which rapidly became the typical centers of English agricultural life."[24] It is essential to Belloc's argument that economic wealth is a source of

21 Belloc, *Servile State*, 82.

22 Belloc, *Servile State*, 82–83.

23 Belloc, *Servile State*, 90.

24 Belloc, *Servile State*, 93.

de facto political power. As such, the dire fiscal situation of the crown resulted in "a Crown at its wit's end for money, and dominated by subjects some of whom were its equals in wealth, and who could, especially through the action of Parliament (which they now controlled), do much of what they willed with government."[25] This is crucial for understanding the rise of aristocratic oligarchy in England, in which "a few wealthy families had got hold of the bulk of the means of production in England, while the same families exercised all local administrative power and were moreover the judges, the higher education, the church, and the generals."[26]

Belloc contends that England embraced capitalism before she embraced industrialism. New inventions such as the steam engine and flying shuttle, which typified the early Industrial Revolution, cannot explain England's transformation: "England, the seed plot of the industrial system, was *already* captured by a wealthy oligarchy *before* the series of great discoveries began."[27] Belloc recognizes that the new productive processes of the eighteenth century had to acquire financing, and because of the concentration of existing wealth in the hands of the aristocracy, the great magnates were an important source of capital. But it did not have to be this way: "There is no conceivable link in reason or experience which binds the capitalization of a new process with the idea of a few employing owners and a mass of unemployed nonowners working at a wage."[28] Had the concentration of wealth during the Reformation not destroyed well-divided property, small owners could have capitalized the new business concerns. Belloc appears to argue that the chief effects were distributional: industrialization would have proceeded with or without the rise of the great landed magnates, but the distribution of the new wealth could have been radically different, benefiting the many instead of just the few.

Instead, the result of industrialization was oligarchical political-economic control:

> That strong central government which should protect the community against the rapacity of a few had gone generations before. Capitalism triumphant wielded all the mechanism of legislation and of information too.

25 Belloc, *Servile State*, 94.

26 Belloc, *Servile State*, 95.

27 Belloc, *Servile State*, 100.

28 Belloc, *Servile State*, 101.

> It still holds them; and there is not an example of so-called social reform today which is not demonstrably . . . directed to the further entrenchment and confirmation of an industrial society in which it is taken for granted that a few shall own, that the vast majority shall live at a wage under them, and that all the bulk of Englishmen may hope for is the amelioration of their lot by regulations and control from above—*but not by property; not by freedom.*[29]

THE INSTABILITY OF INDUSTRIAL CAPITALISM

While the historical narrative is important in contextualizing Belloc's argument, it is not Belloc's substantive contribution. His main concern is demonstrating the fragility of industrial England's precarious equilibrium, characterized by heavily concentrated property alongside mass dispossession. "The capitalist state," Belloc argues, "is unstable, and indeed more properly a transitory phase lying between two permanent and stable states of society."[30] Because capitalism entails dispossessing the masses of property, "there will be under capitalism a conscious, direct, and planned *exploitation* of the majority (the [politically] free citizens who do not own) by the minority who are owners. . . . [T]he possessors can make such terms with the nonpossessors as shall make it certain that a portion of what the nonpossessors have produced shall go to the possessors."[31] This is an extraordinary claim, and one of obvious interest to students of economics.

Capitalism is unstable for two reasons. The first is the "moral strain" it places on society: "This moral strain comes from a contradiction between the realities of capitalist society and the moral base of our laws and traditions."[32] The laws and other institutions supporting property in freedom developed during a time when property was well distributed throughout society. The protection afforded by the English common law for property, both real and personal, stems from widespread access to productive resources. Economically, families with property could resist having terms dictated to them. Well-distributed property means credible alternatives to one-sided commercial deals. These property-supporting institutions were once a bulwark of liberty, but in the grip of industrial capitalism, they

29 Belloc, *Servile State*, 104, my emphasis.

30 Belloc, *Servile State*, 107.

31 Belloc, *Servile State*, 108.

32 Belloc, *Servile State*, 109.

inadvertently became means of perpetuating political and economic injustice. England's "legal machinery has become little more than an engine for protecting the few owners against the necessities, the demands, or the hatred of the mass of their dispossessed fellow citizens. The vast bulk of so-called free contracts are today leonine contracts: arrangements which one man was free to take or leave, but which the other man was not free to take or to leave, *because the second man had for his alternative starvation*."[33] Thus in Belloc's mind, coercion by economic necessity is no less real than coercion by an extortioner. In fact, the prevalence of the former is due to the machinations of the latter: "*Livelihood* is at the will of the possessors."[34] Belloc forcefully argues that "there is acute spiritual conflict, conflict in every man's conscience and ill-ease throughout the commonwealth when the realities of society are divorced from the moral base of its institutions."[35] Such a divorce characterized early twentieth-century England by means of a transformation of liberating distributed property to servile concentrated property.

The second source of capitalism's instability is that "capitalism destroys security. . . . Combine these two elements: the ownership of the means of production by a very few; the political freedom of owners and non-owners alike. There follows immediately from that combination a competitive market wherein the labor of the nonowner fetches just what it is worth, not as full productive power, but as productive power which will leave a surplus to the capitalists."[36] Belloc's subsequent charges are even more severe. He contends that insecurity increases as capitalism—concentration of property—becomes more acute: "If you left men completely free under a capitalist system, there would be so heavy a mortality from starvation as would dry up the sources of labor in a very short time . . . the fact [is] that the possessors have no direct incentive to keep men alive."[37] Thus capitalism, which Belloc regards as synonymous with a *lack* of economic freedom, is incompatible with political freedom.

Belloc also indicts capitalism for a "competitive anarchy of production,"[38] a rebuke that will be familiar to students of late nineteenth- and

33 Belloc, *Servile State*, 111.

34 Belloc, *Servile State*, 111.

35 Belloc, *Servile State*, 112.

36 Belloc, *Servile State*, 112–13.

37 Belloc, *Servile State*, 114–15.

38 Belloc, *Servile State*, 115.

early twentieth-century economic discourse. Belloc argues that the race among producers to extract "surplus value" from workers necessarily creates industrial chaos.[39] Instability and waste are inherent in production when both owners and nonowners are politically free—can supply work and products to the market, or not, as they see fit—but property is restricted to the former. To the extent that capitalism and political freedom conflict, one must give way to the other. Belloc argues that these tensions are slowly being resolved in favor of capitalism, to the detriment of political freedom: "If the full formula of capitalism were accepted by our courts and our executive statesmen, anyone could start a rival business, undersell those trusts and shatter the comparative security they afford to industry within their field. The reason that no one does this is that political freedom is not, as a fact, protected here by the courts in commercial affairs."[40] Belloc is clearly no fan of (monopolistic) capitalism, but neither has he any tolerance for England's oligopolistic halfway house.

RESOLVING THE TENSION: EITHER PROPERTY OR COLLECTIVISM

How can the contradictions of capitalism be resolved? Belloc contends there are only three stable equilibria: "slavery, socialism, and property. . . . To solve capitalism, you must get rid of restricted ownership, or of freedom, or of both."[41] The problem of capitalism is the concentration of the factors of production into few hands and the resultant proletarianization of the masses. Continued concentration of productive power can be resolved only by widely distributing property, or by eliminating property, vesting all productive capacity in the community as a whole. The former is Belloc's distributist state; the latter is a command economy operated by political agents, themselves empowered by the community. However, Belloc also argues that the socialist "solution" is a mirage. Any attempts to implement economic collectivism, operating through the political process, will instead result in increased economic oligarchy: "In the very act of attempting *collectivism*, what results is not collectivism at all, but the servitude of the many, and the confirmation in their present privilege of the

39 Belloc, *Servile State*, 116.

40 Belloc, *Servile State*, 117.

41 Belloc, *Servile State*, 122.

few; that is, the servile state."[42] Furthermore, the attempt of would-be social reformers to move in the direction of capitalism results in "some third thing which the collectivist never dreamt of, or the capitalist either; and that thing is the servile state."[43] Power, Belloc recognizes, has a logic of its own. When used on a society-wide scale, its results often differ from the intentions of those wielding it.

Belloc's final chapter argues that England has already started down the path toward the servile state. At the time, there were several proposals in which Belloc saw the potential for de facto servitude to acquire de jure public sanction. There are two signs of England's progression to servility: first, "the laws and proposals which subject the proletariat to servile conditions; next, the fact that the capitalist, so far from being expropriated by modern 'socialist' experiments, is being confirmed in his power."[44] One example is employer-liability laws. It may seem odd that Belloc worried about the attempt to hold employers responsible for workplace injuries, but the reason becomes clear when viewed in terms of a patron-client relationship. Belloc sees these legal changes as saying to workers, "'You are not a free man making a free contract with all its consequences. You are a worker, and therefore an inferior: you are an *employee*; and that *status* gives you a special position which would not be recognized in the other party to the contract.'"[45] In like measure, Belloc sees various social-welfare proposals, such as mandatory insurance and minimum wages, as inherently servile. Each of these proposals would further enshrine in law the distinction between the employer and employee classes. Legal categories would force patronship on capitalists and clientelism on proletarians, a situation bearing a troubling resemblance to ancient-world servility. Western society once advanced from status to contract; the spirit of these laws pushes it backwards.[46] The final measure is mandatory labor, which Belloc believes is required due to the predictable labor surplus that results from minimum wages. The combination of refusing workers, as a matter of law, the right to withdraw their labor, along with guaranteeing a minimum standard of living, is slavery by another name. That modern servile labor is attached to

42 Belloc, *Servile State*, 127.

43 Belloc, *Servile State*, 138.

44 Belloc, *Servile State*, 171.

45 Belloc, *Servile State*, 177.

46 Belloc, *Servile State*, 179–81.

a business corporation or the state, rather than a private person, does alter its essential servility. Neither a minimum wage nor a positive compulsion to labor had entered English law by the time Belloc wrote his book (September 1912), but Belloc is sure it is only a matter of time.[47]

BELLOC AS ECONOMIST? BELLOC AS PROPHET?

Belloc's analysis is unconventional and challenging. His thesis regarding the erosion of liberty in England is certainly original. Historians and social scientists typically regard postmedieval England as a successful experiment in political and economic freedom, characterized by liberties spreading from elites to ordinary people. Belloc thinks this freedom is a mirage, even though England's laws and institutions appear supportive of private property rights. What good is this protection to the mass of men in society, Belloc wonders, when they are prevented from owning property?

Belloc's analysis is not ironclad. In several places, it conflicts with basic economics. Some parts of his argument are simply incorrect. Belloc, normally a careful thinker, probably made these mistakes because of the assumptions he brings to his analysis. Those assumptions are not necessarily wrong, but they can lead to a rather peculiar interpretation of the facts, as well as an erroneous conception of the social sciences.

Belloc was an admirer of St. Thomas Aquinas, which implies a broadly Aristotelian metaphysical and ethical system. For Thomists, there is no fundamental difference between statements of *is* and statements of *ought*; both are descriptions of reality within a teleological framework that collapses the positive-normative distinction. Modern social scientists understandably chafe at this, but it is important to grapple with Belloc's arguments on his own terms, or else we risk ignoring claims that deserve a hearing. Thus, when Belloc describes a situation as exploitative—see above his remarks regarding capitalists expropriating the surplus value of labor—he is making a statement he regards as factual *and* ethical, because in his system, there is no essential difference between the two. This is how Belloc can write a positive treatise that frequently draws on a normative vocabulary.

47 Belloc, *Servile State*, 182, footnote. We may question Belloc's abilities as a prognosticator—the United Kingdom did not get a national minimum wage law until 1999 and never got anything like compulsory labor—but his analysis of the tendencies in England's political-economic system are interesting nonetheless.

Whether an economist agrees with this system or not, economic analysis can and should be independently applied to assess the robustness of Belloc's claims. The standard economic theory that explains what labor earns in the market (along with capital and land) is marginal productivity theory.[48] In brief, the factors of production receive the value they contribute to the production process. If workers were systematically overcompensated (paid more than the value they add), the firms employing them would forgo profits, which would put them at a disadvantage to their competitors. If workers were systematically undercompensated (paid less than the value they add to the production process), there is an opportunity for firms to hire workers at a slightly higher wage, depriving the underpaying firms of a source of profits and capturing those profits for themselves.

For the above process to work, markets must be competitive, which Belloc would challenge, as would many contemporary economists. There is a basis in price theory for analyzing the effects of imperfect competition on the allocation of resources. The classic work is Joan Robinson's *Economics of Imperfect Competition*, first published in 1933.[49] In output markets, monopolies and oligopolies behave in a manner that imposes costs on the rest of society. Because these firms have market power—the ability to charge prices above the marginal costs of production—their profit-maximizing strategy does not result in an efficient allocation of resources. One consequence is that part of the gains from trade that would accrue to consumers under competitive conditions instead become profits for the firm. Economists usually focus on the social costs of market power, meaning goods that ought to be produced (from an efficiency standpoint) but are not, because firms can only raise prices by restricting output. The transfer of consumers' gains from trade to producers is discussed less frequently, since it is a redistribution of wealth, rather than a destruction of wealth.[50] Belloc

48 Foundational works include John Bates Clark, *The Distribution of Wealth: A Theory of Wages, Interests, and Profits* (London: Macmillan, 1899) and Philip Henry Wicksteed, *The Common Sense of Political Economy* (London: Macmillan, 1910). Marginal-productivity theory is so widely accepted that almost all introductory economics textbooks use it to explain the distribution of income.

49 Joan Robinson, *The Economics of Imperfect Competition* (London: Macmillan, 1933).

50 For an accessible contemporary discussion, see N. Gregory Mankiw, *Principles of Microeconomics*, 9th ed. (Cengage Learning), https://www.cengage.com/c/principles-of-economics-9e-mankiw/9780357038314PF/. Mankiw's book is arguably the world's most successful introductory economics text. Throughout my book, when I make reference to statements that are generally acceptable by economists, readers unfamiliar with economics can refer to Mankiw for an overview.

and those informed by him would obviously be concerned with this transfer, and on ethical grounds, economists cannot object.

Another model pioneered by Robinson and discussed by contemporary economists is the monopsony model. Whereas a monopolist is the sole seller in an output market, a monopsonist is the sole buyer in an input market. The classic example is a labor market in which a single firm hires workers. (As an example, think of a "company town.") Monopsonist market power translates into systematically paying workers less than the value of their marginal product, that is, the value workers add to the production process. This is one way to think about Belloc's claims about labor-value extraction in a way that is intelligible to economists. The overlap is hardly perfect, since economists do not have within their framework anything suggesting workers "deserve" their full marginal value product, or that workers' contributions to production "belong" to them. Nevertheless, to the extent that monopsony power exists throughout the economy, there are price-theoretic arguments supporting the claim that workers are underemployed and undercompensated, compared to the baseline of competitive markets.

How relevant are monopoly and monopsony considerations to real-world markets? Is market power the exception or the rule? Many economists believe the competitive standard is a much lower bar to clear than initially supposed. What is needed is not a very large number of buyers and sellers, readily available information, low costs of contracting, etc., as economists sometimes assume. These features are *sufficient* for competitive markets but not *necessary*. All that is needed for competition is rivalry: Entry by other firms, and even the mere threat of entry by other firms, is enough to discipline existing firms and force them to behave competitively.[51] Contemporary economists disagree over which characterization is most accurate.

What, then, are we to make of Belloc's contention regarding extraction of surplus value? It cannot be dismissed as a mere moral protest, since Belloc clearly stated in his introduction that he was providing a factual account of how capitalist economies operate. Whatever the ethical value of Belloc's position, the claim that capitalists exploit workers through capturing the surplus value of labor—in fact, the very concept of surplus value—is, considered scientifically, uncertain. Perhaps firms can pay workers less than their value added in the short run, but in the long run it is much harder.

51 William J. Baumol, "Contestable Markets: An Uprising in the Theory of Industry Structure," *American Economic Review* 72, no. 1 (1982): 1–15.

Those firms would likely be disciplined by the market process, absent barriers to entry that keep prospective competitors out of the market. As an economist would say, systematic worker undercompensation is "not an equilibrium." If a greedy capitalist tried to exploit his workers in this way, there are plenty of other greedy capitalists waiting in the wings who would be more than happy to profit from this mistake. Belloc would undoubtedly reply that there *are* barriers to entry, even in the long run. For example, legal barriers to entry created by an alliance between political and capitalist elites artificially concentrate markets.[52] And economic barriers to entry result from concentration of property and highly imperfect capital markets, which make it more difficult to finance a small, independent business.[53]

Other claims by Belloc are weaker. His analysis of bargaining between labor and capital has several problems. Belloc seems to regard such bargaining as a bilateral monopoly, as in the case of a monopsonist confronting a labor union, with the lion's share of the power held by the firm. Certainly, there are some scenarios where this is plausible, such as the factory towns of old. But even in this case, we cannot neglect broader market effects. Workers are usually drawn from a wide supply of labor, and businesses from a wide demand for labor. There is surely some substitutability of workers across lines of production, which makes Belloc's take-it-or-leave-it analysis of weak workers and strong employers incorrect. While there is nothing wrong with bargaining models in specific employment contexts, by itself, this does not mean one party can dictate terms to the other.[54] Neither employers nor employees are immune to reprisal. The existence of feasible alternatives makes strong-arm tactics impractical for either party.

We must also realize Belloc's chief predictions did not come to pass. He would probably not be surprised that the welfare state in England, and in all advanced Western democracies, has expanded since he wrote *The Servile State*. Yet his boldest prediction never materialized: compulsory labor. Furthermore, while almost all Western countries have minimum wage laws

52 George Stigler, "The Theory of Economic Regulation," *Bell Journal of Economics and Management Science* 2, no. 1 (1971): 3–21.

53 Joseph E. Stiglitz and Andrew Weiss, "Credit Rationing in Markets with Imperfect Information," *American Economic Review* 71, no. 3 (1981): 393–410.

54 See, for example, the firm–labor union bargaining model in chapter 2 of Robert Gibbons, *Game Theory for Applied Economists* (Princeton, N.J.: Princeton University Press, 1992). Even in the pure bargaining context, the constraints on both the firm and the labor union prevent either party from "imposing their will" on the other.

(though not necessarily at the national level), average wages in these countries are high enough that the minimum wage is not an economically relevant constraint for most of the labor force. Whether or not compulsory labor is even thinkable in liberal democracies, economically there is simply no need for it. Labor-market restrictions, including redistributive policies, that lower the labor force participation rate and reduce the number of desired working hours for those in the labor force, do not create large enough distortions to necessitate the extreme remedies Belloc anticipated. Economic growth in the twentieth century did not stall, and despite popular fears to the contrary, its gains did not solely accrue to "the one percent."

Do these errors relegate Belloc to the "dustbin of history," of interest only to historians of early twentieth-century economic thought? By no means. Belloc's claims about competition and labor extraction are at least debatable. And although Belloc made several other mistakes, they somehow coalesced into an important contribution, as sometimes happens in economics, politics, and philosophy. The most worthwhile reading of Belloc's book is not as an economics treatise. Instead, it is most fruitfully interpreted as a study of the *economic and political prerequisites* of free societies. While Belloc is wrong to dismiss the concept of economic law, meaning the intelligible and predictable processes by which goods and services are produced and distributed, he is correct that the economy is not an autonomous sphere of human conduct that proceeds without recourse to other realms of human action.[55] All commercial systems have noncommercial underpinnings; the rules regarding property ownership, for example, do not have their source in market activity. Markets are institutionally dependent. If we change the underlying rules we can, to a degree, change how markets work.[56] Furthermore, social causality operates in both directions. Political processes set the default conditions for economic processes, and the functioning of economic processes frequently has political implications. Capitalism, as Belloc describes it, *is* a political system just as much as an economic system, and many great industrial concerns did interfere in England's politics to rig the

55 The laws of economics do not deny human creativity or agency. Economic law has plenty of room for institutionally and historically contingent human behavior. The emphasis is on the formal properties of human action under conditions of scarcity at the individual level and the durable patterns of social organization at the societal level. See Peter J. Boettke, *Living Economics: Yesterday, Today, and Tomorrow* (Oakland, Calif.: Independent Institute, 2012).

56 Douglass C. North, *Understanding the Process of Economic Change* (Cambridge: Cambridge University Press, 1999).

rules in their favor, as large firms often do today. It is worth listening to Belloc if only to foster the creative imagination required to consider whether there are viable alternatives to politicized capitalism, which unfortunately seems to be the default situation in actually existing market economies.[57]

Belloc's distributive state, characterized by widespread property ownership, is an idealized social order in which ordinary individuals can resist encroachment on their liberties. Belloc posits a self-enforcing feedback loop between economic freedom and political freedom. Economic freedom means saying no to bad deals, made possible because individuals own sufficient property to support themselves. Its negative component depends on its positive component. Likewise, the negative component of political freedom, the right to withhold one's services and property, depends on its positive component, the right *to* that which one has a claim, established in law and precedent. English institutions, such as the common law, were liberty-affirming because they evolved when individuals enjoyed de facto economic and political freedom. De jure recognition of freedom rested upon, and reinforced, this prior de facto freedom. A society in which the blessings of liberty are widespread will create liberty-respecting formal institutions. Laws will be general, predictable, and nondiscriminatory.[58] These are the essential conditions for the *rule of law*, which is a society's best guarantee of its freedoms.

In contrast, a society where most individuals lack property is unlikely to remain free over time. If I own nothing except my labor, then I am less inclined to preserve institutions that protect general conditions of ownership. Those without property have neither the ability nor the incentive to check encroachments by those with much property. Especially worrisome are the efforts to transform law from a preserver of general interests into an instrument for advancing class-specific interests. This is true even if the material welfare of propertyless laborers improves over time. In terms of consumption, workers in the West are better off than ever. Centuries of economic growth, which was the norm even in the tumultuous twentieth century, created living standards for ordinary individuals that were scarcely imaginable by Belloc and his contemporaries. And yet, this process has

57 Randall G. Holcombe, *Political Capitalism: How Economic and Political Power Is Made and Maintained* (Cambridge: Cambridge University Press, 2018).

58 James M. Buchanan and Roger Congleton, *Politics by Principle, Not Interest: Towards Nondiscriminatory Democracy* (Cambridge: Cambridge University Press, 1998); F. A. Hayek, *The Constitution of Liberty* (Chicago: University of Chicago Press, 1960).

curiously coincided with a massive growth in the size and scope of the state. Government, frequently at the behest of special interests, interferes more and more in our daily lives, and appropriates for itself a larger and larger share of national income. Furthermore, most citizens have almost no control over what happens in their nations' seats of power. Despite free and fair elections with universal suffrage, public policy is increasingly designed and implemented in those organs of government most insulated from popular oversight. Self-government has been in almost continual retreat since Belloc wrote *The Servile State*; managerial-administrative government has taken its place.

Belloc guessed wrong about the form servitude would take, but there is a kind of servitude in the West nonetheless. Living conditions are impressive and are growing more so each year. But perhaps this material prosperity was purchased on crooked terms. After all, the feedback loop between economic and political freedom can work both ways. We may be losing political freedom because we first lost economic freedom. Attempts to address the former without also addressing the latter are akin to bailing out a sinking ship. A society of free and responsible individuals, Belloc argues, first requires individuals within that society to have a tangible stake in preserving it. High wages are not enough. Free societies are composed of citizens, not subjects. The difference is that citizens' worldviews are shaped by the cares and responsibilities of ownership, for which high income per capita is no substitute.

If addressing a deficit of political freedom requires simultaneously addressing a deficit of economic freedom, how should we proceed? Fortunately, Belloc offered some guidance in a subsequent essay, which has some of the ideas we seek. Although it, too, contains several economic errors, its basic message deserves our consideration.

Chapter 4

Belloc's *An Essay on the Restoration of Property*

In the decades after the publication of *The Servile State*, Hilaire Belloc continued to write about the problems of capitalism and the potential distributist solution. *An Essay on the Restoration of Property* is the most important of these writings. Despite its brevity—the 2002 IHS Press edition consists of an eighty-five-page essay plus a four-page preface, not counting introductory material written by others—it is packed with insight. Although Belloc focuses on the possibilities of widely distributing property in England, he also engages in serious conceptual analysis to uncover the fault lines in industrial capitalism. *Essay* is both more imaginative and ambitious than *The Servile State*. Whereas the earlier work often reads like an extended logical proof, the latter feels much more like a treatise at the intersection of politics, philosophy, and economics. Refreshingly, Belloc does not shy away from normative territory in *Essay*, which forces him to distinguish more clearly between description and prescription. This has the fortuitous side effect of making his positive claims more accurate and his normative claims more sympathetic.

Belloc acknowledges in the preface that his presentation is skewed toward the benefits of widely distributed property and does not fully address many of its drawbacks. To his credit, he admits there are problems with a distributist social order. Its members may be "conservative and timid, probably more ignorant, than an economic oligarchy. . . . In Foreign Affairs it is less likely to judge wisely and act rapidly. It may well be suspicious of new inventions and clumsy and recalcitrant at adapting itself to the use of new instruments."[1] But Belloc does not let this dissuade him. He strongly believes there are economic and moral benefits to a distributist state, which he will forcefully defend.

Belloc also wants his readers to understand that his goal is not a society of equalized purchasing power. He would be unimpressed by contemporary

1 Hilaire Belloc, *An Essay on the Restoration of Property* (Norfolk, Va.: IHS Press, [1936] 2009), xxiv.

hang-wringing over income inequality. "The object of those who think as I do in this matter," says Belloc, "is not to restore purchasing power but to restore economic freedom. It is true that there cannot be economic freedom without purchasing power and it is true that economic freedom varies in some degree directly with purchasing power; but it is not true that purchasing power is equivalent to economic freedom."[2] In Belloc's scheme, a wage employee does not possess economic freedom, regardless of how high his wage is. Freedom requires ownership; property provides the security upon which freedom rests.

The best preparation for this essay comes not from Belloc's introductory remarks, however, but from the introduction by the directors of IHS Press. Belloc's faith informs his political economy: "As an integral Catholic, Belloc followed in the footsteps of St. Thomas the *realist*, who spoke of Politics as the moral science 'which considers the proper ordering of men,' and Political Economy as that science 'concerned with the using of money . . . for the good estate of the home.'"[3] For a contemporary economist, this perspective makes reading Belloc simultaneously frustrating and exhilarating.

PROPERTY, WEALTH, AND FREEDOM

As in *The Servile State*, Belloc begins his *Essay* with definitions. Again, we see uncontroversial definitions of concepts such as production and wealth, but we also see bolder statements, as well as ones unique to distributism. A crucial part of Belloc's argument appears quite early: "It is obvious that whoever controls the means of production controls the supply of wealth. If, therefore, the means for the production of that wealth which a family needs are in the control of others than the family, *the family will be dependent upon those others; it will not be economically free*."[4] This echoes a key theme from *The Servile State*: a more expansive definition of economic freedom than that favored by social scientists, rooted in Catholicism's teachings regarding the rights of participation and duties of solidarity.

Belloc more readily admits the limits to economic freedom in *Essay* than in *The Servile State*. He acknowledges that families cannot be completely economically independent, because an extensive division of labor is both socially inevitable and desirable. In the interests of the common good, therefore, too much power to impede the division of labor ought not be

2 Belloc, *An Essay on the Restoration of Property*, xxiv–xxv.

3 Belloc, *An Essay on the Restoration of Property*, xii.

4 Belloc, *An Essay on the Restoration of Property*, 2, my emphasis.

conceded to the state. Families need the ability to check the state's potentially predatory behavior, just as the state needs the ability to check families' potentially antisocial behavior: "The family must have not only power to complain against arbitrary control external to it, but power to make its complaint effective."[5] Unsurprisingly, Belloc locates this check in the institution of private property, provided it is well-distributed throughout society. Freedom, both political and economic, requires widely dispersed property.[6]

Belloc treats the above primarily as a positive claim: Men will not remain economically or politically free unless many families own productive property. It has an associated ethical dimension—private property is conducive to human flourishing and the common good—but Belloc readily admits that men may dislike the attendant responsibilities of property ownership. Whatever one's ethical judgment, however, it remains true that widely dispersed property and freedom go hand-in-hand.

Belloc denies most English families are free in any meaningful sense, despite England's apparent commitments to property rights and the rule of law. As in *The Servile State*, the culprit behind the theft of freedom for the masses is capitalism, by which Belloc means "a state of society in which a minority control the means of production, leaving the mass of citizens dispossessed. Such a dispossessed body of citizens is called a 'proletariat.'"[7] Capitalism causes insecurity and insufficiency for the masses. Belloc notes that alternative social systems *not* commensurate with well-dispersed property can alleviate these problems, but they do so without restoring genuine economic freedom. The first alternative is the servile state, which we have already explored at length. The second is communism, or the command economy. For those who value economic freedom, neither of these will do: "If, then, we regard economic freedom as a good, our object must be to restore property. We must seek political and economic reforms which shall tend to distribute property more and more widely until the owners of sufficient Means of Production (land or capital or both) are numerous enough to determine the character of society."[8]

At this point, Belloc ventures into moral territory. He realizes that well-distributed property cannot persist in a society that does not value freedom.

5 Belloc, *An Essay on the Restoration of Property*, 3.

6 Belloc, *An Essay on the Restoration of Property*, 4.

7 Belloc, *An Essay on the Restoration of Property*, 5.

8 Belloc, *An Essay on the Restoration of Property*, 6.

Belloc vigorously defends the goodness of economic freedom because it comports to human nature. Economic freedom respects free will, as well as diversity of talents and personalities that fosters individuality and channels them towards the common good: "In the absence of economic freedom there must weigh upon any human society a dead and mechanical uniformity, increasingly leaden, and heavy and stifling, in proportion to the absence of freedom."[9] Belloc rejects the claims that man will have genuine economic freedom under command economies, and that economic freedom is a lesser good than economic abundance. There are major problems with widespread public property: "No man feels of public property that it is his own; no man will treat it with the care or affection of a thing that is his own; still less can a man express himself through the use of a thing which is not his own, but shared in common with a mass of other men."[10] As for the possible tension between economic freedom and economic abundance, Belloc argues that "it would still be worthwhile for those of our temper to sacrifice some portion of the material good, and even more worthwhile to permit inequality in distribution, for the sake of economic freedom."[11] Thus, Belloc (indirectly) opposes top-down schemes of economic leveling merely for the sake of outcome equality.

There is another difficulty with redistributive schemes in Belloc's mind. The root problem in England is not dispossession; rather, it is that Englishmen have lost the appetite for freedom. Belloc knows that, by itself, redistributing property will not inaugurate a distributive state: "Of its nature property is the product of human desire; we can help on that desire to achieve its fulfilment, but we cannot create it. *We cannot make owners by merely giving men something to own*."[12] In other words, we cannot neglect the moral and spiritual aspects of ownership. A society of owners means a society of those who *think and act* like owners. Thus, while some state action will be needed to implement and maintain the distributive state—Belloc supports laws that prevent excessive concentrations of property—it will not be enough to rely on enlightened public policy.[13] State support of distributism is necessary but not sufficient.

9 Belloc, *An Essay on the Restoration of Property*, 7.

10 Belloc, *An Essay on the Restoration of Property*, 8.

11 Belloc, *An Essay on the Restoration of Property*, 9.

12 Belloc, *An Essay on the Restoration of Property*, 14–15, my emphasis.

13 Belloc, *An Essay on the Restoration of Property*, 14.

CAPITALISM AND THE DETERMINANTS OF "BIGNESS"

Belloc recognizes that distributists have their work cut out for them. Attempts "to restore the institution of property . . . can only be successful through a deliberate reversal of natural economic tendencies."[14] Prodistributist policy is necessary because widely dispersed property runs against the trends of contemporary economic forces, which heavily favor centralization. Distributists cannot limit themselves to wishful thinking or avoid questions of how well-distributed property can be instituted and maintained by law: "Well-divided property will not spring up of itself in Capitalist society. It must be artificially fostered."[15]

After dispensing with the claims that industrial capitalism is inherent either in the institution of private property itself, or in the nature of industrial machinery,[16] Belloc explores several ways early twentieth-century England selects for concentrated property. He lists seven for special consideration. The first is the increasing prevalence of high fixed costs in modern production methods. The second is the advantage large organizations have in purchasing inputs and acquiring production-relevant information. The third is the advantage large organizations have in securing credit. The fourth is the ability of large firms to practice what economists call "predatory pricing," that is, deliberately pricing below cost to drive competitors out of the market, which can then be monopolized. The fifth is the savings trap, whereby small families and their economic enterprises have a difficult time accumulating capital because their incomes are too low for adequate saving. The sixth is that capitalists will use their wealth to rig the legislative process to favor them over their smaller competitors, who cannot afford to have MPs in their pocket. The seventh and final one is another form of political rigging, but in the judiciary rather than the legislature.[17]

While Belloc admits that fighting these forces is an uphill battle, he refuses to concede the task is hopeless. He knows that economic conditions are institutionally contingent. With different legal institutions, ones supporting well-distributed property, the seven factors he outlined could be

14 Belloc, *An Essay on the Restoration of Property*, 16, emphasis removed for readability.

15 Belloc, *An Essay on the Restoration of Property*, 17.

16 Belloc, *An Essay on the Restoration of Property*, 16–18. Readers of *The Servile State*, as well as the last chapter, will already be familiar with these arguments, so there is no need to repeat them here.

17 Belloc, *An Essay on the Restoration of Property*, 20–22.

checked, and even reversed. It is true that existing commercial institutions "must ultimately produce the rule of ownership by a few," but it is *not* true that societies are helpless before the concentrating forces of industrial capitalism. Man "has always felt this to be a danger, and has instinctively safeguarded itself against that danger by the setting up of institutions for the protection of small property, and that these institutions have never been broken down of themselves, *but always and only under the conscious action of a deliberately hostile act*."[18]

SMALL RETAILERS AND CRAFTSMEN

Now Belloc turns to the difficult problem of how to restore property. Citizens' fundamental attitudes, not merely a few policies, must change: "The profound, ultimate root of the whole affair is a certain mood—an attitude of mind. Where you have a public opinion supporting well-divided property, a state of society that takes well-divided property for granted and therefore a philosophy consonant with well-divided property, institutions or customs conservative of property will arise of their own accord."[19] To get and keep property in the hands of the masses, distributists must cultivate a philosophy of ownership and build a practical political movement, but changing worldviews is very difficult and time consuming. Policy changes must be more modest in their aims but have the advantage quick operability. Thus, the actions of distributist philosophers and distributist statesmen go hand-in-hand.

Belloc divides the problem into three parts: "(a) the restoration of the small cultivator, distributor, and craftsman . . . (b) the division of property in enterprises necessarily large, among many holders in sufficient amount; (c) the confirming of such wholesome division by institutions which shall maintain it and prevent a recurrent degradation of property into capitalism."[20] We should pay careful attention to Belloc's view of the state. At times, Belloc can read like an uncompromising libertarian; at others, a dedicated communitarian. Actually, he is both, depending on the circumstances—or rather he is neither, rejecting these ideological labels in favor of a Catholic approach to social philosophy. The state can be both oppressor and liberator. For Belloc, what matters most is what government does, not what it is: "An

18 Belloc, *An Essay on the Restoration of Property*, 20, my emphasis.

19 Belloc, *An Essay on the Restoration of Property*, 31–32.

20 Belloc, *An Essay on the Restoration of Property*, 34.

action by the State is one thing when it is used to free mankind and to give the citizens economic independence, and exactly the opposite thing when it is used to take that independence away."[21] The state (or as Belloc wistfully reminisces, the king) upholds the common good when it acts as a balance among the various classes and forces in society, especially when it upholds the claims of the small against the great.

The goals of a distributist political program are simple: "We propose to re-establish the peasant, the craftsman, and the small (and secure) retail tradesman."[22] Belloc relegates the peasantry (due to this word's negative connotations, modern readers would be better to think of this as "free yeomanry") to a future chapter. As for the problem of small distributors, Belloc proposes three kinds of graduated taxes on "bigness": "(1) against chain stores; (2) against multiple shops; (3) against large retail turnover."[23]

Belloc dislikes chain shops because they bankrupt small distributors and have too much power when negotiating with producers. A "system of chain shops acting as fishmongers," he contends, is "in a position to dictate prices to the people who send the fish inland from the ports, and to control in great measure the nature and direction of the fisheries."[24] This is in addition to the damage it causes by destroying the economic independence of smaller fishmongers.

As for multiple shops, Belloc recommends the tax to be directly proportional to the "number of categories with which it deals."[25] The quintessential example is a department store. To his credit, Belloc recognizes that deciding what constitutes a "category" is a matter of judgment, and that taxing categories will necessarily extend the state bureaucracy, which itself can stifle independence. He considers this an acceptable risk in exchange for reducing the concentration of property in society.[26] He also recommends a series of licenses for operating certain businesses: "Let there be a licence for carrying on a grocery and fishmongering business; let the license be granted as a matter of right to any applicant; let its cost be insignificant to the man who applies for only one or two licences, but then let it

21 Belloc, *An Essay on the Restoration of Property*, 35.

22 Belloc, *An Essay on the Restoration of Property*, 35.

23 Belloc, *An Essay on the Restoration of Property*, 36.

24 Belloc, *An Essay on the Restoration of Property*, 36–37.

25 Belloc, *An Essay on the Restoration of Property*, 37.

26 Belloc, *An Essay on the Restoration of Property*, 37.

begin to rise more and more steeply as the number of licences applied for increases."[27]

The final proposal, the tax on turnover, is simple enough to sum up in one sentence: "Let there be no tax on turnover up to a certain sufficiently high level, then let it begin and grow steeply until it becomes prohibitive."[28]

Differential taxation disincentivizes concentrations of property. It also generates government revenue, with which it can support distributist efforts.[29] What ought to be done with these resources? Belloc links this to the problem of restoring small artisans, for which he recommends "the re-erection of a small number of craftsman *protected by a charter and guild*."[30] As we will see further, Belloc is a great fan of the guild system. This puts him at odds with many contemporary economists and economic historians. Belloc affirms the necessity of "subsidizing and protecting of the small artisan at the expense of Big Business"[31] along with legal recognition and protection of guilds.

Belloc closes this chapter with an incredibly important statement. In fact, as I will argue later, this statement captures the essence of the distributist project. The above-discussed "enforceable laws and actual institutions which shall artificially advantage the small distributor against the great, and the small craftsman or small user of machinery against the large manufacturer" are, Belloc readily admits, "'uneconomic.' In other words, it will cost effort. . . . A well-made piece of furniture, neither repulsive nor mechanical in design, will cost more than a piece turned out by mass production. *But you are buying something for society at that price, and it is something well worth society's while. . . . That 'something' is citizenship, and the escape from slavery*."[32] This is Belloc at his most economistic, meaning means-ends consistent. He knows his proposals will diminish what we now call economic efficiency, but this does not trouble him. His goals are loftier.

Restoring small property by taxing bigness and subsidizing smallness might work for some industries, but what do we do about industries with

27 Belloc, *An Essay on the Restoration of Property*, 38.

28 Belloc, *An Essay on the Restoration of Property*, 38.

29 However, there is a trade-off here Belloc does not discuss. The more taxes thwart concentrated property, the less revenue the state gets; the more revenue the state gets, the less the taxes have thwarted concentration. Navigating this tradeoff means deciding the relative importance of the two goals.

30 Belloc, *An Essay on the Restoration of Property*, 40.

31 Belloc, *An Essay on the Restoration of Property*, 41.

32 Belloc, *An Essay on the Restoration of Property*, 41, my emphasis.

inherently large-scale production methods? Belloc believed that "Vast areas of modern production and exchange will necessarily concern great units and great units alone. How shall these be dealt with? How shall well-divided property re-arise in those fields of economic effort where the small unit can in the nature of modern things have no place?"[33]

WRESTLING WITH AMALGAMATION

Belloc next considers distributist proposals for production processes that "cannot of their nature be worked 'severally.'"[34] This phenomenon, which Belloc refers to as amalgamation, has two causes. The first is "*from the nature of the instrument used* . . . the classical example is the railway system."[35] The second is "because the elimination of competitive costs, and even the greater perfection of methods accompanying amalgamation, tend to produce such great units."[36] The latter is artificial and hence susceptible to policy changes. Amalgamation is not a law of economics, except in the trivial sense that certain results are the predictable consequences of specific institutions. Change the "rules of the game," and you can get very different outcomes.[37]

In the first case, "where the large unit is inevitable, we must have control either for the purpose of creating well-distributed property in the shares thereof, or for the purpose of managing the use of it as a communal concern."[38] In the second case, where the problem is "not due to the nature of the instrument but to unchecked competition . . . we must penalize amalgamation and support division of units."[39] Belloc again recommends differential taxation. In either case, wherever the unit of production is amenable to separately ownable shares, the goal should be "creating the largest possible number of shareholders and at preventing the growth of large blocs of shares under one control."[40]

The reader may be surprised Belloc recommends communal (state) ownership for certain production processes. To be clear, Belloc understands

33 Belloc, *An Essay on the Restoration of Property*, 42.

34 Belloc, *An Essay on the Restoration of Property*, 43.

35 Belloc, *An Essay on the Restoration of Property*, 43.

36 Belloc, *An Essay on the Restoration of Property*, 44.

37 Belloc, *An Essay on the Restoration of Property*, 45.

38 Belloc, *An Essay on the Restoration of Property*, 46.

39 Belloc, *An Essay on the Restoration of Property*, 46.

40 Belloc, *An Essay on the Restoration of Property*, 46.

the difficulties and risks associated with this. He grants that "ownership by the State is better avoided wherever possible,"[41] but then immediately afterwards contends that "State ownership is better . . . than ownership by a few rich individuals, or even the ownership by many small shareholders who are at the mercy of a few rich ones."[42] State ownership always runs the risk of "inefficiency and corruption." Better than state ownership, therefore, is "State *protection* by charter for the purpose of preventing irresponsible monopoly."[43]

As for graduated taxation, its goal is not solely penalizing bigness; it should also promote "setting up of smaller units held in shares and controlled by Guild or company monopoly."[44] Belloc suggests taxes to prevent the rise of large blocs of shareholders who can muscle out smaller shareholders, to limit how many shares can be owned by any individual, and to implement a capital tax on industrial (nonagricultural) shares. Importantly, capital taxes must take the place of income taxes, or else large holdings will still have an advantage.[45]

The biggest obstacle to any of these proposals is capitalist-financed political opposition: "The forces against even the partial success of such an attempt are ubiquitous and highly organized."[46] But the stakes are too high to surrender: "Either we restore property or we restore slavery, to which we have already gone more than halfway in our industrial society."[47] Even if England musters the political will, Belloc is concerned that capitalist domination has already eliminated a viable foundation for economic freedom. "True and full economic freedom is only present when a man himself possesses and himself uses the instruments of his craft."[48] Widely distributing ownership shares, rather than the factors of production themselves, seems a poor substitute. "But a policy of emancipation must deal with things as they are."[49] A small craftsman who also possesses some wealth in public

41 Belloc, *An Essay on the Restoration of Property*, 48.

42 Belloc, *An Essay on the Restoration of Property*, 48.

43 Belloc, *An Essay on the Restoration of Property*, 48.

44 Belloc, *An Essay on the Restoration of Property*, 51.

45 Belloc, *An Essay on the Restoration of Property*, 51.

46 Belloc, *An Essay on the Restoration of Property*, 54.

47 Belloc, *An Essay on the Restoration of Property*, 54.

48 Belloc, *An Essay on the Restoration of Property*, 55.

49 Belloc, *An Essay on the Restoration of Property*, 55.

bonds and distributed industrial shares is more independent than he would be otherwise. Thus, while Belloc cares most about productive property, circumstances compel him to also address pecuniary wealth.

In passing, Belloc also responds to the counterargument that breaking up big businesses imposes economic costs on society. Once again, he shows he cares little for cheap consumer goods. Instead, his object is liberty: "Production and distribution may be rendered somewhat cheaper" by leaving things as they are, and "the work may even be somewhat more efficiently done, *but the price you have to pay in the loss of freedom is a great deal too high*."[50]

LAND AND ECONOMIC FREEDOM

Now Belloc addresses the restoration of property in land, which he regards as the foundation for distributist political economy. Although Belloc previously argued that pecuniary security was preferable to pecuniary insecurity, he regards this as a poor substitute for security in property itself. "When men have become wage slaves," Belloc asserts, "they think in terms of income. When they are economically free they think in terms of property."[51] This is a difference in worldview that is essential to Belloc's thesis, and as I will argue further, the chief reason why we ought to take him seriously. For proletarians, property is valuable only because it can produce income for consumption. For free (propertied) men, income cannot provide security *unless it results from securely held property*. Historically, the most important form of securely held property was land. which explains Belloc's belief that well-distributed land is key to well-distributed property in general.

Medieval Europe is Belloc's ideal type for a society with widely distributed land. The themes in this section of his essay will be familiar to readers of *The Servile State*. Belloc reasserts the de facto security of medieval serfs, who could not be evicted from their land so long as they performed their customary duties. The rise of the free peasantry during the Middle Ages is an even better example in Belloc's mind, one worthy of serving as a model for a property-owning society. The decline of well-distributed property began with the confiscation of church property by the crown and the eventual passing of this property to the realm's great magnates. Belloc also discusses the Statute of Frauds, passed by Parliament during the reign of Charles II. Among other things, this statute mandated that property holdings could not be considered

50 Belloc, *An Essay on the Restoration of Property*, 50, my emphasis.

51 Belloc, *An Essay on the Restoration of Property*, 56.

valid unless they were formally specified. Many holdings in England were customary, however, having no formal title. Thus, an important step in the formalization and modernization of property rights, in Belloc's mind, was actually a means of expropriation of the small by the great.[52]

Belloc's program for land restoration rests on two distinctions: the first between urban and rural (agricultural) land, and the second between land occupied by its owners and land occupied by tenants. His recommendation for the latter is simple: "There must be a radical difference in the burdens imposed upon land occupied, as land (according to our view) should be occupied, by a human family living thereon, and land occupied by others from whom the owner draws tribute."[53] The motivation for this is the restoration of "the simple principle that a man living under his own roof, and on his own land, shall have the advantage over a man who uses his property only to exploit others."[54] His recommendation for the rural-urban distinction is more nuanced, in part because it is often difficult to ascertain under which category a given piece of land falls. Belloc concludes the best way forward is the regular registration and inspection of land and, in doubtful cases, classifying a piece of land as rural.[55] This matters because in Belloc's program, urban leases must include a provision permitting tenants to purchase the land by installment. Leases that do not include this provision will be declared null and void.[56]

While the restoration of land is crucially important, Belloc is ambivalent about its possibilities. Freedom must be widely desired before it can be restored, and Belloc worries that you simply "cannot make a peasant direct out of a townsman."[57] Most would rather have comfortable insecurity than rugged security: "The land will supply under well divided property no more than a modest sustenance under normal conditions. The man with a small freehold which he cultivates himself with the aid of his family must not expect to be better off and usually will not be so well off, reckoning in cash values, as the wage slave of a corresponding station in society."[58]

52 Belloc, *An Essay on the Restoration of Property*, 57.

53 Belloc, *An Essay on the Restoration of Property*, 59.

54 Belloc, *An Essay on the Restoration of Property*, 59.

55 Belloc, *An Essay on the Restoration of Property*, 59.

56 Belloc, *An Essay on the Restoration of Property*, 60.

57 Belloc, *An Essay on the Restoration of Property*, 60.

58 Belloc, *An Essay on the Restoration of Property*, 61.

Assuming the will can be mustered, what political means should be used? An important principle is the "burden laid upon the land of the small owner must be light, the tribute he has to pay—wherein I include usury in all its forms—must be a minimum."[59] It follows that "everything should be done by artifice of law to make it easy for the smaller man to buy land from the richer man, and difficult for the larger man to buy land from the smaller man."[60] This includes Belloc's familiar standby, the differential tax. Ultimately, "any such attempt to re-erect a peasantry in a society where the idea of peasantry has almost disappeared must be based upon subsidy, that is, upon gift. . . . It *must* begin as a social luxury and, while it remains in that initial 'luxury' state, it must like all luxuries be extravagantly paid for."[61]

While Belloc has much to say about the revival of a free peasantry, he is uninterested in legislating for this new (old?) class. This is unsurprising given Belloc's views on freedom and self-governance: "A free peasantry once established will see to itself. Make it unfree by too close a supervision from any form of bureaucracy, and the moral motive power will be maimed."[62] State power should only be the spark that lights the fire. Afterwards it can and must burn of itself; otherwise, there is no point to restoring widely distributed land.

TAXATION

Belloc recommends differential taxation several times as a remedy for the excessive concentration of property. He is not fond of high taxation in general, however: "High taxation is incompatible with the general institution of property."[63] Taxation is excessive whenever it significantly impinges on the productive choices of households, but he acknowledges such choices are a continuum, and that it is likely impossible to specify ex ante when taxation becomes "high." This does not bother him, however, because he "knows it when he sees it."[64]

59 Belloc, *An Essay on the Restoration of Property*, 63. Due to Belloc's conception of ownership, he regards many modern financial instruments used to purchase land as illegitimate. For example, a mortgage holder is not a true owner, whatever the property registers may say. De facto, the land is owned and controlled by large financiers.

60 Belloc, *An Essay on the Restoration of Property*, 64.

61 Belloc, *An Essay on the Restoration of Property*, 65.

62 Belloc, *An Essay on the Restoration of Property*, 64.

63 Belloc, *An Essay on the Restoration of Property*, 66.

64 Belloc, *An Essay on the Restoration of Property*, 66–67.

Intriguingly, Belloc thinks that well-distributed property is itself a defense against excessive taxation. The reason is simple: small property holders will resist high taxation more strongly, because you "can take away, annually, half the income of a very rich man and yet leave him very rich, but if you take away half that of a small man you ruin him."[65] This claim resembles economists' arguments about the marginal utility of income and tax rates. Because the marginal unit of purchasing power is allocated towards higher-valued uses for those with less purchasing power, it makes intuitive sense that they would resist attempts to confiscate this purchasing power more strongly, ceteris paribus.[66]

Hence Belloc is confident in the "general principle that high taxation can be levied with more success in proportion as property is ill-distributed; high taxation is incompatible with a wide and equitable distribution of ownership."[67] By implication, it will be quite difficult to restore property when taxes are already high. It follows that tax policy ought to be restructured away from revenue considerations alone, instead serving as an instrument to promote and defend well-distributed property. Belloc adds that there are several related institutions and policies that must prevail to restore property: economic security, sound money (preferably commodity-based), the dismantling of the administrative-managerial state, and legal protections for the small against the great. All of these are complements to moderate taxation, not substitutes for it.[68]

Belloc dislikes taxation as a means of equalizing economic outcomes. He recognizes that even in a distributist state, economic activity will naturally result in differential rewards for various activities: "It is not a bad thing but a good thing that rents, the dwelling house, the income from investment, and the rest, should be upon various scales, for such variety corresponds to the complex reality of human society. What *is* a bad thing is that the destitute wage slaves—a proletariat—should form the determining member of society, and that real production and thrift and personal effort—in other words, work and citizenship—should be encouraged."[69] Instead of a society of proletarians

65 Belloc, *An Essay on the Restoration of Property*, 67.

66 However, this argument may rely on interpersonal utility comparisons, which are controversial at best.

67 Belloc, *An Essay on the Restoration of Property*, 68–69.

68 Belloc, *An Essay on the Restoration of Property*, 69.

69 Belloc, *An Essay on the Restoration of Property*, 70.

and capitalists, Belloc earnestly desires a large and secure middle class, a concern that has occupied philosophers going back to Aristotle. High taxation destroys the middle class, which has insidious political consequences. Because the middle class is "the spokesman for property, property lies undefended when a middle class fails."[70] If excessive taxation remains in force, "we shall end with a state of society wherein there will stand contrasted a few very great fortunes on one side and a proletarian mass upon the other, with all hope for the reconstruction of property abandoned."[71]

RESTORING PROPERTY: WHOLESALE, BANKING, AND GUILDS

Belloc finishes his essay by discussing how wholesale and banking can be brought within the domain of distributed property. He also considers the role of guilds in a distributist state. Belloc thinks wholesale is a problem because it has "been captured by highly centralized capitalism,"[72] but he does not offer much specific advice on this question. Instead, he reaffirms general principles for legally protecting small concerns against large ones in the hopes that an environment conducive to distributed property will impede wholesalers relative to smaller distributors and shopkeepers. The only possibility in the short run "until we are strong enough to affect the mass of it, is to guard the small man jealously from discrimination by the wholesale provider."[73]

Next Belloc conducts a deeper analysis of guilds. He strongly believes any attempt to restore property "must take the form of the Guild: not the unprotected guild arising spontaneously . . . but of the Guild *chartered and established by positive law*."[74] Belloc credits trade unions "for the partial protection of a minority of the population" but clearly views these as insufficient.[75] Guild restoration must start small, in specific professions, to build the political and economic power to scale up. There is no use in hoping top-down political efforts will help in this matter. Parliament cannot be called upon because large-scale representative bodies "are necessarily the organs

70 Belloc, *An Essay on the Restoration of Property*, 72.

71 Belloc, *An Essay on the Restoration of Property*, 74.

72 Belloc, *An Essay on the Restoration of Property*, 75.

73 Belloc, *An Essay on the Restoration of Property*, 77.

74 Belloc, *An Essay on the Restoration of Property*, 77.

75 Belloc, *An Essay on the Restoration of Property*, 78.

of plutocracy. . . . No approach to the guild system, even as a modest and partial experiment, can be expected until political power is decentralized and re-arranged according to economic classes and interests."[76] Eventually, once the bottom-up system has achieved a degree of political and economic power, legal chartering can be the next step. In fact, Belloc regards success at regulating production in this manner as a sign of the broader social persuasiveness of the distributist ideal. One of his remarks will certainly shock modern economists: "If people could not obtain properly made craftsman furniture, *save from a man admitted to the Guild and subject to its rules*, we should know that in that one small department we have achieved success."[77]

As for banking and credit, Belloc begins with this curious declaration: "Dealing with the function of credit is not fundamental to the restoration and maintenance of property. Credit is not a vital element of all societies; it is not a permanent and general social, economic, or political problem."[78] Belloc is probably making a historical claim: Only recently have financial markets developed sufficiently to support advanced credit structures. Immediately afterwards, he acknowledges that historical novelty and economic importance are not the same thing. Belloc sharply castigates the monopolizing tendencies of English banking. He regards the banks as controlling the supply of liquidity and credit, thus wielding enormous de facto power over production decisions everywhere in the economy: "It is no use attempting to restore the institution of property here in England now until we have given the small owner some power of reaction against this universal master."[79] Rather than a direct assault on big finance, Belloc recommends defensive action in the form of establishing "small co-operative credit institutions duly chartered and legally protected from attack."[80] Ideally, these cooperatives should be popularly controlled and associated with (or otherwise connected to) a guild.[81]

Here Belloc ends his essay defending distributism against both capitalism and socialism. Belloc reminds his readers that, important as his recommendations are, specific transition plans are not the crux of distributist

76 Belloc, *An Essay on the Restoration of Property*, 78.

77 Belloc, *An Essay on the Restoration of Property*, 79, my emphasis.

78 Belloc, *An Essay on the Restoration of Property*, 80.

79 Belloc, *An Essay on the Restoration of Property*, 80–81.

80 Belloc, *An Essay on the Restoration of Property*, 80–81.

81 Belloc, *An Essay on the Restoration of Property*, 82.

political economy. The "main task" is "not that of elaborating machinery for the reaction toward right living, but of forwarding the spirit of that reaction in a society which has almost forgotten what property and its concomitant freedom means."[82] Belloc's proposals are primarily valuable as a means of reviving a *worldview* of freedom. That being said, it does matter for our purposes whether Belloc's recommendations are means-ends consistent. This is the main consideration for economists in their role as comparative institutional analysts. We must delve deeper into the specifics of Belloc's proposals, to find out what in his analysis is enduring and has relevance for us today.

BELLOC AS COMPARATIVE INSTITUTIONAL ANALYST

But we cannot conduct this evaluation according to the standards of welfare economics. That kind of political economy, whether in its early twentieth-century or modern form, is alien to Belloc's project. To judge whether he was means-ends consistent, we must first keep in mind *his* ends, not ours.

Toward the conclusion of his essay, Belloc reminds his readers what is at stake. The goal is a social order that respects human freedom, where *freedom* takes its specific meaning from Catholic social teaching. Existing institutions are wolves in sheep's clothing: "The only difference between a herd of subservient Russians and a mob of free Englishmen pouring into a factory of a morning, is that the latter are exploited for private profit, the former by the State in communal fashion."[83] Hence, the attempt to escape the servility of private and public tyranny: "We are attempting a radical change. We are attempting a reactionary revolution: perhaps impossible. Thus even where we have to accept centralized power we shall try to get the profits payable severally to very many citizens, and we shall try to make small industry preferred in the use of that power and to prevent its being centralized for the advantage of large units."[84]

In general, Belloc is a much more subtle and interesting political economist in *Essay* than in *The Servile State*. Numerous objections that could be raised against Belloc's economics in the latter do not work in the former, and this is because Belloc is more careful in distinguishing his positive and normative claims in *Essay*. Numerous times, Belloc admits that his proposals

82 Belloc, *An Essay on the Restoration of Property*, 82.

83 Belloc, *An Essay on the Restoration of Property*, 76.

84 Belloc, *An Essay on the Restoration of Property*, 76.

may result in increased prices and decreased output, but the apparent social costs are illusory, because they purchase something even more precious: a free society.

There are still numerous claims that are vulnerable to counterarguments drawn from modern economics. Consider two of them from Belloc's list of the factors that promote amalgamation. The least plausible is the predatory-pricing argument. The claim that large firms can temporarily price below cost to drive out competitors and monopolize markets has significant intuitive appeal, but most economists, even those who have major reservations about the efficiency of markets, think this claim is meritless.[85] To begin, it is almost impossible to distinguish empirically any instance of supposed predatory pricing. Cost conditions are not as obvious as many noneconomists think, making it difficult to ascertain where price is in relation to cost. Another problem is that there are frequently legitimate reasons, unrelated to attempts to corner a market, for firms to price below costs temporarily. A simple example is a fall in demand for the firm's product, which often results in a lower price for the firm's product without similarly bringing down costs. In addition to these problems, there is an analytically prior objection to predatory pricing. It simply is not in firms' interests to attempt it. So long as markets are contestable—meaning entry and exit are not limited by law, but are open to any firm or firms that wish to compete—taking a loss to reduce present competition does nothing to stave off the threat of *future* competition.[86] If a large firm ruined smaller firms through predatory pricing, raising prices afterwards would create room for new firms to undercut the attempted monopolist. In fact, economists so disdain predatory pricing that they frequently use it in introductory courses as a textbook example of "cheap talk." Predatory pricing is cutting off one's nose to spite one's face. It is a poor pricing strategy because it lacks credible commitment.

Also problematic is Belloc's description of what we might call the dilemma of small savings. Admittedly, it is more difficult for a poor household to save a given fraction of its income than a rich household. It is also

85 Aaron Director, a University of Chicago law professor who was one of the pioneers of law and economics as a field, usually gets the credit for inoculating economists against predatory pricing. The canonical article is John S. McGee, "Predatory Price Cutting: The Standard Oil (N.J.) Case," *Journal of Law and Economics* 1 (1958): 137–69, which was heavily influenced by Director.

86 For contestable markets in general, in addition to the paper cited in the previous chapter, see William Baumol, John Panzar, and Robert Willig, *Contestable Markets and the Theory of Industry Structure* (New York: Harcourt Brace, 1988).

more difficult for small firms to reinvest out of earnings in their production processes than large firms. But these barriers are by no means insurmountable. The same counterarguments could be raised against the dilemma of small savings as were raised against the poverty trap in development economics.[87]

Development economists once believed that poor countries (those with very low per capita incomes) were trapped in poverty. Development requires capital accumulation, which in turn requires abstaining from consumption in favor of saving and investment. This is hard to do at low income levels. There is an element of economistic logic to this story. In fact, some economists still find significant merit in poverty traps as explanatory phenomena, so Belloc is not totally at odds with the economics profession.[88]

But affirming the poverty trap leads to a paradox. At one time, per capita incomes *in all countries* were very low. Some countries managed to grow, and grow extraordinarily, despite initial poverty. Go far enough back, and everybody was poor. Thus, we cannot explain poverty today by pointing to poverty yesterday. In like manner, every industrial conglomerate was once a small firm, with all the cash flow difficulties that entails. Some enterprises do not survive; some grow and become quite large. The problem of business reinvestment out of small revenues is no different than the problem of savings out of small income: While undoubtedly difficult for the individuals and organizations in those positions, they do not tilt the playing field of the economic system as a whole. While there are some exceptions, economists today generally do not find these kinds of explanations convincing.

Finally, a word should be said about Belloc and guilds. Belloc is clearly a fan, applauding and recommending them several times. He even calls for legal protections. To be fair to Belloc, several contemporary economists have pointed to the longevity of European trade guilds as evidence for them

87 William Easterly, "Reliving the 1950s: The Big Push, Poverty Traps, and Takeoffs in Economic Development," *Journal of Economic Growth*, 11, no. 4 (2006): 289–318; Easterly, *The White Man's Burden: Why the West's Efforts to Aid the Rest Have Done So Much Ill and So Little Good* (New York: Penguin Press, 2006); and Peter Tamas Bauer, *From Subsistence to Exchange and Other Essays* (Princeton, N.J.: Princeton University Press, 2000).

88 See Jeffrey Sachs, John McArthur, Guido Schmidt-Traub, Margaret Kruk, Chandrika Bahadur, Michael Faye, and Gordon McCord, "Ending Africa's Poverty Trap," *Brookings Papers on Economic Activity* 2004, no. 1 (2004): 117–240; Jeffrey Sachs, *The End of Poverty: Economic Possibilities for Our Time* (New York: Penguin House, 2006); and Costas Azariadis and John Stachurski, "Poverty Traps," in *Handbook of Economic Growth*, ed. Philippe Aghion and Steven Durlauf (Amsterdam: Elsevier, 2006), 295–384.

serving some useful purpose.[89] Examples include instilling valuable skills and mediating disputes involving the effects of technological change on livelihoods. On this point, there is a way to reconcile Belloc's arguments with the conversations economists and economic historians are currently having. Nevertheless, for a social critic so obviously concerned with the perils of monopoly, Belloc's fondness for guilds borders on the excessive. After all, a legally privileged guild is just a different form of monopoly.[90] It more resembles a cooperative than a hierarchical firm does, but the essence of monopoly lies in producers' ability to exclude competitors from the market using legal force. If monopoly per se is objectionable, then the internal structure of the monopolizing organization should be a secondary concern. Whether the organization has a horizontal or vertical decision process matters less than whether it has a legal corner on the market. Belloc would probably reply that legal protection is justified due to the internal distributional properties of the guild: Rather than profits accruing to relatively few owners of property within a firm, they are dispersed to relatively more numerous owners of property within a guild. Furthermore, legal charters do provide security. Firms in today's markets looking for the same legal privileges, such as local transportation monopolies held by taxi companies, would not fight for them so hard if they did not confer a secure revenue stream. It thus makes sense to interpret Belloc as opposed to the legal privileges that emerge under industrial capitalism, rather than legal privileges in general.

These are just some of the tensions between Belloc and contemporary economics. There are undoubtedly many more, but this is ultimately a minor concern. Again, it is not helpful to judge Belloc primarily based on means-ends consistency, according to the accumulated economic knowledge we now possess. Instead, the most profitable reading of Belloc is as a social philosopher whose concern is freedom and human flourishing. The last chapter ended with Belloc's intriguing claim that economic freedom, which has significant affirmative content, makes societies prosperous. It is

89 See, for example, Charles Hickson and Earl Thompson, "A New Theory of Guilds and European Economic Development," *Explorations in Economic History* 28, no. 2 (1991), 127–67; S. Epstein, "Craft Guilds, Apprenticeship, and Technological Change in Preindustrial Europe," *Journal of Economic History* 58, no. 3 (1998): 684–713; and the essays in S. Epstein and Maarten Praak, *Guilds, Innovation, and the European Economy, 1400–1800* (Cambridge: Cambridge University Press, 2008).

90 Among economic historians, Sheilagh Ogilvie is the preeminent guild skeptic. See her book, *The European Guilds: An Economic Analysis* (Princeton, N.J.: Princeton University Press, 2019), for a thoroughly researched analysis.

not enough for the legal system to prevent force and fraud in commercial life. If a free society is to remain free, it must guarantee access to the factors of production to a wide segment of society. Those who refuse the burdens of ownership will also shirk the responsibilities of maintaining rights-respecting institutions. Political freedom and economic freedom are necessarily complementary. Only societies that embody an ownership-centric worldview will cultivate a liberty-centric worldview. This thesis is most fully developed in *Essay*, and in a way, it is frequently amenable to the economic way of thinking.

Recall Belloc's quote about the prices of consumer goods in a distributist state. He concedes that "enforceable laws and actual institutions which shall artificially advantage the small distributor against the great, and the small craftsman or small user of machinery against the large manufacturer" will result in higher prices. But the subsequent argument strikes at the heart of the matter: "You are buying something for society at that price, and it is something well worth society's while. . . . That 'something' is citizenship, and the escape from slavery."[91] Or again, from the next chapter: "Production and distribution may be rendered somewhat cheaper" under capitalism than a distributist state, and "the work may even be somewhat more efficiently done, but the price you have to pay in the loss of freedom is a great deal too high."[92] One way of interpreting Belloc is that he means the low prices for consumer goods under capitalism do not reflect the full costs of their production. We may be giving up fewer economic resources to produce these goods under capitalism than distributism, but we are consuming more *political* resources, and this is not reflected in the pricing process. Low capitalist prices do not take account of the fact that the production methods used, by concentrating property in the hands of the few, result in a widespread loss of freedom. Economists are quite familiar with this kind of reasoning. It implies that Belloc's argument can be understood as an *externality* argument. An externality exists whenever economic activity creates costs and benefits for bystanders that parties to the economic activity do not consider.[93] The classic example is pollution: Because nobody has a property right to clean air, producers face no private costs from creating pollution as a byproduct for making and selling their goods. Pollution is still an economic

91 Belloc, *An Essay on the Restoration of Property*, 41.

92 Belloc, *An Essay on the Restoration of Property*, 50.

93 Arthur Cecil Pigou, *The Economics of Welfare* (London: Macmillan, 1920).

bad, however, and its existence makes those in society worse off. The solution to the problem of pollution (a negative externality) is to find some way of forcing producers to bear the full costs of their activities: both the private costs associated with using up resources and the social costs associated with creating an economic bad as a byproduct. Interestingly, the textbook economic answer to pollution is a special tax on producers, with the price of the tax reflecting the damage done to society by pollution. This is precisely what Belloc recommends in the case of production by large corporations that have concentrated property. Belloc's differentiated and graduated taxes on all forms of bigness are analogous to corrective taxes on activities that create pollution.

Capitalist economies have political externalities: this is Belloc's claim expressed as concisely as possible. If the costs to human freedom, and hence human flourishing, were reflected in prices, consumers would be much less likely to purchase goods produced by capitalist methods. Similar goods produced by distributist methods entail higher economic costs, but lower political costs, since widely dispersed property supports liberty. Belloc's project can be viewed as an attempt to grapple with the fact that the market cannot put a price on human freedom.

Chapter 5

Chesterton's *What's Wrong with the World*

CHESTERTON AS POET AND PROPHET

G. K. Chesterton was an English writer, literary and art critic, and lay theologian. He was born on May 29, 1874, in London. He attended University College London, studying art and literature, but never completed a degree in either subject. Involved in writing and the publishing business his whole life, his literary output is prodigious: He was the author of eighty books and more than four thousand shorter works, including essays, poems, and plays. Known as the "prince of paradox," Chesterton delighted in posing seemingly contradictory arguments to his readers and then showing how a particular view of life—typically the ideals of Christianity, which Chesterton saw most fully realized in Catholicism—resolved those contradictions in a way that was both intellectually and emotionally satisfying. His social criticism and Christian apologetic works were widely read and discussed during his own time, and he significantly influenced the next generation of English Christian intellectuals, most notably C. S. Lewis.

Chesterton was himself inspired by Belloc in both his religious and social views. Belloc's guidance was an important factor in Chesterton's conversion to Catholicism, as well as his advocacy for an economic system that avoided the inhumane excesses of capitalism and socialism. George Bernard Shaw, Chesterton's private friend and public enemy, often referred to the two as a single entity, creating the term "Chesterbelloc" to describe the pair and their views. Along with Belloc, Chesterton is an indispensable part of distributist thought. Any survey that purports to be representative must engage them both.

Belloc's influence on Chesterton is more apparent in Chesterton's *The Outline of Sanity*, which is the focus of the next chapter. *What's Wrong with the World*, the topic of this chapter, contains many distributist themes, but it is more attributable to Chesterton's concern with the family than any explicit coupling with distributism. *What's Wrong with the World* is about home economics in its truest sense: the permanence of the ideal of the family and the productive household. The family conjoined with the productive household is the center of reality, from which one can descend into the internal workings of the household or ascend into the external workings of the polity. But the center remains fixed. Even if the reader is skeptical of some of Chesterton's "downstream" arguments, provided the reader appreciates the importance of the family as the premier social institution, Chesterton would be satisfied.

Somehow, Chesterton manages to be cheerful and curmudgeonly at the same time. Even when he calls down fire and brimstone on modern pieties, it is impossible to imagine him without a smile on his face. Readers of both Belloc and Chesterton will immediately notice their significant stylistic differences. Chesterton's writings are decidedly more poetic. As is fitting given his lifelong love for arts and letters, he uses artistic impression as part of his arguments. There is a whimsical, sometimes ethereal, quality to Chesterton's prose that makes reading him an adventure. This also makes him quite difficult to excerpt, which in part accounts for this (and the next) chapter's length. I hope some of these impressions come through in my discussion of his views, but this is a poor substitute for reading Chesterton in his own words. Rather than trying to recreate the experience of reading Chesterton, I focus on the analytical value of his arguments, which fits better with my overall project. I encourage readers who are interested in experiencing the aesthetic, not just the logical, aspects of Chesterton's positions to read him for themselves.

THE PRIMACY OF THE IDEAL

Chesterton's first task is convincing his readers that the conventional wisdom about curing what ails society is not only wrong but backward. Most would-be societal physicians try to cure social diseases by diagnosing first and treating second: "But it is the whole definition and dignity of man that in social matters we must actually find the cure before we find the disease."[1] In other words, the only way to improve a bad society is to first figure out what a good society looks like. Only then is it safe to act. The problem, of course, is that the "good society" is the most hotly debated (and least settled) question in social philosophy. The quarrel "is not merely about the difficulties, but about the aim. We agree that it [the problem] is evil; it is

1 G. K. Chesterton, *What's Wrong with the World* (New York: Dover Publications, [1910] 2007), 3.

about the good that we should tear each other's eyes out."[2] Nonetheless, the "only way to discuss the social evil is to get at once to the social ideal."[3] The hard way is the only way.

Chesterton knows that insisting on the ideal "exposes one to the cheap charge of fiddling while Rome is burning."[4] The quest for the ideal is impractical, many would say. Chesterton thinks this is raving nonsense: "When things will not work, you must have the thinker, the man who has some doctrine about why they work at all. It is wrong to fiddle while Rome is burning; but it is quite right to study the theory of hydraulics while Rome is burning."[5] This explains why Chesterton is not terribly optimistic about conventional political solutions: Politicians are too practical. But if "our statesmen were visionaries something practical might be done. If we asked for something in the abstract we might get something in the concrete."[6]

Obstinate pragmatism is sometimes hypocrisy in disguise: "The old hypocrite . . . was a man whose aims were really worldly and practical, while he pretended that they were religious. The new hypocrite is one whose aims are really religious, while he pretends that they are worldly and practical."[7] People keep their radical ideals under wraps, fearing that genuine social renewal may prove offensive, divisive, and perhaps even destructive. They are happy to offer a twelve-point plan or a reform pamphlet but afraid to espouse a creed. This does not eliminate the need for a creed, however; it only forces men to pretend they do not have one. Chesterton insists that "the only adequate answer is, that there is a permanent human ideal that must not be either confused or destroyed. . . . It is man, says Aristotle, who is the measure. It is the Son of Man, says Scripture, who shall judge the quick and the dead."[8] There is no getting around asking "what is the need of normal men, what is the desire of all nations, what is the ideal house, or road, or rule, or republic, or king, or priesthood," so we had best be honest and get on with it.[9]

2 Chesterton, *What's Wrong with the World*, 5.

3 Chesterton, *What's Wrong with the World*, 6.

4 Chesterton, *What's Wrong with the World*, 8.

5 Chesterton, *What's Wrong with the World*, 9.

6 Chesterton, *What's Wrong with the World*, 11.

7 Chesterton, *What's Wrong with the World*, 13.

8 Chesterton, *What's Wrong with the World*, 19.

9 Chesterton, *What's Wrong with the World*, 19.

Many men are afraid of extremes and hence afraid of ideals. Interestingly, this fear of universals also results in a disdain for particulars. Rather than searching human history for a worthy ideal, they obsess over the future because they think it will help them evade the burden of purpose: "There have been so many flaming faiths that we cannot hold; so many harsh heroisms that we cannot imitate; so many great efforts of monumental building or of military glory which seem to us at once sublime and pathetic. The future is a refuge from the fierce competition of our forefathers."[10] But this leads us to a paradox: historically, "there is no Revolution that is not also a Restoration . . . all the men in history who have really done anything with the future have had their eyes fixed upon the past."[11] Modern reformers delude themselves that they can fix things without revolutionary reactionism. They think improvement must be forward-looking, in the spirit of the times. These are the men who always say, "'You can't put the clock back.' The simple and obvious answer is, 'You can.' A clock, being a piece of human construction, can be restored by the human finger to any figure or hour. In the same way society, being a piece of human construction, can be reconstructed upon any plan that has ever existed."[12] With this passage, Chesterton reveals he is no conventional Burkean conservative.

Chesterton rejects the argument that the ideals of the past have been tried and found wanting. Instead, the "lost causes are exactly those which might have saved the world,"[13] precisely because they were lost. It is the winners of history that are discredited by their success, not the losers by their failures. After all, the winners brought about the current state of affairs. It is only the failed causes—those that moved men to action but tragically were left incomplete—that are worth taking up. "History does not consist of completed and crumbling ruins," Chesterton explains; rather, "it consists of half-built villas abandoned by a bankrupt builder. This world is more like an unfinished suburb than a deserted cemetery."[14]

Chesterton has spent thirty pages telling us what he is against, but what is he for? His answer is deceptively simple. His goal is "the principle of domesticity; the ideal house, the happy family, the holy family of his-

10 Chesterton, *What's Wrong with the World*, 21.

11 Chesterton, *What's Wrong with the World*, 22.

12 Chesterton, *What's Wrong with the World*, 25.

13 Chesterton, *What's Wrong with the World*, 27.

14 Chesterton, *What's Wrong with the World*, 32.

tory."[15] For Chesterton, property and family are two complementary institutions. One is barely conceivable without the other. For ordinary families, their property is more than just their livelihoods: it is their means of self-expression, their operative material for cultivating virtue, and their opportunity to enrich their souls:

> For the mass of men the idea of artistic creation can only be expressed by . . . the idea of property. The average man cannot cut clay into the shape of a man; but he can cut earth into the shape of a garden; and though he arranges it with red geraniums and blue potatoes in alternate straight lines, he is still an artist; because he has chosen. . . . Property is merely the art of the democracy. It means that every man should have something that he can shape in his own image, as he is shaped in the image of Heaven.[16]

Chesterton's defense of property would make free-marketeers uneasy, however. For Chesterton, property implies limitation. Excessive holdings of property by any one individual, family, or corporate body undermine the institution of property itself: "One would think, to hear people talk, that the Rothschilds and the Rockefellers were on the side of property. But obviously they are the enemies of property, because they are the enemies of their own limitations."[17] These brief sentences convey Chesterton's essential objection to capitalism. There is much more that he will say about this later.

Chesterton's views on the family help us understand why propertied families are necessary for a good society. A distributive state, with widely dispersed property holdings, is Chesterton's goal, but he understands this cannot be achieved or preserved unless the family is a widely held normative ideal. It must be treated as part of the fabric of reality, rather than a conscious principle of social organization. For Chesterton, "this institution of the home is the one anarchist institution. That is to say, it is older than law, and stands outside the State."[18] The family is prior to politics. In fact, the family is the foundation of politics. Family complements property because both couple fulfillment with restraint. Just as a man may own something, but not anything, a man may marry a woman, but not any woman. There is freedom here, but it is the freedom of limits, not license. Our right

15 Chesterton, *What's Wrong with the World*, 34.

16 Chesterton, *What's Wrong with the World*, 35.

17 Chesterton, *What's Wrong with the World*, 36.

18 Chesterton, *What's Wrong with the World*, 38.

to choose what we own or whom we marry is meaningful because it is also a choice to bind ourselves. The renunciatory freedom of property and family rests on the principle "that in everything worth having, even in every pleasure, there is a point of pain or tedium that must be survived, so that the pleasure may revive and endure. . . . All human vows, laws, and contracts are so many ways of surviving with success this breaking point, this instant of potential surrender."[19]

Chesterton knows he is fighting against long odds. Then as now, it was fashionable to reject domesticity as boring, oppressive, or both. He insists the opposite is nearer to the truth: For men of ordinary means, "the home is the only place of liberty. Nay, it is the only place of anarchy. It is the only spot on earth where a man can alter arrangements suddenly, make an experiment or indulge in a whim. . . . For a plain, hard-working man the home is not the one tame place in the world of adventure. It is the one wild place in the world of rules and sets and tasks."[20] Whether "we can give every Englishman a free home of his own or not, at least we should desire it; and he desires it. . . . He does not merely want a roof above him and a chair below him; he wants an objective and a visible kingdom; a fire at which he can cook what food he likes, a door he can open to what friends he chooses."[21]

Chesterton's opponents refused to recognize this is a widely shared desire and a worthy ideal. Instead, they insisted on relegating men to slums or shepherding them into soulless planned domiciles, but "the healthy human soul loathes them both."[22] Conservatives and liberals bicker over unpalatable alternatives, never thinking "for an instant what sort of house a man might probably like for himself. In short, they did not begin with the ideal; and, therefore, were not practical politicians."[23] The goal is neither the street nor the workhouse but the *home*: "A house of his own being the obvious ideal for every man, we may now ask . . . why he hasn't got it," and how he might get it.[24]

Wherever else this ideal might exist, Chesterton is convinced it does not exist in England: "Burke, a fine rhetorician, who rarely faced realities,

19 Chesterton, *What's Wrong with the World*, 39–40.

20 Chesterton, *What's Wrong with the World*, 44.

21 Chesterton, *What's Wrong with the World*, 45.

22 Chesterton, *What's Wrong with the World*, 49.

23 Chesterton, *What's Wrong with the World*, 49.

24 Chesterton, *What's Wrong with the World*, 49.

said (I think) that an Englishman's house is his castle. This is honestly entertaining; for as it happens the Englishman is almost the only man in Europe whose house is not his castle."[25] Why is England "the last of the true oligarchies of Europe; and why does there seem no very immediate prospect of our seeing the end of it"?[26] The answer most would give—the aristocracy's excessive traditionalism—is dead wrong: "Who would dream of looking among aristocrats anywhere for an old custom? One might as well look for an old costume! The god of aristocrats is not tradition, but fashion, which is the opposite of tradition."[27] Chesterton's political sociology is concisely summarized as follows: "Thus they were on the side of the Reformation against the Church, of the Whigs against the Stuarts, of the Baconian science against the old philosophy, of the manufacturing system against the operatives, and (to-day) of the increased power of the State against the old-fashioned Individualist. In short, the rich are always modern; it is their business."[28] More recently, in the "nineteenth century the great nobles who became mine-owners and railway directors, earnestly assured everybody that they did not do this from preference, but owing to a newly discovered Economic Law."[29] As the previous quote suggests, Chesterton denigrates modern (marginalist-subjectivist) economics, which asserted the existence of universal forces that transcended historical particulars. This latter theme is prominent throughout distributist writings.

Since we know the ideal, we can recognize the problem: "The ordinary Englishman has been duped out of his old possessions, such as they were, and all in the name of progress."[30] Duped how? "He has been offered bribes of worlds and systems: he has been offered Eden and Utopia and the New Jerusalem, and he only wanted a house; and that has been refused him."[31] Neither Manchesterism nor Marxism can give man what he wants, and what he wants is expressed by the "idea of private property universal but private,

25 Chesterton, *What's Wrong with the World*, 49.

26 Chesterton, *What's Wrong with the World*, 52.

27 Chesterton, *What's Wrong with the World*, 52.

28 Chesterton, *What's Wrong with the World*, 53.

29 Chesterton, *What's Wrong with the World*, 54. Chesterton rightly pushes back against a deterministic interpretation of economic law. But we do not need to reject economic law as a meaningful concept. Indeed, we cannot do the kind of social and political analysis distributists call for without it. See p. 61, n. 149.

30 Chesterton, *What's Wrong with the World*, 55.

31 Chesterton, *What's Wrong with the World*, 56–57.

the idea of families free but still families, of domesticity democratic but still domestic, of one man one house—this remains the real vision and magnet of mankind."[32] Since we now understand what a healthy society looks like, we can prescribe a course of treatment and, just as importantly, counsel which treatments to avoid.

DELEGATION IS THE DEATH OF DEMOCRACY

The next group of essays, titled "Imperialism, or the Mistake about Man," gives the reader the impression they will encounter an antimilitaristic screed. Chesterton does castigate imperialism, but in a way that results in a much broader critique of modernity. His objections are not just to imperialism but to all forms of hierarchy and specialization that stifle camaraderie and solidarity among men.

On imperialism specifically, Chesterton decries it because it "consoles men for the evident ugliness and apathy of England with legends of fair youth and heroic strenuousness in distant continents and lands."[33] Imperialism redirects the impulse of social improvement away from man's native patrimony toward the conquest of distant lands and peoples, to the detriment of all. To put it another way, imperialism "is the attempt of a European country to create a kind of sham Europe which it can dominate, instead of the real Europe, which it can only share."[34]

To show how this is contrary to human flourishing, Chesterton will "cast back and begin anew with a more general discussion of the first needs of human intercourse."[35] He starts with an extensive discussion of comradeship. To Chesterton, comradeship entails three great social virtues. First is "a sort of broad philosophy like the common sky, emphasizing that we are all under the same cosmic conditions."[36] Second, "it recognizes this bond as the essential one; for comradeship is simply humanity seen in that one aspect in which men are really equal."[37] Third, comradeship insists on the importance of material creation, on "the body and its indispensable satisfaction."[38] The

32 Chesterton, *What's Wrong with the World*, 58.

33 Chesterton, *What's Wrong with the World*, 62.

34 Chesterton, *What's Wrong with the World*, 63.

35 Chesterton, *What's Wrong with the World*, 64.

36 Chesterton, *What's Wrong with the World*, 68.

37 Chesterton, *What's Wrong with the World*, 68.

38 Chesterton, *What's Wrong with the World*, 69.

thrust of these three elements is that no "man must be superior to the things that are common to all men. This sort of equality must be bodily and gross and cosmic. Not only are we all in the same boat, but we are all sea-sick."[39]

To Chesterton, comradeship "is the life within all democracies and attempts to govern by debate; without it the republic would be a dead formula."[40] By extension, camaraderie is the spirit of those who hold the most important things among them in common. The enemy of comradeship, and hence democratic self-rule, "is civilization. Those utilitarian miracles which science has made . . . must be individualistic and isolated. A mob can shout round a palace; but a mob cannot shout down a telephone. The specialist appears, and democracy is half spoilt at a stroke."[41] Chesterton clarifies, however, that he does not oppose all forms of specialization or hierarchy. Oligarchy, or even despotism, has a place in grave situations where time is of the essence: "If the house has caught fire a man must ring up the fire engines; a committee cannot ring them up. If a camp is surprised by night somebody must give the order to fire; there is no time to vote it."[42] In this simple and compelling logic, Chesterton anticipates much of the literature on efficient hierarchy and optimal vote thresholds for collective action.[43] But his purpose is to make a humane, prescriptive case for democracy rather than a descriptive one only. In fact, Chesterton sees even in command-and-control scenarios a certain republican spirit: "Discipline does not involve the Carlylean notion that somebody is always right when everybody is wrong, and that we must discover and crown that somebody. On the contrary, discipline means that in certain frightfully rapid circumstances, one can trust anybody so long as he is not everybody."[44] Even men under military discipline express democratic truths: "The essence of an army is the idea of official inequality, founded on unofficial equality. The Colonel is obeyed not because he is the best man, but because he is the Colonel."[45]

39 Chesterton, *What's Wrong with the World*, 69.

40 Chesterton, *What's Wrong with the World*, 72.

41 Chesterton, *What's Wrong with the World*, 75.

42 Chesterton, *What's Wrong with the World*, 76.

43 Cf. James M. Buchanan and Gordon Tullock, *The Calculus of Consent: Logical Foundations of Constitutional Democracy* (Ann Arbor: University of Michigan Press, 1962); Ronald Coase, "The Nature of the Firm," *Economica*, 4, no. 16 (1937): 386–405; and Oliver Williamson, *Markets and Hierarchies: Analysis and Antitrust Implications* (New York: Free Press, 1983).

44 Chesterton, *What's Wrong*, 77.

45 Chesterton, *What's Wrong*, 78.

The two aspects of man, specialism and sociality, point to subordination and equality, respectively. So long as these are kept in balance, men can flourish both individually and collectively, but Chesterton does not see that balance in early twentieth-century England. To Chesterton, "the peculiar peril of our time, which I call for argument's sake Imperialism or Caesarism, is the complete eclipse of comradeship and equality by specialism and domination."[46] In politics and economics, whenever balance is lost and hierarchy engulfs equality, an essential feature of human sociality is threatened.

This argument has constitutional implications. "There are only two kinds of social structure conceivable," Chesterton tells us: "personal government and impersonal government. If my anarchic friends will not have rules—they will have rulers. Preferring personal government, with its tact and flexibility, is called Royalism. Preferring impersonal government, with its dogmas and definitions, is called Republicanism."[47] While acknowledging royalism has its place, Chesterton is a republican through and through. The appeal of republicanism is that men "feel that rules, even if irrational, are universal; men feel that law is equal, even when it is not equitable. There is a wild fairness to the thing—as there is in tossing up."[48] The problem with modern social arrangements is that they lack this institutionalized recognition of fair play. It does not matter much whether the hierarchy is that of a business or a bureau: both are impatient with the rowdy camaraderie of liberty, equality, and fraternity. Advocates of specialization and subordination would no doubt reply, "Specialists must be despots; men must be specialists. You cannot have equality in a soap factory; so you cannot have it anywhere. . . . We live in a commercial civilization; therefore we must destroy democracy."[49] This is another version of the "ship of state" analogy that admirers of the regimented society have used ever since Plato. Chesterton concedes not an inch to this tradition: "A ship still remains a specialist experiment . . . in such particular perils the need for promptitude constitutes the need for autocracy. But we live and die in the vessel of the state; and if we cannot find freedom, camaraderie and the popular element in the state, we cannot find it at all."[50]

46 Chesterton, *What's Wrong*, 78–79.

47 Chesterton, *What's Wrong*, 79.

48 Chesterton, *What's Wrong*, 79.

49 Chesterton, *What's Wrong*, 80–81.

50 Chesterton, *What's Wrong*, 81.

To conclude, Chesterton reiterates, "this is what is wrong. This is the huge modern heresy of altering the human soul to fit its conditions, instead of altering human conditions to fit the human soul. If soap-boiling is really inconsistent with brotherhood, so much the worse for soap-boiling, not for brotherhood. If civilization really cannot get on with democracy, so much the worse for civilization, not for democracy."[51] In this section, Chesterton may prove too much, or else not enough. If men can be disciplined-yet-democratic in an army or a fire department, why does this not extend to a government bureau or a factory floor? Chesterton has conceded specialization under the division of labor has its place, while simultaneously making an eloquent case that specialization can be dehumanizing. Adam Smith recognized this as well.[52] Chesterton's intuitions do him credit, and he is correct to regard with suspicion his contemporaries' call for a planned society. The minute would-be planners try to turn a nation into a barracks, it loses its organic vitality and begins to decay.

DOMESTICITY AND COMPLEMENTARITY

Since the theme of *What's Wrong with the World* is household economy, Chesterton naturally discusses the division of labor between men and women. Chesterton's opinions, which were contrary to public trends even in the early twentieth century, may seem quirky or anachronistic now, and perhaps even offensive. Nevertheless, we cannot understand Chesterton's arguments about the importance of the household for shaping the character of persons and societies without engaging these arguments. Even if we do not find him persuasive, the principles on which he grounds his arguments can illuminate other discussions.

A crucial public issue in Chesterton's time was women's suffrage, which he uses as a hook for his own discussions. As he often does, Chesterton takes a position that manages to offend all parties: without finding any principled problem with women's suffrage, he nonetheless finds quite a few with suffragettes. His objection to the suffragettes "is not that they are Militant Suffragettes . . . it is that they are not militant enough."[53] Advocates of women's suffrage "do not create a revolution; what they do create is anarchy;

51 Chesterton, *What's Wrong*, 81–82.

52 Adam Smith, *An Inquiry into the Nature and Causes of the Wealth of Nations*, ed. Edwin Cannan (London: Methuen, 1904), bk. 5, chap. 1.

53 Chesterton, *What's Wrong*, 85.

and the difference between these is not a question of violence, but a question of fruitfulness and finality. Revolution of its nature produces government; anarchy only produces more anarchy."[54] In other words, Chesterton objects to the substitution of a means for an end. This is the same problem he identified at the beginning of the book, and it motivates his discussion of women's issues and household economy in the pages to follow.

Chesterton seems to digress, discussing the relationship between contingent social practices (traditions and customs) and universal values, but in reality, he is subtly directing his readers. It is "the great mark of our modernity," Chesterton asserts, "that people are always proposing substitutes for . . . old things; and these substitutes always answer one purpose where the old thing answered ten."[55] He contrasts "ancient and universal things and the modern and specialist things."[56] Balancing them "has been the vision of many groups of men in many ages. It was the Liberal Education of Aristotle; the jack-of-all-trades artistry of Leonardo da Vinci and his friends; the august amateurishness of the Cavalier Person of Quality like Sir William Temple or the great Earl of Dorset."[57] Achieving balance between the universal and eternal on the one hand, and the particular and transient on the other, is the chief accomplishment of the household, accomplished through a division of labor along sexual lines. According to Chesterton, men are naturally specialists: "What makes it difficult for the average man to be a universalist is that the average man has to be a specialist; he has not only to learn one trade but to learn it so well as to uphold him in a more or less ruthless society."[58] In contrast, women serve as the source of breadth and liberality within the household: "Tradition has decided that only half of humanity should be monomaniac. It has decided that in every home there shall be a tradesman and a Jack-of-all-trades. But it has also decided, among other things, that the Jack-of-all-trades shall be a Jill-of-all-trades. It has decided, rightly or wrongly, that this specialism and this universalism shall be divided between the sexes. Cleverness shall be left for men and wisdom for women. For cleverness kills wisdom; that is one of the few sad and certain things."[59]

54 Chesterton, *What's Wrong*, 86.

55 Chesterton, *What's Wrong*, 89.

56 Chesterton, *What's Wrong*, 89.

57 Chesterton, *What's Wrong*, 92.

58 Chesterton, *What's Wrong*, 92.

59 Chesterton, *What's Wrong*, 93.

The household can only serve as the cornerstone of a free and prosperous society if it reconciles the universal and the particular, ameliorating each's vices with the other's virtues. Society must "permit the existence of a partly protected half of humanity; a half which the harassing industrial demand troubles indeed, but only troubles indirectly. In other words, there must be in every centre of humanity one human being upon a larger plan; one who does not 'give her best,' but gives her all."[60] In brief, to Chesterton, "woman stands for the idea of Sanity; that intellectual home to which the mind must return after every excursion on extravagance."[61] It is evident from the next comparison that Chesterton does not think this a lesser function, but a necessary and complementary one: "To correct every adventure and extravagance with its antidote in common sense is not (as the moderns seem to think) to be in the position of a spy or a slave. It is to be in the position of Aristotle or (at the lowest) Herbert Spencer, to be a universal morality, a complete system of thought."[62]

Chesterton acknowledges the sexual division of labor is contingent, and thus could be altered, but he does not find the possibility particularly interesting. "The advanced person will at once begin to argue," Chesterton writes with an almost-perceptible groan, "about whether these instincts are inherent and inevitable in woman or whether they are merely prejudices produced by her history and education. Now I do not propose to discuss whether woman could not be educated out of her habits. . . . I will not exhaust my intelligence by inventing ways in which mankind might unlearn the violin or forget how to ride horses; and the art of domesticity seems to me as special and as valuable as all the ancient arts of our race."[63] For Chesterton, a certain amount of givenness is implied by human nature. This is the part that most readers today will find objectionable. To what extent it is essential to his thesis we can explore later.

Now Chesterton returns to castigating the moderns, especially the suffragettes. He is chiefly annoyed because, by "the beginning of the twentieth century, within the last few years, the woman has in public surrendered to the man."[64] Surrendered how? "She has seriously and officially owned that

60 Chesterton, *What's Wrong*, 95.

61 Chesterton, *What's Wrong*, 97.

62 Chesterton, *What's Wrong*, 98. See also n. 124.

63 Chesterton, *What's Wrong*, 112–13.

64 Chesterton, *What's Wrong*, 116.

the man has been right all along; that the public house (or Parliament) is really more important than the private house; that politics are not (as woman had always maintained) an excuse for pots of beer, but are a sacred solemnity to which new female worshippers may kneel; that the talkative patriots in the tavern are not only admirable but enviable; that talk is not a waste of time, and therefore (as a consequence, surely) that taverns are not a waste of money."[65] Chesterton seems genuinely surprised by this: "Suddenly, without warning, the women have begun to say all the nonsense that we ourselves hardly believed when we said it. The solemnity of politics; the necessity of votes . . . all these flow in a pecullid [sic] stream from the lips of all the suffragette speakers. I suppose in every fight, however old, one has a vague aspiration to conquer; but we never wanted to conquer women so completely as this. We only expected that they might leave us a little more margin for our nonsense; we never expected that they would accept it seriously as sense."[66] A bold claim, and one many would reject, but Chesterton sees this point as sufficiently obvious that he states it without defense. Instead, he wishes to take "a little wider and freer sweep of thought and ask ourselves what is the ultimate point and meaning of this odd business called voting."[67]

That "wider and freer sweep" takes the form of a disquisition on government: "Seemingly from the dawn of man all nations have had governments; and all nations have been ashamed of them. Nothing is more openly fallacious than to fancy that in ruder or simpler ages ruling, judging, and punishing, appeared perfectly innocent and dignified. These things were always regarded as penalties of the Fall; as part of the humiliation of mankind, as bad in themselves."[68] Government operates coercively, plain and simple. It is "a necessary but not a noble element."[69] Democratic government "is not only coercive, but collective."[70] In democratic nations, coercion "is a collective coercion. The abnormal person is theoretically thumped by a million fists and kicked by a million feet. If a man is flogged, we all flogged him; if a man is hanged, we all hanged him. This is the only possible mean-

65 Chesterton, *What's Wrong*, 116.

66 Chesterton, *What's Wrong*, 117.

67 Chesterton, *What's Wrong*, 118.

68 Chesterton, *What's Wrong*, 119.

69 Chesterton, *What's Wrong*, 120.

70 Chesterton, *What's Wrong*, 121.

ing of democracy, which can give any meaning to the first two syllables [demos] and also to the last two [kratos]."[71]

Chesterton acknowledges that by keeping the vote from women, society does "keep her out of the collective act of coercion; the act of punishment by a mob."[72] But for him, this is a feature, not a bug. The purpose of democracy is to give the public a stake in collective action, which includes coercive acts of enforcement and punishment. Voting is inseparable from this: "If votes for women do not mean mobs for women they do not mean what they were meant to mean. A woman can make a cross on a paper as well as a man. . . . But nobody ought to regard it merely as making a cross on a paper; everyone ought to regard it as what it ultimately is, branding the fleur-de-lys, making the broad arrow, signing the death warrant. Both men and women ought to face more fully the things they do or cause to be done; face them or leave off doing them."[73]

But now Chesterton makes a curious turn; he suggests that keeping women out of government enables the principle of *anarchy*—being anterior to and outside the state—to have its place in the household, and through it society at large. This counteracts the tendency of popular governments to politicize all aspects of life. To "hear people talk to-day," Chesterton laments, "one would fancy that every important human function must be organised and avenged by law; that all education must be state education, and all employment state employment; that everybody and everything must be brought to the foot of the august and prehistoric gibbet." But the family, for its perpetuation, must have some anchor that keeps it with one foot outside the state: "The huge fundamental function upon which all anthropology turns, that of sex and childbirth, has never been inside the political state but always outside it. The state concerned itself with the trivial question of killing people, but wisely left alone the whole business of getting them born."[74] If the family grounds politics without becoming political, it preserves the balance between the universal and the particular, and hence between society and the state.

Ultimately women's suffrage does not concern Chesterton. He took it as a "test case . . . because it is topical and concrete," not because he thinks

71 Chesterton, *What's Wrong*, 122.

72 Chesterton, *What's Wrong*, 123.

73 Chesterton, *What's Wrong*, 124.

74 Chesterton, *What's Wrong*, 124.

it is the locus of a great social conflict.[75] The philosophical and anthropological assumptions behind these arguments are his real interest. Chesterton's goal was determining what contemporary proposals implied, in light of enduring principles of domestic economy. The most important question is whether "we can recover the clear vision of woman as a tower with many windows, the fixed eternal feminine from which her sons, the specialists, go forth; whether we can preserve the tradition of a central thing which is even more human than democracy and even more practical than politics; whether, in a word, it is possible to re-establish the family, freed from the filthy cynicism and the cruelty of the commercial epoch."[76] Since this is where he thinks the stakes are highest, it is also where we should direct the bulk of our attention, engagement, and critique.

EDUCATING FOR HUMANITY

Having considered the relationship of the household to the commonwealth, and the bonds within the household itself, Chesterton turns to the connection between the household and social continuity. His object is education, especially what children are taught to venerate or despise. He begins with another disguised digression. Once Chesterton accused his personal friend and political enemy George Bernard Shaw of being a Calvinist. Despite his religious nonconformity, Shaw heartily agreed, saying that "Calvin was quite right in holding that, 'If once a man is born it is too late to damn or save him.'"[77] Chesterton finds this viewpoint false and repulsive. "Now all our sociology and eugenics and the rest of it are not so much materialist as confusedly Calvinist," Chesterton laments; "they are chiefly occupied in educating the child before he exists."[78] It is against this view of man, and its implications for education, that Chesterton takes up his sword.

First Chesterton considers, and quickly dismisses, the (pseudo)science of genetic determinism. Chesterton knows education matters only if you can mold a child's mind, making him different than otherwise. The genetic determinists of the early twentieth century thought this was impossible to take seriously, whereas Chesterton thought it impossible to take seriously the genetic determinists. Nobody "has ever been able to offer any theories of

75 Chesterton, *What's Wrong*, 133.

76 Chesterton, *What's Wrong*, 136.

77 Chesterton, *What's Wrong*, 139.

78 Chesterton, *What's Wrong*, 140.

moral heredity which justified themselves in the only scientific sense; that is, that one could calculate on them beforehand."[79] This is why "no one is mad enough to legislate or educate upon dogmas of physical inheritance; and even the language of the thing is rarely used except for special modern purposes, such as the endowment of research or the oppression of the poor."[80]

"After all the modern clatter of Calvinism therefore," he continues, "it is only with the born child that everybody dares to deal; and the question is not of eugenics but education."[81] While Chesterton is equally wary of environmental determinism as genetic determinism, he nonetheless recognizes that "it is not a question of heredity but of environment," and environment means education.[82] The question then becomes, what environment ought we create for our children in their formative periods? How should we educate them?

Chesterton's answer (unsurprisingly) runs contrary to the spirit of the times. His theory of education is that it is inherently *dogmatic*: "Gibbon thought it frightfully funny that people should have fought about the difference between the 'Homoousian' and the 'Homoiousian.' The time will come will laugh louder to think that men thundered against Sectarian education and also against Secular Education; that men of prominence and position actually denounced the schools for teaching a creed and also for not teaching a faith."[83] In other words, those who think it matters not one iota what one is taught, so long as one is taught how to think, fail to understand the nature of education: "It is quaint that people talk of separating dogma from education. Dogma is actually the only thing that cannot be separated from education. It *is* education. A teacher who is not dogmatic is simply a teacher who is not teaching."[84]

But we cannot hand down principles if we remain obsessed with process: "The fashionable fallacy is that by education we can give people something that we have not got. . . . These pages have, of course, no other general purpose than to point out that we cannot create anything good until we have conceived it. It is odd that these people, who in the matter of heredity

79 Chesterton, *What's Wrong*, 143.

80 Chesterton, *What's Wrong*, 144.

81 Chesterton, *What's Wrong*, 145.

82 Chesterton, *What's Wrong*, 145.

83 Chesterton, *What's Wrong*, 147.

84 Chesterton, *What's Wrong*, 149.

are so sullenly attached to law, in the manner of environment seem almost to believe in miracle."[85] The crucial point is that all education is education *for something*. This has major implications for the household and the commonwealth: "We cannot teach citizenship if we are not citizens; we cannot free others if we have forgotten the appetite for freedom. Education is only truth in a state of transmission: and how can we pass on truth if it has never come into our hand?"[86]

Ultimately "you cannot anyhow get rid of authority in education; it is not so much (as the poor Conservatives say) that parental authority ought to be preserved, as that it cannot be destroyed."[87] Nor does it help to draw an artificial distinction between *educators*, who are dogmatic, and *instructors*, who are mere providers of information: "The only result of all this pompous and precise distinction between the educator and the instructor is that the instructor pokes where he likes and the educator pulls where he likes. Exactly the same intellectual violence is done to the creature who is poked and pulled."[88] Chesterton uses the word "violence" with great care and precision: "Education is violence because it is creative. It is creative because it is human. It is as ruthless as playing the fiddle; as dogmatic as drawing a picture; as brutal as building a house."[89] This is why education is so important: it places just as great a burden on the parent as the child. Those who are brave enough to educate must assume "the responsibility of affirming the truth of our human tradition and handing it on with a voice of authority, an unshaken voice."[90]

The truths instilled by education must help make sense of the world. Education means acquiring a sociocultural worldview that provides a way to interpret and judge. Educators "have the heavy business of turning drunkards into wine tasters."[91] This analogy captures Chesterton's beliefs that true education includes instilling prudence and discernment, and even a kind of healthy ascetism, so long as that ascetism is joyful rather than dour. But true education is in short supply in Chesterton's time: "We are

85 Chesterton, *What's Wrong*, 150.

86 Chesterton, *What's Wrong*, 151.

87 Chesterton, *What's Wrong*, 153.

88 Chesterton, *What's Wrong*, 153.

89 Chesterton, *What's Wrong*, 154.

90 Chesterton, *What's Wrong*, 154.

91 Chesterton, *What's Wrong*, 164.

not like children who have lost their paint-box and are left alone with a grey lead pencil. We are like children who have mixed all the colours in the paint-box together and lost the paper of instructions."[92]

Education is enculturation, and the "true task of culture to-day is not a task of expansion, but very decidedly of selection—and rejection. The educationist must find a creed and teach it. Even if it be not a theological creed, it must still be as fastidious and as firm as theology."[93] Chesterton then examines the educational landscape of Britain, focusing on the differences between public and state schools.[94] His initial remarks show his views on education are rooted in the same principles as his writings on the nature of self-governance: "I do not propose (like some of my revolutionary friends) that we should abolish the public schools. I propose the much more lurid and desperate experiment that we should make them public. I do not wish to make Parliament stop working, but rather to make it work; not to shut up churches, but rather to open them; not to put out the lamp of learning or destroy the hedge of property; but only to make some rude effort to make the universities fairly universal and property decently proper."[95]

Chesterton begins his critique of the public schools by acknowledging their one virtue. This system "may not work satisfactorily, but it works; the public schools may not achieve what we want, but they achieve what they want."[96] The purpose of the public school system is to churn out well-mannered gentlemen who will occupy the commanding heights of the empire. Chesterton objects because it works too well. Yet at least this system has a plan, and is functioning according to that plan. The state schools, in contrast, have no plan, no purpose, and no standards. Advocates of popular education claim their system creates something better than a gentleman: "The popular educationists would say that they had the far nobler idea of turning out citizens. I concede that it is a much nobler idea, but where are the citizens?"[97]

92 Chesterton, *What's Wrong*, 165.

93 Chesterton, *What's Wrong*, 166.

94 This distinction may confuse American readers. In the United Kingdom, "public school" means something much more like what Americans mean by "private school." The public schools are public in the sense that anybody may enroll, provided one pays tuition and meets the admission standards. State schools, in contrast, are funded not by tuition fees but by taxes. They more closely resemble what Americans call public schools.

95 Chesterton, *What's Wrong*, 166.

96 Chesterton, *What's Wrong*, 169.

97 Chesterton, *What's Wrong*, 170.

The failure of the public school system is "its utterly blatant and indecent regard of the duty of telling the truth."[98] Nobody could help but notice that Eton, Harrow, and Winchester produce (after a detour through Oxbridge) a disproportionate share of high government officials, both in Parliament and in the civil service. But the average English schoolboy who matriculates from these institutions "is never taught to desire the truth. From the very first he is taught to be totally careless about whether a fact is a fact; he is taught to care only whether the fact can be used on his 'side' when he is engaged in 'playing the game.' . . . England is the country of the Party System, and it always has been chiefly run by public school men. Is there anyone out of Hanwell who will maintain that the Party System, whatever its conveniences or inconveniences, could have been created by people particularly fond of truth?"[99] While a public-school man is certainly "kind, courageous, polite, clean, companionable," he lacks the one thing needful, because "in the most awful sense of the words, the truth is not in him."[100]

The state schools, in contrast, are a mess not because they have a bad map but because they have no map at all. Chesterton reminds us that "progress ought to be based on principle," but "our modern progress is mostly based on precedent. We go, not by what may be affirmed in theory, but what has been already admitted in practice."[101] Rather than stake out a bold position on educating for citizenship, the state schools "have no definite ideal of their own," which is why "they so openly imitate the ideals of the public schools."[102] Furthermore, despite their claim to popular support, they actually insulate themselves from public opinion as much as possible. This is demonstrated by the fact that the "only persons who seem to have nothing to do with the education of the children are the parents."[103] In fact, those who make up the state school system seem to go out of their way to teach children to despise fathers and folkways. Too many schoolmasters "think it not merely natural but simply conscientious to eradicate all these rugged legends of a laborious people, and on principle to preach soap and Socialism against beer and liberty. . . . Modern

98 Chesterton, *What's Wrong*, 175.

99 Chesterton, *What's Wrong*, 176. Hanwell is an insane asylum.

100 Chesterton, *What's Wrong*, 177.

101 Chesterton, *What's Wrong*, 181–82.

102 Chesterton, *What's Wrong*, 182.

103 Chesterton, *What's Wrong*, 185.

education means handing down the customs of the minority, and rooting out the customs of the majority."[104]

To sum up, Chesterton claims that England educates for oligarchy and servility because it is not brave enough to educate for democracy and liberty. Privileging the household is all well and good, but unless education helps the next generation steward its inheritance, there will be no permanence in the commonwealth.

"THE HUMAN AND SACRED IMAGE"

In the concluding group of essays, Chesterton returns to first principles. To motivate his most important argument, he discusses the legacies of Robespierre and the French Revolution as compared to Burke and the English reaction against it. Chesterton makes it exceedingly difficult to classify him as a garden-variety conservative: He criticizes Burke and praises Robespierre. "The Revolution appealed to the idea of an abstract and eternal justice," he explains, "beyond all local custom of convenience. If there are commands of God, then there must be rights of man."[105] Chesterton castigates Burke as a kind of Darwinian before Darwin: "Man, said Burke, in effect must adapt himself to everything, like an animal; he must not try to alter everything, like an angel."[106] In contrast, he sees in Robespierre and his comrades a flaming faith in absolute, non-negotiable right, which also fueled the lives and missions of some of the church's greatest saints.

Chesterton disdains arguments that instrumentalize the social order, especially ones that deny a fixed human nature. When "one begins to think of man as a shifting and alterable thing, it is always easy for the strong and crafty to twist him into new shapes for all kinds of unnatural purposes."[107] To Chesterton, the otherwise-admirable prudence of Burke too easily drifts toward the abominable reification of society: "In resisting this horrible theory of the Soul of the Hive, we of Christendom stand not for ourselves, but for all humanity; for the essential and distinctive human idea, that one good and happy man is an end in himself, that a soul is worth saving."[108]

104 Chesterton, *What's Wrong*, 187.

105 Chesterton, *What's Wrong*, 195.

106 Chesterton, *What's Wrong*, 196.

107 Chesterton, *What's Wrong*, 196.

108 Chesterton, *What's Wrong*, 200.

Next, Chesterton takes on the socialists. Despite their prominence, as well as their insistence that they can offer humanity what it needs, socialists do not offer a plan that comports with human nature. They "have no firm instinctive sense of one thing being in its nature private and another public, of one thing being necessarily bond and another free. That is why piece by piece and quite silently, personal liberty is being stolen from Englishmen, as personal land has been silently stolen ever since the sixteenth century."[109] Chesterton is far from saying all public things must give way to private things, but he does insist that some things are properly public and others properly private. With respect to private things, Chesterton contends "that the communal ideal is not conscious of their existence, and therefore goes wrong at the very start, mixing a wholly public thing with a highly individual one."[110] Man needs not just a shelter but a *home*, and socialism cannot distinguish between the two.

Of course, Chesterton admits, the Tories are just as bad. While appearing to be implacable enemies of socialism, they have conceded everything of importance while play-fighting on margins of no importance. Chesterton is particularly hard on the Tories for failing to defend the family, because they refuse to acknowledge families require productive and independent households:

> For the plain truth to be told pretty sharply to the Tory is this, that if *he* wants the family to remain, if he wants it to be strong enough to resist the rending forces of our essentially savage commerce, he must make some very big sacrifices and try to equalize property. The overwhelming mass of the English people at this particular instant are simply too poor to be domestic. They are as domestic as they can manage, they are much more domestic than the governing class; but they cannot get what good there was originally meant to be in this institution, simply because they have not got enough money.[111]

Chesterton sees the battle between Tories and socialists as little more than a pantomime, disguising the awful possibility that they "are secretly in partnership; that the quarrel they keep up in public is very much of a put-up job; and that the way in which they perpetually play into each other's

109 Chesterton, *What's Wrong*, 203.

110 Chesterton, *What's Wrong*, 205–6.

111 Chesterton, *What's Wrong*, 208.

hands is not an everlasting coincidence."[112] Whether they are in active cahoots or tacit symbiosis, the truth remains that "between them they still keep the common man homeless."[113] Whatever the way forward, it will not be with either of these parties and their brittle, undignified conception of a humane life.

Chesterton leaves his readers with a principle and a parable. The principle is the necessity of the distributive state, founded on the productive household. There is no escaping the fact that "the strong centres of modern English property must swiftly or slowly be broken up, if the idea of property is to remain among Englishmen. There are two ways in which it could be done, a cold administration by quite detached officials, which is called Collectivism, or a personal distribution, so as to produce what is called Peasant Proprietorship. I think the latter solution the finer and more fully human, because it makes each man (as somebody blamed somebody for saying of the Pope) a sort of small god."[114]

A parable neatly expresses everything that repels Chesterton about contemporary England: "A little while ago certain doctors and other persons permitted by modern law to dictate to their shabbier fellow-citizens, sent out an order that all little girls should have their hair cut short."[115] Of course, in practice, this only applies to "all little girls whose parents were poor."[116] Long hair, at least among the poor, fosters lice, so the well-to-do of England apparently decided "that poor people must not be allowed to have hair, because in their case it must mean lice in the hair."[117] This is yet another example of how England's social reformers have put the cart before the horse: "It never seems to strike these people that the lesson of lice in the slums is the wrongness of slums, not the wrongness of hair."[118] Once again the well-to-do have forgotten "that the body is more than raiment; that the Sabbath was made for man; that all institutions shall be judged and damned by whether they have fitted the normal flesh and spirit."[119]

112 Chesterton, *What's Wrong*, 210.

113 Chesterton, *What's Wrong*, 211.

114 Chesterton, *What's Wrong*, 212.

115 Chesterton, *What's Wrong*, 213.

116 Chesterton, *What's Wrong*, 213.

117 Chesterton, *What's Wrong*, 213.

118 Chesterton, *What's Wrong*, 214.

119 Chesterton, *What's Wrong*, 215.

And so Chesterton takes his stand:

> Now the whole parable and purpose of these last pages, and indeed of all these pages, is this: to assert that we must instantly begin all over again, and begin at the other end. I begin with a little girl's hair. That I know is a good thing at any rate. Whatever else is evil, the pride of a good mother in the beauty of her daughter is good. It is one of those adamantine tendernesses which are the touchstones of every age and race. If other things are against it, other things must go down.[120]

To Chesterton, a series of inescapable conclusions follows from this, each as forceful as a blow:

> Because a girl should have long hair, she should have clean hair; because she should have clean hair, she should not have an unclean home; because she should not have an unclean home, she should have a free and leisured mother; because she should have a free mother, she should not have a usurious landlord; because there should not be an usurious landlord, there should be a redistribution of property; because there should be a redistribution of property, there shall be a revolution.[121]

FOCUSING ON THE FAMILY

To recapitulate: Chesterton believes the modern faith in the inevitability of progress is absurd. Progressives reify change, but they rarely know toward what kind of society they wish to progress. Chesterton offers a vision: the economically independent household, grounded in the family, with sufficient property to maintain itself. This is the cornerstone of a free state. Productive households promote liberty, equality, and democracy. The household is society's refuge against despotism, which looms when specialization and hierarchy go too far.

The household embodies a crucial balance between generalist and specialist forces. The family, formed from the natural complementarities between man and woman, maintains this balance. The family functions best, within itself and in relation to other households, when it divides labor along lines of sex: Men are specialists and focus on production outside the household, while women are generalists and focus on production within the household.

120 Chesterton, *What's Wrong*, 215.

121 Chesterton, *What's Wrong*, 215–16.

The family is also how society regenerates itself. It is the first and most important locus of education for future generations. Modern education seems intent on severing the bond between parents and children, but such efforts make society vulnerable to servility. The household is the only classroom that can educate for liberty. Ultimately, the family, conjoined with the productive household, is the only institution that can ground both public and private life. The economically free household and the politically free state are mutually supportive, but the former is necessary for the latter. Politics cannot rebuild fractured households and broken families. At best, it can set the background conditions against which families and productive households organically form.

Chesterton's focus on the family as the foundation of the distributive state reflects Catholic social teaching on the rights of workers, the importance of subsidiarity, and the inherent dignity of the human person. *What's Wrong* can be viewed as an extended argument for why the family and the productive household (really a single institution in Chesterton's mind; while it is possible to separate them, it is unthinkable to him that any good could come of it) must exist for a free and equal state. Top-down political programs are not substitutes for the family. Chesterton would argue any attempts to construct something like a distributive state through conventional political means would backfire. The concentration of power necessary for such a program is dangerous. Trying to force it would further entrench the power of unaccountable oligarchs in both commercial and political organizations. Politics has an important role to play in promoting and maintaining a distributive state, but the necessary political action must occur through deliberation among citizens who stand on a level playing field, which requires productive households.

Chesterton's discussion of household specialization contains many themes emphasized by modern economists. In some ways, Chesterton anticipates the arguments from the subfield of "family economics." There is a clear affinity between his arguments for how tasks are allocated within the family (the division of labor between household production and market production) and the economic approach to the family, which focuses on comparative opportunity costs as the determinant for who performs which tasks.[122]

122 Gary Becker authored many of the classic works on this subject. Particularly relevant are "A Theory of the Allocation of Time," *Economic Journal* 75, no. 299 (1965): 493–517, and *A Treatise on the Family* (Cambridge, Mass.: Harvard University Press, 1981). See Martin Browning, Pierre-Andre Chiappori, and Yoram Weiss, *Economics of the Family* (New York: Cambridge University Press, 2014) for a recent overview.

However, his contention that the division of household production along traditional sexual lines is an immutable pattern of human sociality is too hastily reached. While this division is assumed in much of the literature that comprises the Western canon—it is explicitly present in Xenophon's writings in the mid-fourth century BC, for example—subjecting it to the economic way of thinking shows that it is not an unchangeable natural law. If the allocation of tasks within the household depends on comparative opportunity costs, especially in terms of time, then we would expect social forces that alter these costs to affect the household division of labor, and following the end of the Second World War, marriage rates (and divorce rates), women's labor force participation, and the share of household income earned by women have all undergone marked changes in response to novel economic conditions. Perhaps Chesterton would view this as a bad thing, and a further step along the road to servility. Nonetheless the changes must be accounted for, and Chesterton's framework, while it hints at an explanation, is incomplete.

On this point, it is worth revisiting an odd quote. Chesterton contends, "The solemnity of politics; the necessity of votes . . . all these flow in a peculid [sic] stream from the lips of all the suffragette speakers. I suppose in every fight, however old, one has a vague aspiration to conquer; but we never wanted to conquer women so completely as this. We only expected that they might leave us a little more margin for our nonsense; we never expected that they would accept it seriously as sense."[123] The last two sentences are particularly strange. Chesterton sometimes confuses his own perspective with the perspective of the general public. To his claim that "we [men] never expected they would accept it seriously as sense," we can only reply: "Yes, we did!" Going back to Plato, the assumption was that public things were more important than private things. The production of goods and the organization of households fell under the category of the menial or servile arts. Those with liberal and magnanimous characters devoted their attention to statesmanship, leaving the lesser tasks to those whose natures were suited to them. Obviously, it was the men who devoted themselves to great public matters, while women were expected to handle minor private matters. Chesterton should be commended for denying public things are more important than private things, and hence (on his typology), the sphere

123 Chesterton, *What's Wrong*, 117.

of men is more important than the sphere of women.[124] But he still accepts that these spheres are separate and rarely overlap.

Chesterton's metaphysic of sex and gender is not necessary for his arguments about the private and public role of the family to succeed. Importantly, Chesterton identifies specific functions the family must perform, both inside the household and outside it, to reconcile liberty and equality. These functions (household production, market production, education, etc.) are separable from the persons who fulfill them. In terms of ascertaining the affinities between distributism and contemporary political economy, the functions should be the object of attention.

Nevertheless, Chesterton makes a seminal contribution to distributist thought by placing the productive household at the center of a free society, and the family at the center of the household. If society is a wheel and various social arenas (markets, politics, civil society) are its spokes, then the family is the hub. The wheel can still work passably well if one, or several, of its spokes are broken. But if the hub is broken, the wheel cannot work. Families without sufficient property to maintain the productive household, or productive households unanchored to the past and future by the family, are like broken hubs. Chesterton's other writings, which more directly engage political and economic problems, should be read with this in mind. The centrality of the family to the common good is the strongest link between distributism and Catholic social teaching. It is also the key for understanding distributist views on liberty, equality, and democracy.

124 In fact, Chesterton strongly suggests the private (domestic) sphere is more important than the public (economic, political) sphere. This goes beyond the "necessary and complementary" (see note 62) relations of man and woman. The flourishing household is the ultimate end.

Chapter 6

Chesterton's *The Outline of Sanity*

HUMANITY IN ECONOMY AND POLITY

The Outline of Sanity is a compilation of several essays Chesterton wrote on political and economic topics, edited and expanded to create a coherent narrative. Although Chesterton harshly criticizes the state of Western society and culture, especially in England, *The Outline of Sanity* "is *not* another book about the dissolution of the West. It is rather a book that pulls plug on the lies; it indicates clearly what does and does not constitute a worthwhile society; it draws lines and makes distinctions."[1] That is, it is primarily a positive treatise. It tears down only to make it easier to build up.

The Outline of Sanity is as much about politics as economics. Chesterton attacks monopolization (which entails both bigness and standardization) in markets and government. Whether private or public, Chesterton argues monopoly's goal "is the centralization of Life, both in its parts and as a whole. Its purpose is social control, the modern phrase for the age-old institution of Slavery." The use of the normatively charged term "Slavery" is intentional: Chesterton clearly builds on Belloc's *The Servile State*, offering a complementary perspective on the problems addressed previously by Chesterton's mentor. Chesterton agrees with Belloc and the body of Catholic social thought that "political and social freedom without economic freedom is a *cruel illusion*."[2] Furthermore, economic freedom requires independence: not just the liberty to refrain, but the liberty to undertake. For those who desire true freedom, both capitalism and socialism must be rejected in favor of distributism.

Given the contemporary urge to classify him as a reactionary, it is important to remember Chesterton is a liberal and a democrat through and through. His understanding of liberalism and democracy are idiosyncratic—Chesterton wouldn't be Chesterton without such quirks—but that does not lessen his devotion. This is not important only for intellectual

1 G. K. Chesterton, *The Outline of Sanity* (Norfolk, Va.: IHS Press, [1926] 2001), 9.

2 Chesterton, *The Outline of Sanity*, 20.

history. Understanding where Chesterton is coming from, and what his ideals are, is critical to interpreting him correctly. It's worthwhile to reproduce a few paragraphs from another work of his, *Orthodoxy*, which sheds light on these issues.

First, Chesterton has the following to say about democracy, and why it is an ultimate human ideal:

> This is the first principle of democracy: that the essential things in men are the things they hold in common, not the things they hold separately. And the second principle is merely this: that the political instinct or desire is one of these things which they hold in common. Falling in love is more poetical than dropping into poetry. The democratic contention is that government (helping to rule the tribe) is a thing like falling in love, and not a thing like dropping into poetry. It is not something analogous to playing the church organ, painting on vellum, discovering the North Pole (that insidious habit), looping the loop, being Astronomer Royal, and so on. For these things we do not wish a man to do at all unless he does them well. It is, on the contrary, a thing analogous to writing one's own love-letters or blowing one's own nose. These things we want a man to do for himself, even if he does them badly. I am not here arguing the truth of any of these conceptions; I know that some moderns are asking to have their wives chosen by scientists, and they may soon be asking, for all I know, to have their noses blown by nurses. I merely say that mankind does recognize these universal human functions, and that democracy classes government among them. In short, the democratic faith is this: that the most terribly important things must be left to ordinary men themselves—the mating of the sexes, the rearing of the young, the laws of the state. This is democracy; and in this I have always believed.[3]

Next, Chesterton offers a fascinating perspective on the relationship between democracy and tradition. Many of his fashionable contemporaries thought tradition was undemocratic, but Chesterton disagrees:

> But there is one thing that I have never from my youth up been able to understand. I have never been able to understand where people got the idea that democracy was in some way opposed to tradition. It is obvious

3 G. K. Chesterton, *Orthodoxy* (New York: John Lane, 1908), 83. Personally, this is one of the most powerful affirmations of democracy I have read. A dozen scholarly monographs do not contain the profundity of this paragraph.

> that tradition is only democracy extended through time. It is trusting to a consensus of common human voices rather than to some isolated or arbitrary record. The man who quotes some German historian against the tradition of the Catholic Church, for instance, is strictly appealing to aristocracy. He is appealing to the superiority of one expert against the awful authority of a mob. It is quite easy to see why a legend is treated, and ought to be treated, more respectfully than a book of history. The legend is generally made by the majority of people in the village, who are sane. The book is generally written by the one man in the village who is mad. Those who urge against tradition that men in the past were ignorant may go and urge it at the Carlton Club, along with the statement that voters in the slums are ignorant. It will not do for us. If we attach great importance to the opinion of ordinary men in great unanimity when we are dealing with daily matters, there is no reason why we should disregard it when we are dealing with history or fable. Tradition may be defined as an extension of the franchise. Tradition means giving votes to the most obscure of all classes, our ancestors. It is the democracy of the dead. Tradition refuses to submit to the small and arrogant oligarchy of those who merely happen to be walking about. All democrats object to men being disqualified by the accident of birth; tradition objects to their being disqualified by the accident of death. Democracy tells us not to neglect a good man's opinion, even if he is our groom; tradition asks us not to neglect a good man's opinion, even if he is our father. I, at any rate, cannot separate the two ideas of democracy and tradition; it seems evident to me that they are the same idea. We will have the dead at our councils. The ancient Greeks voted by stones; these shall vote by tombstone. It is all quite regular and official, for most tombstones, like most ballot papers, are marked with a cross.[4]

Tradition, democracy, the human things—in Chesterton's mind, these are inexorably linked. With this appreciation of Chesterton's views on political philosophy, we are prepared to begin our investigation of Chesterton's political economy. There is much in *The Outline of Sanity* that will make the modern economist sneer, and many of these things are, in fact, unsupportable based on our knowledge of price theory. Dismissing him out of hand, however, is impermissible; with Chesterton, there are whole worlds lurking beneath the surface.

4 Chesterton, *Orthodoxy*, 84.

FIRST THINGS FIRST

Unsurprisingly, Chesterton begins with definitions and first principles. Immediately, he captures the reader's attention by highlighting the tensions between private *property* and private *enterprise*.[5] This seems strange to modern economists, and probably would to economists in Chesterton's day as well. Such an opposition is less perplexing given what we know from Belloc's work, but it nonetheless highlights the paradoxical quality of Chesterton's writing, a quality in which he revels. Right away, Chesterton expresses his disapproval of the "extension of business rather than the preservation of belongings";[6] this is probably the most concise way of expressing his point.

Like Belloc, Chesterton has an idiosyncratic definition of capitalism, by which he means "that economic condition in which there is a class of capitalists, roughly recognizable and relatively small, in whose possession so much of the capital is concentrated as to necessitate a very large majority of the citizens serving those capitalists for a wage."[7] Chesterton equates capitalism with proletarianism; widespread wage labor is a direct consequence of the accumulation and concentration of capital. Socialism, in contrast, "is a system which makes the corporate unity of society responsible for all its economic processes, or all those affecting life and essential living." When anything of importance is controlled by the state, citizens are reduced to subjects. Following their economic dispossession, the people are stripped of their right to resist tyranny: "Opposition and rebellion depend on property and liberty. They can only be tolerated where other rights have been allowed to strike root, besides the central right of the ruler."[8] Thus, we see a de facto link between economic and political freedom, as in Belloc's works. Finally, as opposed to capitalism and socialism, Chesterton stands for a "policy of small distributed property,"[9] which we know as distributism.

Chesterton touches on several familiar themes. First, distributism is desirable because it preserves the balance of forces conducive to a free state.[10] Second, capitalism is not a natural step in economic progression; it

5 Chesterton, *Outline*, 25.

6 Chesterton, *Outline*, 25.

7 Chesterton, *Outline*, 27.

8 Chesterton, *Outline*, 29.

9 Chesterton, *Outline*, 29.

10 Chesterton, *Outline*, 30–32.

develops where men have already been dispossessed of their traditional lands and liberties. England, for example, "became a capitalist country because it had long been an oligarchical country."[11] Where widely distributed property exists from time immemorial, public opinion and law blend together at a deep level, presenting a potent obstacle to any would-be oligarch. Attempted centralization is met with immediate outcry: "When it is really thought hateful to take Naboth's vineyard, as it is to take Uriah's wife, there is little difficulty in finding a local prophet to pronounce the judgment of the Lord."[12]

Next, Chesterton tries to pin down the sources of capitalist instability: "Now the capitalist system, good or bad, right or wrong, rests upon two ideas: that the rich will always be rich enough to hire the poor; and the poor will always be poor enough to want to be hired."[13] But this is a shaky foundation, because the average capitalist "is always trying to cut down what his servant demands, and in doing so is cutting down what his customer can spend. As soon as his business is in any difficulties . . . he tries to reduce what he has to spend on wages, and in doing so reduces what others have to spend."[14] This argument will immediately resonate with students of macroeconomics. Those who think aggregate demand instability is intrinsic to capitalism, as did Keynes and his school, will nod their heads approvingly. On the other hand, those who focus on relative prices rather than economic aggregates to explain the trade cycle will not see much merit in this explanation.

Whatever the economic mechanisms at work, Chesterton regards it as self-evident that capitalism has failed and that an alternative is needed. He does not have much patience for rebuttals that industrial capitalism, now that it has arrived, will inevitably continue. Capitalists "are always telling us that in resisting capitalism and commercialism we are like Canute rebuking the waves; and they do not even know that the England of Cobden is already as dead as the England of Canute."[15] In fact, he is confident that a healthy polity will sprout as soon as we start pulling the weeds of industrialism and commercialism.[16] Yet Chesterton is no utopian. He does not believe

11 Chesterton, *Outline*, 34.

12 Chesterton, *Outline*, 35.

13 Chesterton, *Outline*, 41.

14 Chesterton, *Outline*, 43.

15 Chesterton, *Outline*, 46.

16 Chesterton, *Outline*, 51.

implementing distributism will end social strife: "We do not say . . . [man] will be always be perfectly happy or perfectly good; because there are other elements in life besides the economic; and even the economic is affected by original sin."[17] He does believe, however, that there are better and worse ways of constituting society such that men can "get on reasonably well with each other."[18] Distributism can better help men "get on"; capitalism and socialism cannot.

Chesterton closes his introductory section with a blistering indictment of the dehumanizing tendencies of collectivism, both private and public. Their chief sins are bureaucracy and standardization, which destroy the humane diversity of civilization. In this regard, capitalism and socialism are flip sides of the same coin: "It would make no difference," Chesterton claims, "to the clerk if his job became a part of a Government department tomorrow. He would be equally civilized and equally uncivic if the distant and shadowy person at the head of the department were a Government official."[19] These systems equally have proletarianized English society. A modern Englishman "lives in a house he does not own, that he did not make, that he does not want. He moves everywhere in ruts; he always goes up to his work on rails. He has forgotten what his fathers, the hunters and the pilgrims and the wandering minstrels, meant by finding their way to a place. He thinks in terms of wages; that is, he has forgotten the real meaning of wealth. His highest ambition is concerned with getting this or that subordinate post in a business that is already a bureaucracy."[20] In contrast, a distributist polity is lively and robust because it is not one coordinated thing but rather many cooperating things:

> We do not propose that in a healthy society all land should be held in the same way; or that all property should be owned on the same conditions; or that all citizens should have the same relation to the city. *It is our whole point that the central power needs lesser powers to balance and check it*, and that these must be of many kinds: some individual, some communal, some official and so on. Some of them will probably abuse their privileges; but we prefer that risk to that of the State or the Trust, which abuses its omnipotence.[21]

17 Chesterton, *Outline*, 53.

18 Chesterton, *Outline*, 53.

19 Chesterton, *Outline*, 59.

20 Chesterton, *Outline*, 62.

21 Chesterton, *Outline*, 63, my emphasis.

It is tempting to dismiss the above as a medieval wish-list, and Chesterton readily admits influence of medievalism on his thought. But he is no mere romantic in love with the past. His goal is not reaction, but balance: "So, from our social garden, we should not necessarily exclude every modern machine anymore than we should exclude every medieval monastery."[22] Why industrial capitalism upsets balance, and what can be done about it, Chesterton considers in subsequent sections.

BIG BUSINESS: ATTACK ON FREEDOM

Chesterton is an opponent of bigness in all its forms, including big business. He views the large commercial organizations of early twentieth-century capitalism as exploitative, irresponsible, and hostile to true human freedom. He even denies their supposed economic benefits: "I think the big shop is a bad shop. I think it bad not only in a moral but a mercantile sense; that is, I think shopping there is not only a bad action but a bad bargain."[23] This criticism extends even to the apparent gains from some degree of hierarchical-managerial control: "I deny that its large organization is efficient. Large organization is loose organization . . . it is not true that you must have a long rigid line of people trimming hats or tying bouquet, in order that they may be trimmed or tied neatly. The work is much more likely to be neat if it is done by a particular craftsman for a particular customer with particular ribbons and flowers."[24] Big business really benefits only big businessmen.

Chesterton's first recommendation is deceptively simple: "Very little is left free in the modern world; but private buying and selling are still supposed to be free . . . nobody is yet driven by force to a particular shop."[25] Given this freedom, the way to break the power of the big shops is . . . to stop shopping there. If Englishmen "came to the conclusion that big shops ought to be boycotted, we could boycott them as easily as we should (I hope) boycott shops selling instruments of torture or poisons for private use in the home. In other words, this first and fundamental question is not a question of necessity but of will."[26]

22 Chesterton, *Outline*, 65.

23 Chesterton, *Outline*, 67.

24 Chesterton, *Outline*, 68.

25 Chesterton, *Outline*, 71.

26 Chesterton, *Outline*, 72.

The most immediate objection to the above—indeed, to any distributist proposal—is its impracticability. It requires changing men's fundamental commercial and political habits. Chesterton would happily admit the conclusion while denying the premise. Restoring widely divided property will undoubtedly be difficult. That the task is hard, however, is no reason to abstain from trying. In fact, the difficulty of the task suggests the importance of starting immediately. "I knew a hundred correspondents," Chesterton recounts, who "would call me utopian; and say it was obvious my scheme could not work, because I could only describe it when it was working. But what they really mean by my being utopian would be this: that until the scheme was working, there was no work to be done."[27] Chesterton replies: there is plenty of work to be done. So start working!

In addition to voluntary boycott, Chesterton is optimistic about (some) political proposals to implement well-distributed property. These actions, while nominally restricting rights of property, in fact expand those rights. The view that the existing distribution of property is a result of private choice, which public authority ought to respect, Chesterton believes is absurd. He scoffs at "the nonsense whereby men, who are more powerful than emperors, pretend to be private tradesmen. . . . [Proposals] will assert that those who are in practice public men must be criticized as potential public evils."[28] Specific proposals in which Chesterton finds merit include:

1. The taxation of contracts so as to discourage the sale of small property to big proprietors and encourage the breakup of big property among small proprietors
2. Something like the Napoleonic testamentary law and the destruction of primogeniture
3. The establishment of free law for the poor, so that small property could always be defended against great
4. The deliberate protection of certain experiments in small property, if necessary, by tariffs and even local tariffs
5. Subsidies to foster the starting of such experiments
6. A league of voluntary dedication, and any number of other things of the same kind[29]

27 Chesterton, *Outline*, 74.

28 Chesterton, *Outline*, 78.

29 All six quoted from p. 79.

To further demonstrate the feasibility of distributist reform, Chesterton explores one additional proposal: a law requiring all shops to close for a weekly holiday, with an exemption for proprietorships (the owner is the sole employee). When the proposal had received some public attention, even at one point being discussed within Parliament, "the Minister in charge of the matter actually replied, with a ghastly innocence, that it was impossible; for it would be unfair to the big shops."[30] So much for the inevitability of bigness. "Apparently Big Business must be accepted because it is invulnerable, and spared because it is vulnerable."[31] If the political establishment is worried, bigness must not be unavoidable after all. Chesterton thinks, in addition to showing the invincibility of bigness to be a mirage, that such a law would help to restore an ownership mentality among ordinary families:

> I am sure if they could trade on the general holiday, it would not only mean that there would be more trade for them, but that there would be more of them trading. It might mean at last a large class of little shopkeepers; and that this is exactly the sort of thing that makes all the political difference, as it does in the case of a large class of little farmers. It is not in the merely mechanical sense a matter of numbers. It is a matter of the presence and pressure of a particular social type. It is not a question merely of how many noses are counted; *but in the more real sense of whether the noses count.*[32]

The change in the character of the state, with a significantly larger number of independent proprietors contributing to public opinion, would also lessen the appeal of socialism. Men secure in what is their own do not foment revolutions. Such men instinctively understand "why the things we produce ourselves are precious like our own children, *and why we can pay too dearly for the possession of luxury by the loss of liberty.*"[33]

Chesterton closes his jeremiad against big business by pointing out again the folly of resigned acceptance of capitalism. It is, in fact, possible to protect private property while punishing monopoly: "The modern commercial combine has a great many points in common with a big balloon. It is swollen and yet it is swollen with levity; it climbs and yet drifts; above all, it is full of gas, and generally of poison gas. But the resemblance most relevant here is that

30 Chesterton, *Outline*, 83.

31 Chesterton, *Outline*, 83.

32 Chesterton, *Outline*, 83, my emphasis.

33 Chesterton, *Outline*, 84, my emphasis.

the smallest prick will shrivel the biggest balloon."[34] As long as anybody fights for small property, those who would corner markets are vulnerable: "Ahab has not his kingdom so long as Naboth has his vineyard."[35]

Chesterson believed that attempted monopolization should be punished as a crime: "The commonsense of Christendom, for ages on end, has assumed that it was as possible to punish cornering as to punish coining."[36] When people say they cannot imagine punishing private commercial activity, what they "really mean is that they cannot imagine cornering being treated like coining. They cannot imagine attempted forestalling or, indeed, any activity of the rich, coming into the realm of the criminal law at all. . . . The laughter that leaps up spontaneously at the suggestion is itself a proof that nobody takes seriously, or thinks of taking seriously, the idea of rich men and poor being equal before the law."[37] It is not disembodied economic forces but mistaken impressions of unfeasibility and undesirability that stop men from fighting monopolies and busting trusts.

In making his argument, Chesterton propounds some questionable claims about the practice of dumping and the operation of credit markets, as does Belloc before him, but we do not need to reconsider those errors. What is important and enduring is the spirit that permeates his closing remarks. England

> shall never have a real civic sense until it is once more felt that the plot of three citizens against one citizen is a crime, as well as the plot of one citizen against three. In other words, private property ought to be protected against private judgement. But private property ought to be protected against public crime, just as public order is protected against private judgment. But private property ought to be protected against much bigger things than burglars and pickpockets. It needs protection against the plots of a whole plutocracy. It needs defence against the rich, who are now generally the rulers who ought to defend it . . . if they had served their God as they have served their Pork King and their Petrol King, the success of our Distributive democracy would stare at the world like one of their flaming sky signs and scrape the sky like one of their crazy towers.[38]

34 Chesterton, *Outline*, 89.

35 Chesterton, *Outline*, 89.

36 Chesterton, *Outline*, 90.

37 Chesterton, *Outline*, 92.

38 Chesterton, *Outline*, 94.

LIVING WITH THE LAND

Chesterton next turns to the issue that, more than any other, seems to delight the distributist intellect: the restoration of a free yeomanry. Especially in Chesterton's writing, there is a quasiphysiocratic emphasis on land as an object of veneration. Living with the land helps men to remember that they are stewards, not masters. It also prevents them from confusing the ends of economic activity with the means. Most importantly, making land a central part of his analysis is necessary for Chesterton's eagerly sought equilibrium of social power. "But," he affirms,

> even my ideal . . . would be what some call a compromise. Only I think it more accurate to call it a balance. For I do not think that the sun compromises with the rain when together they make a garden; or that the rose that grows there is a compromise between green and red. But I mean that my utopia would contain different things of different types holding on different tenures; that as in a medieval State there were some peasants, some monasteries, some common land, some private land, some town guilds, and so on, so in my modern State there would be some things nationalized, some machines owned corporately, some guilds sharing common profits, and so on, as well as many absolute individual owners.[39]

Restoring peasant proprietors would revive a class of citizens with a vested interest in tradition and continuity. Chesterton is not a conservative—not a conventional one, at least—but there is plenty of time-tested common sense in him that recognizes that tradition is a guardian of liberty. He also believes, even amidst English industrial capitalism, there are still realistic prospects for the economically dispossessed to "take to the land": "A man in England might live on the land, if he did not have rent to pay to the landlord and wages to pay to the labourer. He would therefore be better off, even on a small scale, if he were his own landlord and his own labourer."[40] Lastly, peasant proprietors have a strong, if inchoate, appreciation for the institution of private ownership, meaning "in so far as the peasant proprietor is certainly tenacious for the peasant property . . . he does, in fact, constitute a solid block of private property which can be counted on to resist Communism."[41]

39 Chesterton, *Outline*, 98.

40 Chesterton, *Outline*, 99.

41 Chesterton, *Outline*, 100.

Chesterton admits that returning to the land is challenging. Hopefully, the reader can predict by now that Chesterton does not admit this as a valid counterargument: "We cannot pretend to be offering merely comforts and conveniences. Whatever our ultimate view of labour-saving machinery, we cannot offer our ideal as a labour-saving machine. There is no more question of comfort than there is for a man in a fire, a battle, or a shipwreck. There is no way out of the danger except the dangerous way."[42] As if relishing his defiance of modern sensibilities, Chesterton calls for "independent individual action on a large scale."[43] It will not do to wait for state support: "The fulfilment of parliamentary promises grows rather slower than grass; and if nothing is done before the completion of what is called a constitutional process, we shall be about as near to Distributism as a Labour politician is to Socialism."[44] The best way forward is to live out the ideal. Positive law will follow.

Chesterton is pragmatic enough to anticipate a significant obstacle: Living off the land is quite laborious: "The responsibility of small farms, for the sake of self-sufficiency, of real property," is not taken on lightly.[45] "It is impossible to disguise that the man who gets the land, even more than the man who gives up the land, will have to be something of a hero. . . . We are not asking people to cut a coupon out of a newspaper, but to carve a farm out of a trackless waste; and if it is to be successful, it must be faced in something of the stubborn spirit of the old fulfilment of a vow."[46]

To find volunteers, Chesterton recommends searching the ranks of the economically dispossessed. He sees a healthy amount of vitality and desire for independence in England's urban proletariat. Whereas other commenters write them off as an underclass, Chesterton sees in them the seeds of social revival.[47] If fishermen could conquer an empire, perhaps it is not so farfetched that laborers could conquer a plot of land. His proposals could not be seriously entertained without believing that a proletarian is the moral peer of a prince and is equally capable of living a dignified life.

While state support cannot substitute for a widespread popular movement, it can complement it: "Though much could be done by volunteers . . .

42 Chesterton, *Outline*, 103.

43 Chesterton, *Outline*, 104.

44 Chesterton, *Outline*, 104.

45 Chesterton, *Outline*, 105.

46 Chesterton, *Outline*, 105.

47 Chesterton, *Outline*, 108–9.

there is nothing in our social philosophy that forbids the use of the State power where it can be used."[48] At minimum, proletarians will need some way of acquiring the land they wish to work. If Brown the proletarian wishes to buy some land, and Smith the absentee landlord wishes to be relieved of his currently vacant plot, it seems "within the resources of civilization to enable Brown to buy from Smith what is now of very little value to Smith and might be of very great value to Brown."[49] A state subsidy could be immensely helpful in this regard.

Chesterton finishes his discussion on land reform by considering some broader aspects of the division of labor. Restoring widespread landownership is both easier and harder than acquiescing to capitalism or socialism: "It is more easy because it need not be crushed by complexities of cosmopolitan trade. It is harder because it is a hard life to live apart from them."[50] While modern economists marvel at the wonders afforded by specialization under the division of labor, Chesterton is less sanguine. "A system based entirely on the division of labor is in one sense literally half-witted," Chesterton warns us. "That is, each performer of half an operation does really use only half of his wits. . . . The community is at present very defective because there is not in the core of it . . . any one man who represents the two parties to a contract. Unless there is, there is nowhere a full understanding of those terms: self-support, self-control, self-government."[51]

These are difficult words for economists to swallow. They are most profitably read in the spirit of Belloc's remarks on the divergence between procommerce and proliberty social orders.[52] To Chesterton, the problem with the overly specialized man is that "he does not know the causes of things; and that is why . . . *he can be too much dominated by despots and demagogues* . . . he does not protest too much, because he cannot; and he cannot because he does not know enough about the causes of things—about the primary forms of property and production, or the points where man is nearest to his natural origins."[53] Even a free yeoman "will have but a partial experience if he grows things in the country solely in order to sell

48 Chesterton, *Outline*, 109.

49 Chesterton, *Outline*, 110.

50 Chesterton, *Outline*, 112.

51 Chesterton, *Outline*, 113–14.

52 See also Adam Smith's similar remarks in *Wealth of Nations* (bk. 5, chap. 1).

53 Chesterton, *Outline*, 115, my emphasis.

them to the town."[54] Free societies thus require at least some degree of autarky: "It seems to me a very good thing, in theory as well as practice, that there should be a body of citizens primarily concerned in producing and consuming and not in exchanging."[55] The supporting idea is once again that economically free men produce politically free societies. To be clear, Chesterton does not advocate a return to widespread barter or local exchange, nor does he propose that a majority of citizens be cut off from the division of labor: "I do not say that the State needs only the man who needs nothing from the State. But I do say that this man who supplies his own needs is very much needed."[56]

MACHINERY AND FREEDOM

Next Chesterton considers the challenge modern machinery poses to distributism. His ambivalence toward machines—economists would call this "capital," meaning the produced factors of production—is obvious, but it would be an oversimplification to dismiss him as a Luddite. Instead, he insists that, like all other aspects of economic life, machinery must be judged not according to its efficiency in producing output but in promoting human flourishing. Once again, Chesterton refuses to countenance any claims about the inevitability of modern production methods: "Before we begin any talk of the practical problem of machinery, it is necessary to leave off thinking like machines. It is necessary to begin at the beginning and consider the end. Now we do not necessarily wish to destroy every sort of machinery. But we do desire to destroy a certain sort of mentality. And that is precisely the sort of mentality that begins by telling us that nobody *can* destroy machinery. Those who begin by saying that we *cannot* abolish the machine, that we must use the machine, are themselves refusing to use the mind."[57]

"The aim of human polity," Chesterton tells us, "is happiness . . . the making glad of the heart of man, is the secular test and the only realistic test. . . . There is no obligation on us to be richer, or busier, or more efficient, or more productive, or more progressive, or in any way worldlier or wealthier, if it does not make us happier."[58] Here it must be noted that Chesterton

54 Chesterton, *Outline*, 117.

55 Chesterton, *Outline*, 117.

56 Chesterton, *Outline*, 118.

57 Chesterton, *Outline*, 123.

58 Chesterton, *Outline*, 123.

does not mean by "happiness" mere subjective satisfaction. Happiness for Chesterton is objective, as it was for Aristotle and St. Thomas Aquinas. It means human flourishing: a life well-lived according to right reason. This represents another significant departure from economic thought but one we must grapple with if we are to understand Chesterton on his own terms. His commitment to this conception of the human good is uncompromising: "If we can make men happier, it does not matter if we make them poorer, it does not matter if we make them less productive, it does not matter if we make them less progressive, in the sense of changing their life without increasing their liking for it."[59] Chesterton does not say, "nor perhaps should every say, that machinery has been proved to be practically poisonous in this degree."[60] That is, he does not convict machinery of undermining human happiness in all cases, but he certainly claims the right to judge, and to render a guilty verdict if the facts support it.

Chesterton makes a concrete suggestion that is also promoted by Belloc: "In so far as the machine cannot be shared, I would have the ownership of it shared; that is, the direction of it shared and the profits of it shared. But when I say 'shared' I mean it in the modern mercantile sense of the word 'shares.'"[61] This is already done in modern industrial concerns; Chesterton's objection is that it is not done enough, or rather widely enough. To the extent large machinery is required for a production process, his preference "would be that any such necessary machine should be owned by a small local guild, on principles of profit-sharing, or rather profit-dividing: but of real profit-sharing and real profit-dividing, not to be confounded by capitalist patronage."[62]

While Chesterton sees modern machinery as a challenge for the distributist state, he does not think achieving the latter requires abolishing the former. He sympathizes with the concerns of uncompromising antimachinists, but he thinks they make the same spiritual mistake as Panglossian promachinists: "It seems to me quite as materialistic to be damned by a machine as saved by a machine. It seems to be quite as idolatrous to blaspheme it as to worship it."[63] Machinery can be a boon so long as its ownership (and its

59 Chesterton, *Outline*, 125.

60 Chesterton, *Outline*, 125.

61 Chesterton, *Outline*, 125–26.

62 Chesterton, *Outline*, 126.

63 Chesterton, *Outline*, 129.

attendant benefits) are widely distributed, but this requires man's attitude toward machinery to change. In brief, man ought to treat machinery imaginatively, rather than practically. If we value machinery as a marvel of applied science, we can have a healthy relationship with it. Instead of the machine "being a giant to which the man is a pygmy, we must at least reverse the proportions until man is a giant to whom the machine is a toy."[64] If man could treat machinery with the same wonder and levity as a boy does his toys, then machinery could be just as conducive to health and happiness as child's play. The problem machinery raises for the well-being of the individual, and hence the vitality of the polity, is that "an essential and not accidental character of machinery [is] that it is an inspiration for the inventor but merely a monotony for the consumer."[65]

In monotony lies the death of variety and joy, without which no distributist state is feasible. "Inventions have destroyed invention," Chesterton laments.[66] Detached from a healthy sense of life, modern production methods have turned man from a subject into an object. As a result, "we are not getting the best out of men. We are certainly not getting the most individual or the most interesting qualities out of men."[67] The claim that machinery is a neutral agent, producing more outputs with fewer inputs and thus affording man greater leisure, does not withstand scrutiny in Chesterton's paradigm: "If by machinery saving labour, and therefore producing leisure, be meant the machinery that now achieves what is called mass production, I cannot see any vital value in the leisure; because there is in that leisure nothing of liberty."[68] Because of the moral aspects of production, no amount of quantitative production will suffice for a qualitative value-judgment on machinery.

A final concern Chesterton raises about machinery is its inegalitarian potential. The context for these objections is some remarks made by Henry Ford, who claimed that many men were suitable only for monotonous production on the assembly line. Modern production methods, precisely because they discouraged individuality and variety, supposedly contributed to social pacification by providing remunerative employment for "inferior"

64 Chesterton, *Outline*, 133.

65 Chesterton, *Outline*, 134.

66 Chesterton, *Outline*, 138.

67 Chesterton, *Outline*, 138–39.

68 Chesterton, *Outline*, 139.

individuals. While this view now strikes us as odious, it was not uncommon among the liberal, especially the Progressive, politicians and businessmen at the time. Chesterton, an unterrified defender of the *imago Dei*, rightly replies, "I shall begin to take seriously those classifications of superiority and inferiority, when I find a man classifying himself as inferior."[69] In other words, Chesterton denies that modern production methods select for a class of natural plebes to take orders and a class of natural aristocrats to give them. The cream does not necessarily rise to the top: "Anybody who knows anything of modern business knows that there are any number of such men who remain in subordinate and obscure positions because their private tastes and talents have no relation to the very stupid business in which they are engaged."[70]

Because Chesterton sees variety and independence as necessarily entwined, he worries about mass production:

> The condition in which . . . secondary talents do to some extent come out is the condition of small independence. The peasant almost always runs two or three sideshows and lives on a variety of crafts and expedients. The village shopkeeper will shave travelers and stuff weasels and grow cabbages and do half a dozen such things, keeping a sort of balance in his life like the balance of sanity in the soul. The method is not perfect; but it is more intelligent than turning him into a machine in order to find out whether he has a soul above machinery.[71]

Chesterton's final word on the subject is "that it is quite right to use the existing machines in so far as they do create a psychology that can despise machines; but not if they create a psychology that respects them." Chesterton's issue is not with "Mr. Ford's car," but "Mr. Ford's creed. If accepting the car means accepting the philosophy I have just criticized, the notion that some men are born to make cars, or rather small bits of cars, then it will be far more worthy of a philosopher to say frankly that men never needed to have cars at all."[72] Everything hinges not on whether man uses machines but on whether using them makes him machinelike.

69 Chesterton, *Outline*, 145.

70 Chesterton, *Outline*, 147.

71 Chesterton, *Outline*, 147.

72 Chesterton, *Outline*, 147–48.

DISTRIBUTISM AND NATIONALISM

The next section deals with cultural aspects of political-economic systems. It must be remembered that when Chesterton wrote his books and essays, England was in possession of a world-spanning empire. Colonial questions were often at the forefront of policy debates. Chesterton thus cannot avoid discussing colonial issues, such as emigration. Interestingly, this does not render Chesterton's analysis less relevant to contemporary discussions. Although many of his concerns are anachronistic, his overall perspective endures, and this is particularly evident today.

At the time of this writing, many Western nations are grappling with resurgent populist and nationalist politics. These political programs are amplified by distributional tensions. Due to perceptions of rising inequality and the hollowing out of working- and middle-class populations, calls for national solidarity and economic security frequently go together. Whether or not these positions are feasible, or even desirable, as major shifts in public opinion, they cannot be ignored. Chesterton's perspective on these issues, much of which reads like it was written for today, warrants special attention.

Chesterton takes the existence of empire as given; although he is no imperialist, he does recognize that there is no immediate possibility of retreating from England's longstanding foreign policy. His concern is "our owning an Empire and not of an Empire owning us."[73] Given significant population flows between the homeland and its colonies, Chesterton wishes that "England shall remain English. . . . It may have been wrong to be an Empire, but it does not rob us of our right to be a nation."[74] Chesterton's views overlap, to some degree, with "Little Englanders" or "England Firsters." He insists "our first step should be to discover how far the best ethical and economic system can be fitted into England, before we treat it as an export and cart it away to the ends of the earth."[75] Before England governs foreign nations, Chesterton believes, she ought to learn how to govern herself.

Chesterton thinks colonial policy is downstream from domestic policy. One issue he discusses at length is emigration to the colonies. This naturally raises questions concerning the ability of England to "export" her institutions, but whether it is possible for Englishmen to take England with them

73 Chesterton, *Outline*, 152.

74 Chesterton, *Outline*, 152.

75 Chesterton, *Outline*, 152.

is the wrong question. The right one is whether they love England enough to try, and love requires loyalty: "I put first the statement that real colonial settlement must be not only stable but sacred. I say the new home must be not only a home but a shrine. And that is why I say it must be first established in England, in the home of our fathers and the shrine of our saints, to be a light and an ensign to our children."[76] Or to put it another way: "I ask for nothing better than a man should be English in England. But I think he will have to be something more than English (or at any rate something more than 'British') if he is to create a solid social equality outside England."[77]

Lest there be any doubt as to Chesterton's motivations, he dispels them by asserting, "I am a nationalist; England is good enough for me. I would defend England against the whole European continent. With even greater joy would I defend England against the whole British Empire."[78] Hence, Chesterton believes there is a tension between nationalism (and even patriotism) and empire. This tension is particularly evident when the worldviews of the colonizers clash with those of the colonized. Chesterton insists that, whatever else is mixed, the expedients of empire cannot justify renouncing what makes England, England. In terms of English pioneers and land policy, Chesterton laments that none of the men helming the ship of state "ever conceived him [the pioneer] as having any strong sense of private property. There was in the vague idea of his gaining something for the Empire always, if anything, the idea of his gaining what belonged to someone else."[79] Imperialist exploitation abroad can subtly promote proletarianism at home. To prevent empire from swallowing England, what is needed "is the ideal of Property, not merely Progress—especially progress over other people's property. Utopia needs more frontiers, not less. And it is because we were weak in the ethics of property on the edges of Empire that our own society will not defend property as men defend a right. The Bolshevist is the sequel and punishment of the Buccaneer."[80]

Chesterton continues his discussion of nationalism and distributism by exploring the situation of French Canadians. In Chesterton's mind, these settlers embody the spirit of imagination and practicality that is required

76 Chesterton, *Outline*, 154.

77 Chesterton, *Outline*, 154.

78 Chesterton, *Outline*, 155.

79 Chesterton, *Outline*, 157–58.

80 Chesterton, *Outline*, 158.

for social property. Chesterton notes that "a number of sly critics . . . would point the finger of detection at me and cry, as if they had caught me in something very naughty, 'You believe in the French Canadians because they are Catholics'; which is on one sense not only true, but very nearly the whole truth. But in another sense it is not true at all; if it means that I exercise no independent judgment in perceiving that this is really what we do want."[81] Chesterton makes two points here that may be difficult for contemporary readers to grasp. First, he denies religion is a private matter that ought to have no bearing on public affairs. One's ultimate view of life, Chesterton insists, is necessarily expressed in the institutions that constitute collective action and give it meaning. Second, economic and political questions necessarily bleed into religious questions. Just as religious neutrality is a mirage, it is impossible to insulate discussions of how goods ought to be produced and distributed from reference to some ultimate end.

Chesterton goes on to quote an article written by a man from Toronto about the situation of French Canadians. Chesterton is in complete agreement with the spirit of the gentleman's remarks: "'Though I [the Canadian man] am not a religious man myself, I must confess I think religion has a good deal to do with it. These French Canadians are more Catholic than the Pope. You might call a good many of them desperately ignorant and desperately superstitious. They seem to be to be a century behind the times *and a century nearer happiness*."[82] Chesterton praises the attitude in the article as "a tribute to Frenchmen as colonists as because it is a tribute to colonists as pious and devout people. But what concerns me most of all in the general discussion of my own theme is the insistence on stability. They are staying on the soil; they are a social organism; they are held together as a unit. That is the new note which I think is needed in all talk of colonization, before it can again be any part of the hope of the world."[83]

"It is only religion," Chesterton insists, that can "give a sort of accumulated power of culture and legend to something that is crude or incomplete. . . . In a sense a new world can be baptized as a new baby is baptized, and become a part of an ancient order not merely on the map but in the mind."[84] Only while holding fast to an ultimate end, which religion alone can pro-

81 Chesterton, *Outline*, 161.

82 Chesterton, *Outline*, 162, my emphasis.

83 Chesterton, *Outline*, 164.

84 Chesterton, *Outline*, 165.

vide, can man embrace what is new and make it his own, without forgetting the permanent things. Holding on to this spirit, "it would be possible for people to cultivate the soil as they cultivate the soul. . . . In the most exalted phrase, we need a real presence. In the most popular phrase, we need something that is always on the spot."[85]

Now Chesterton links this insight with distributism: "But its practical relation to the reconstruction of property is that, unless we understand this spirit, we cannot now relieve congestion with colonization."[86] In other words, population issues, both at home and abroad, are secondary. What matters most is restoring veneration for the kind of society in which every man can be secure in what is his own. Chesterton acknowledges there is more than a touch of romanticism in his remarks but believes that distributists are hardly the only ones to indulge such visions:

> If we are indeed presenting impossible portraits of an ideal humanity, we are not alone in that. Not only the Socialists but also the Capitalists parade before us their imaginary and ideal figures, and the Capitalists if possible more than the Socialists. . . . But we do not blame either the Capitalists or the Socialists for setting up a type or talismanic figure to fix the imagination. We do not wonder at their presenting the perfect person for our admiration; we only wonder at the person they admire . . . ours is much more of a reality as well as a romance than the dreams of the other romantics. There cannot be a nation of millionaires, and there has never yet been a nation of utopian comrades; but there have been any number of nations of tolerably content peasants.[87]

Thus, maintaining well-distributed property overseas is the same kind of problem as maintaining it in the homeland. If it has failed abroad, it is because the supposed exigencies of empire have infected minds and manners at home. Extending England's reach to other nations has come at the cost of the English nation: a vision of what England is, why it matters, and why it is worth keeping. The solution to this ultimately lies in the realm of ideas; we must get "men to think, not merely of a place which they would be interested to find, but of a place where they would be contented to stay."[88]

85 Chesterton, *Outline*, 166.

86 Chesterton, *Outline*, 166.

87 Chesterton, *Outline*, 167.

88 Chesterton, *Outline*, 168.

To make other places like home, Englishmen must first make no place like home. But this cannot happen without religion, because only religion can instill an enduring respect for man's ultimate end as well as foster individual and social charity to ensure he has the earthly goods that can help him achieve this end.

RESUMÉ

Chesterton's arguments are rarely straightforward. He revels in exploring tangents, seemingly without rhyme or reason, then suddenly demonstrates that these secondary issues are in fact crucial for his thesis. If reading Belloc suggests the precision of a military march, reading Chesterton suggests a meandering walk in the woods. He acknowledges that following his train of thought can be difficult, and that for him to "turn this sort of mixture of a gossip and a gospel into anything like a grammar of Distributism has been quite impossible."[89] The best he can do is collect the various strands of his argument into a rough map, leaving the reader with a clearer view of the way forward.

"If we proceed as at present in a proper orderly fashion," Chesterton says to begin his recapitulation, "the very idea of property will vanish. It is not revolutionary violence that will destroy it. It is rather the desperate and reckless habit of not having a revolution."[90] Capitalism and socialism both are destructive of true property. These social systems "are both powers that believe only in combination; and have never understood or even heard that there is any dignity in division. They have never had the imagination to understand the idea in Genesis and the great myths; that Creation itself was division."[91] Furthermore, they are flip sides of the same coin: "There is no longer any difference in tone and type between collectivist and ordinary commercial order; commerce has its officialism and Communism has its organization. Private things are already public in the worst sense of the word; that is, they are impersonal and dehumanized. Public things are already private in the worst sense of the word; that is, they are mysterious and secretive and largely corrupt."[92]

The solution to the twin tyrannies is "to restore that long-forgotten thing called Self-Government: that is, the power of the citizen in some

89 Chesterton, *Outline*, 172.

90 Chesterton, *Outline*, 172.

91 Chesterton, *Outline*, 172.

92 Chesterton, *Outline*, 174.

degree to direct his own life and construct his own environment; to eat what he likes, to wear what he chooses, and to have (what the Trust must of necessity deny him) a range of choice."[93] First, the most important things to change are not laws and statutes but hearts and minds. There must be a transformation in the attitudes and habits of the masses. Proletarians are dispossessed not only because they have been robbed but because they do not realize they have been robbed. Restoring well-distributed property "is a thing that could be done by people. It is not a thing that can be done to people. . . . But it must be done in the spirit of a religion, of a revolution, and (I will add) of a renunciation. They must want to do it as they want to drive invaders out of a country or to stop the spread of a plague."[94]

Second, building a distributist polity "would have to be done step by step and with patience and partial concessions . . . it would never do for us to give very violent shocks to the sentiment of property, even where it is very ill-placed or ill-proportioned; for that happens to be the very sentiment we are trying to revive."[95] The right kind of revolution is not that of France or Russia, or even America. Instead, it is the kind by which Christianity supplanted paganism: cheerful, patient, long-suffering, and above all hopeful. It will be slow, often messy, always imperfect. But the way to correct wrong turns is not to abandon the destination but to backtrack to the correct path and try again.

State policy is not the primary means for achieving distributism, but it can play a supporting role: "The State might do a great deal in the first stages, especially by education in the new and necessary crafts and labours, by subsidy or tariff to protect distributive experiments and by special laws, such as the taxation of contracts. All these are covered by what I call the second principle, that we may use intermediate or imperfect instruments; but it goes along with the first principle, that we must be perfect not only in our patience, but in our passion and our enduring indignation."[96] As for state policy toward attempted monopolization, "that falls under the first of my two principles. It is simply a question of whether we have the moral courage to punish what is certainly immoral. There is no more doubt about these operations . . . than there is about piracy on the high seas. It is merely

93 Chesterton, *Outline*, 175.

94 Chesterton, *Outline*, 175.

95 Chesterton, *Outline*, 177.

96 Chesterton, *Outline*, 179.

a case of a country being so disorderly and ill-governed that it becomes infested with pirates."[97]

"Men must realize the new meaning of the old phrase, 'the sacredness of private property.'"[98] Chesterton insists sustaining this sentiment requires religious sanction. It cannot be denied "that there is a doctrine behind the whole of our political position. It is not necessarily the doctrine of the religious authority [Catholicism] which I myself receive; but it cannot be denied that it must in a sense be religious. That is to say, it must at least have some reference to an ultimate view of the universe and especially of the nature of man."[99] Chesterton believes the social teaching of the Catholic Church to be a straight road to distributism, although it may not be the only road: "The old morality, the Christian religion, the Catholic Church . . . really believed in the rights of men. That is, it believed that ordinary men were clothed with powers and privileges and a kind of authority."[100]

In contrast, the philosophy that has replaced Christianity leads only to servitude: "Now in these primary things in which the old religion trusted a man, the new philosophy utterly distrusts a man. It insists that he must be a very rare sort of man to have any rights in these matters; and when he is the rare sort, he has the right to rule others even more than himself. . . . They are not in revolt against the King. They are in revolt against the Citizen."[101] The rising managerial-administrative class, whether in the service of a government bureau or a private industrial combine, "cannot trust the normal man to rule in the home, and most certainly do not want him to rule in the State. They do not really want to give him any political power. *They are willing to give him a vote, because they have long discovered that it need not give him any power.* They are not willing to give him a house, or a wife, or a child, or a dog, or a cow, or a piece of land, because these things really do give him power."[102]

"Now we wish it to be understood," he continued, "that our policy is to give him power by giving him these things. We wish to insist that this is the real moral division underlying all our disputes, and perhaps the only one

97 Chesterton, *Outline*, 178.

98 Chesterton, *Outline*, 180.

99 Chesterton, *Outline*, 180.

100 Chesterton, *Outline*, 180–81.

101 Chesterton, *Outline*, 181.

102 Chesterton, *Outline*, 181, my emphasis.

really worth disputing. . . . We alone . . . have the right to call ourselves democratic. A republic used to be called a nation of kings, and in our republic the kings really have kingdoms."[103] True defenders of self-government are "quite content to dream of the old drudgery of democracy, by which as much as possible of a human life should be given to every human being."[104] Economic security, political liberty, and a humane social order, each of which presupposes and reinforces the others, cannot be achieved so long as men are not secure in what is theirs by right.

CHESTERTON'S ERRORS, CHESTERTON'S PRESCIENCE

Chesterton's style is very different than Belloc's, but the takeaway is the same. He makes concrete, verifiable claims as to the operation of economic systems and the prerequisites to a free and humane society. As with Belloc, he errs on the first while speaking meaningfully about the second.

It is neither necessary nor profitable to document the errors in detail. Briefly going over two of the more egregious will suffice. First, Chesterton's claims about the economic inadequacy of the "big shops" are incorrect. His complaint is captured in the previous quotation: "I think the big shop is a bad shop. I think it bad not only in a moral but a mercantile sense; that is, I think shopping there is not only a bad action but a bad bargain."[105] Economists cannot argue, qua economists, about ends, but we certainly can about means, and that is precisely what Chesterton is talking about here. Both theoretically and historically, there are economic gains to bigness. By organizing hierarchically, firms can produce a given amount of output more cheaply; provided there are fixed costs of production, firms can economize on those costs more effectively on a per-unit basis by spreading the costs over a larger range of output. Chesterton's claims about organization decreasing efficiency simply do not make sense. There are undoubtedly situations where it is *less* efficient to organize hierarchically, or to produce a large amount of output, in which case nobody will profit from doing it, but the economic benefit of bigness in certain circumstances, speaking strictly in terms of forgone resources, is undisputable. Lower prices tell the story. Admittedly, they may not tell the *whole* story. In fact, it is a key distributist insight that they are not the whole story—we are unknowingly giving

103 Chesterton, *Outline*, 182.

104 Chesterton, *Outline*, 182.

105 Chesterton, *Outline*, 67.

something else up even more precious for low consumer-goods prices. But there is a huge difference between saying that something is inefficient and saying that something is efficient but bad for freedom.

Chesterton recognizes this at some level, which is why in his chapter on big business he feels the need to explain why consumers shop at the big shops if they are bad shops. His answer is a combination of monopoly power and the psychological aspects of modern advertising. This is an unconvincing argument. Like Belloc, Chesterton does not understand the difference between a monopolized market and a market that currently has one or a few firms in it. Entry barriers, especially legal barriers, are crucial for monopolies. If big shops are profiting, and they are not legally protected, the simplest explanation is that they make things people want to buy and sell them those things at prices they can afford.[106]

As for psychological manipulation of consumers, it is a weak leg to stand on. If buyers can be influenced by a poster or a slogan, might they not be equally influenced by one of Chesterton's charming essays? In this same section, Chesterton also asserts that there is quite a bit of grumbling against big shops, and hence his argument about big shops being bad bargains is supported by consumer dissatisfaction. This is trying (but failing) to have it both ways. For grumble though they may, consumers are still consuming. They may wish the quality were higher, or the price were lower, as all of us do whenever we buy anything, but commerce operates within constraints. Unless the constraints change, the products of human behavior within those constraints, such as the prices and quality of goods, will remain the same. Wishing for additional benefits without incurring additional costs is not much use. Complaints by themselves do not constitute evidence. Thinking they do fails to engage the reality of trade-offs.

Second, at times, Chesterton apparently misunderstands the most basic function of economic systems. These mix-ups could be deliberate, in order to make an artful or rhetorically clever point. This is not necessarily duplicitous given Chesterton's preferred mode of engaging his audience. Perhaps if pressed he would qualify his views. Nevertheless, those views are very much in need of qualification. Consider this "critique" of economists' perspective on the division of labor:

106 This lapse in means-ends reasoning is not very damaging to Chesterton's cause. So what, he could reply, if big shops are giving people what they want? The point is that they should not want these things if the cost is lack of self-government and economic security.

> The whole of industrial society is founded on the notion that the quickest and cheapest thing is to carry coals to Newcastle; even if it be only with the object of afterwards carrying them from Newcastle. It is founded on the idea that rapid and regular transit and transport, perpetual interchange of goods, and incessant communication between remote places, is of all things the most economical and direct. But it is not true that the quickest and cheapest thing, for a man who has pulled an apple from an apple tree, is to send it in a consignment of apples on a train that goes like a thunderbolt to a market at the other end of England. The quickest and cheapest thing for a man who has pulled a fruit from a tree is to put it in his mouth. He is the supreme economist who wastes no money on railway journeys.[107]

Frankly, this is absurd. Chesterton inappropriately analogizes a Robinson Crusoe economy to one with millions of people. Consequently, he overlooks the role of *prices* in guiding resource allocation. But this passage displays an even more elementary error. It completely ignores the fact that there are conflicting claims over how a good, such as an apple, can be used; that we need some system for adjudicating these conflicts; and that widespread voluntary exchange can ameliorate such conflicts.

When Chesterton errs, he errs badly. Belloc sometimes misses the mark; Chesterton not only misses the mark, however, but fires in the wrong direction. This is a feature of his argumentative style. In making prosaic arguments poetic, he helps us imagine a different world. Sometimes he becomes so absorbed in his vision, however, that he forgets where it ends and reality begins. Nonetheless, the broader point of Belloc's writings also characterizes Chesterton's. His errors of economic reasoning in what economists would now call price theory do not invalidate his sociopolitical critique. At several points, he makes the same higher-level argument we encountered before: There is an unacknowledged trade-off between concentration of productive property and human freedom. We are not paying the full price of our actions in the marketplace. Lower prices are indirectly subsidized by social and political capital consumption: "The things we produce ourselves are precious like our own children, and . . . we can pay too dearly for the possession of luxury by the loss of liberty."[108]

The themes developed by Belloc are given deeper expression by Chesterton. This can be seen in selections from previous quotes. First, there is

107 Chesterton, *Outline*, 134.

108 Chesterton, *Outline*, 84.

the relationship between economic security and political liberty: "Opposition and rebellion depend on property and liberty. They can only be tolerated where other rights have been allowed to strike root, besides the central right of the ruler."[109] Second is the threat to liberty from the collusion of big business and big government: "Private things are already public in the worst sense of the word; that is, they are impersonal and dehumanized. Public things are already private in the worst sense of the word; that is, they are mysterious and secretive and largely corrupt."[110] Third is the historical experience of Christendom, especially the High Middle Ages, as the proving grounds for distributism: "My utopia would contain different things of different types holding on different tenures; that as in a medieval State there were some peasants, some monasteries, some common land, some private land, some town guilds, and so on, so in my modern State there would be some things nationalized, some machines owned corporately, some guilds sharing common profits, and so on, as well as many absolute individual owners."[111] Fourth is the necessary connection between the church's social teachings and a variegated society of well-divided property: "The old morality, the Christian religion, the Catholic Church . . . really believed in the rights of men. That is, it believed that ordinary men were clothed with powers and privileges and a kind of authority."[112]

We fail to appreciate all Chesterton has to offer if we view his philosophy solely through the lens of economics. Of course, price theory should be brought to bear on his arguments. Chesterton would be the first to admit that mistaken means result in mistaken ends, but his enduring message speaks to the relationship between economic freedom and political freedom, rightly conceived. This freedom is not solely negative. It includes an element of security, which necessarily entails positive claims. When society gives men their due, they have a stake in the social and political infrastructure by which they secure their rights. Economic justice and political justice are mutually reinforcing components of social justice, understood in the context of Catholicism's teachings on human dignity. On this point, Belloc the logician and Chesterton the aesthetician speak with one voice.

109 Chesterton, *Outline*, 29.

110 Chesterton, *Outline*, 174.

111 Chesterton, *Outline*, 98.

112 Chesterton, *Outline*, 180–81.

Chapter 7

Extensions: Distributism and Contemporary Political Economy

WHAT WE'VE LEARNED FROM BELLOC AND CHESTERTON

It will be helpful to summarize the arguments thus far. Hilaire Belloc, the first of the two thinkers we surveyed, is the more rigorous and analytical. In his *The Servile State*, which is best understood as a positive work at the intersection of politics and economics, Belloc argues the tendencies of early twentieth-century England, under industrial capitalism, threaten to extinguish human liberty. The reason is the economic system prevents a widespread distribution of property, leading to an erosion of economic independence. Basing his analysis on economic history, Belloc views the rise of a free peasantry in the High Middle Ages as emblematic of a distributive state. This ideal type forms the pattern of a society that resists the pull of both privatized and socialized collectivism. The England of Belloc's day, however, is caught in an unstable equilibrium that must eventually yield to one of these two poles. From *The Servile State*, we discover the hypothesis that there is a causal link running from economic freedom to political freedom.

The Servile State does not consider whether a free society is desirable or good, but the next of Belloc's works does. His *An Essay on the Restoration of Property* is an investigation into the workings and maintenance of the "good society," as embodied in a distributive state. Belloc distinguishes in *Essay* between purchasing power and independence. The former does not guarantee the latter. Indeed, an omnicompetent state may provide each of its subjects a comfortable living, but this is not the kind of life Belloc believes is proper for man. Belloc's alternative is economic security conferred by independent ownership of productive resources. Perhaps the most intriguing aspect of *Essay* is Belloc's suggestion, reinterpreted through the lens of modern public economics, that there is a *negative political externality* associated with the ordinary operation of the market mechanism. Markets select for low-cost production processes, which may require a concentration of capital detrimental to the maintenance of economic independence. This diminishes political freedom, but this loss is not reflected in the pricing process.[1] The complicated interplay between economic and political institutions may be such that there is a trade-off between the efficient operation of a capitalist system and the maintenance of widespread human freedom—and by extension, a limited state.

Now we turn to G. K. Chesterton, whose works are more artistic and speculative. The first of Chesterton's books, *What's Wrong with the World*, is a defense of the traditional family and the productive household. The answer to the question in the work's title is, "Whatever infringes on the rights of the family." The family's proper sphere has both economic and political dimensions. Economically, the family serves as the primary non-market institution that makes market activity possible. Politically, the family serves as a prepolitical locus of loyalty that grounds more socially distant loyalties, such as those to the community and the state. The division of labor within and across the household, itself a kind of "moral economy," is the single most important consideration in Chesterton's scheme for reconciling order and liberty.

Chesterton's collection of essays, *The Outline of Sanity*, is more difficult to summarize due to its eclectic character, yet it does have a coherent theme that ties the arguments together. As with Belloc, Chesterton in *Outline* posits an inherent link between political and economic liberty, and the link is bidirectional. For this reason, Chesterton excoriates both big business and big government—in his mind, flip sides of the same coin—and praises middling enterprises, which are the constitutional bedrock of a free state. He develops and applies this "small is beautiful" philosophy to several topics, such as landownership, technology, and foreign policy. Chesterton's goal is preserving self-governance, as well as keeping social affairs within an appropriate scale to strengthen and complete, rather than swallow and destroy, human persons. This requires discovering the prerequisites of an open, as opposed to a monopolized, society and then maintaining that openness while forestalling monopolization.

Finally, we must keep in mind the intellectual context behind these writings. Belloc's and Chesterton's projects are not scholarly, in the sense that they are not academic. The authors are not trying to "advance the sciences" or "expand the frontiers of knowledge" of politics and economics. Even when they limit themselves to positive analysis, it is in the service of

1 In the language of economists, it is a technological externality, not a pecuniary one.

a broader, normative project: fleshing out the social institutions most likely to honor Catholic social teaching. Both men were devout Catholics and self-consciously promoted the lessons of the great social encyclicals. Belloc and Chesterton are trying to move from the status quo to a society that respects the dignity of the human person, the universal destination of goods, the rights and duties of labor and capital, and the subsidiary rights of local communities within a balanced polity. Unless we keep this in mind, we run the risk of criticizing them on intellectual margins that are irrelevant to their purpose.

However, Belloc and Chesterton do have several interesting things to say that speak to ongoing scholarly controversies in politics and economics. That their intention was not to carry forward a research program does not prevent us from asking whether a contemporary research program in distributism is viable. As a matter of fact, there are several literatures in political economy where Belloc's insights in *The Servile State* and *Essay* and Chesterton's in *What's Wrong* and *Outline* become relevant. Furthermore, distributist ideas show promise in helping us understand several political-economic phenomena.

But if adjudicating academic controversies was not Belloc's nor Chesterton's purpose, why go in this direction? The simplest answer is that even if distributism was not intended to be a progressive research program, it is still interesting and valuable that it can be. Building bridges between distributism and contemporary political economy could bring scholars in the relevant fields to new vistas. It may foster greater engagement by economists with ethics and theology, and greater attention paid by ethicists and theologians to economics. And since the motivations behind even positive research programs are not value free—we are all searching for the "good society," in one way or another—it behooves us to look for complementarities where few scholars have explored.[2]

In this chapter, I focus on three areas to which applying distributist insights can be particularly fruitful. While there are probably many more,

2 Distributism's potential as a research program does not relegate it to credentialed academics at "research universities." In addition to the researcher's goal of accumulating knowledge, distributist scholarship can pursue the traditional holistic ends of liberal education. Distributism benefits from an interdisciplinary approach that combines the precision of the social sciences with the imagination of humane learning. The boundaries between scholarship, teaching, and character formation are imprecise, and artificially delineating them obscures the truth that motivates them. Although dated, Cardinal Newman's *The Idea of a University* ([1852] San Francisco: Ignatius Press, 2010) remains a compelling argument for the academic-institutional context conducive to a distributist revival.

these three have the most obvious potential. The relevant literatures in political economy are state capacity and economic development, the determinants of economic and political freedom, and alternative approaches to normative economics. I discuss each in turn.

ECONOMY, STATE, AND THE WEALTH OF NATIONS

State Capacity: A Summary

Why are some countries rich and others poor? This question has been central to economics since Adam Smith published his *Inquiry into the Nature and Causes of the Wealth of Nations* in 1776. Most economists believe good institutions—social rules that protect private property rights, constrain the state, and uphold the rule of law—caused the massive increase in economic prosperity, beginning in the nineteenth century, that Western nations have enjoyed.[3] Countries that remain poor lack institutions that perform these important functions. In fact, their institutions frequently do the opposite. Now scholars of economic development are asking the natural follow-up question: Where do good institutions come from?

The most notable literature that tries to answer this question is the *state capacity* literature. Wealthy countries usually have open-access institutions: rather than monopolized political and economic processes, these nations have a strong central state that preserves a level playing field among political-economic contenders.[4] In addition, wealthy countries have efficient legal and fiscal bureaucracies for upholding the rule of law and harnessing the resources to finance important public goods.[5] The implication is that states play a crucial, and perhaps even necessary, role in helping their citizens attain lasting economic prosperity. This is somewhat counterintuitive: Usually strong states are viewed as impediments to economic progress,

3 Douglass C. North, *Institutions, Institutional Change, and Economic Performance* (Cambridge: Cambridge University Press, 1990).

4 Daron Acemoglu and James Robinson, *Why Nations Fail: The Origins of Power, Prosperity, and Poverty* (New York: Crown Publishing Group, 2012); Douglass C. North, John Joseph Wallis, and Barry R. Weingast, *Violence and Social Orders: A Conceptual Framework for Interpreting Recorded Human History* (Cambridge: Cambridge University Press, 2009).

5 Timothy Besley and Torsten Persson, *Pillars of Prosperity: The Political Economics of Development Clusters* (Princeton, N.J.: Princeton University Press, 2011); Besley and Persson, "State Capacity, Conflict, and Development," *Econometrica* 78, no. 1 (January 2010): 1–34; and Besley and Persson, "The Origins of State Capacity: Property Rights, Taxation, and Politics," *American Economic Review* 99, no. 4 (2009): 1218–44.

rather than enablers of that progress. It is easy to come up with many examples of heavy-handed states wreaking economic destruction. This is the paradox of state capacity: states must be strong enough to prevent societies from devolving into a collection of petty despotisms, yet they must also be limited so that their own actions do not themselves become tyrannical. Daron Acemoglu and James Robinson, in an influential recent work, present a tripartite scheme for addressing this problem: absent Leviathan, despotic Leviathan, and shackled Leviathan.[6] When Leviathan is absent, as in ancient tribal societies, society is subject to the chaos of tribal elites jockeying for power, status, and resources. Economic development cannot occur in such a messy and uncertain environment. But a despotic Leviathan also prevents wealth creation. An autocrat can be just as destructive as a coterie of chieftains. Only in the middle path—the "narrow corridor"—in which Leviathan is strong yet constrained can generalized economic prosperity emerge.

Noel Johnson and Mark Koyama, who have written an excellent review and analysis of the state-capacity literature, get at the heart of the issue: "Powerful states can also impede economic growth and produce economic stagnation. The link between greater state capacity and sustained economic growth is contingent: it depends on whether state policies complement markets and market-supporting institutions. The experience of the twentieth century teaches that attempts to build state capacity in the absence of the rule of law or a market economy have failed to generate sustained economic growth."[7]

What institutional mechanisms can perform the requisite constraining yet empowering role? The state capacity literature has yet to answer this question. Something must simultaneously bind and loose the state so it has the information and incentives to govern wisely. Or, as immortalized by James Madison in *Federalist No. 51*, "You must first enable the government to control the governed; and in the next place oblige it to control itself." Whatever accomplishes this balancing act cannot itself be state capacity. Power cannot be the source of its own constraints. For Acemoglu and Robinson, the crucial factor is society: the network of voluntary institutions between the market and the state, which serve as a countervailing source of social authority, thereby preventing the monopolization of power. Other

6 Daron Acemoglu and James A. Robinson, *The Narrow Corridor: States, Societies, and the Fate of Liberty* (New York: Penguin Press, 2019); cf. also James M. Buchanan, *The Limits of Liberty: Between Anarchy and Leviathan* (Chicago: University of Chicago Press, 1975).

7 Noel D. Johnson and Mark Koyama, "States and Economic Growth: Capacity and Constraints," *Explorations in Economic History* 64 (April 2017): 1–20, at 3.

scholars have come up with their own, and oftentimes related, answers. Peter Boettke and Rosolino Candela point to important episodes from comparative historical political economy to argue for political constraints that are themselves anterior to the state.[8] Ennio Piano argues similarly, from the standpoint of the Virginia school of political economy.[9] And Vincent Geloso and I have suggested the balance of power *between* states is an important yet neglected feature determining how state capacity is built and wielded.[10] Whatever the mechanisms, the major task facing the state-capacity literature is explaining how and why government power is used in a manner that is both productive and protective, but not predatory.[11]

Here is where distributism can contribute. There are two aspects to the state-capacity question. The first is historical: How did productive and protective, yet not predatory, states arise in the first place? The second is contemporary: How can states wield their protective and productive powers, while forestalling their predatory powers, to bolster political liberty and economic flourishing? Belloc and Chesterton offer intriguing suggestions for both.

Distributism and State Capacity

Belloc's arguments concerning the evolution of medieval European governance institutions can also explain the development of state capacity, as well as its responsible use. The fall of the Roman Empire and the spread of Christianity contributed to the transformation of the villa worked by slave labor to manor-estates worked by serfs. This in turn gave way to peasant proprietorship. As Belloc tells the story, the reason laborers' bargaining power rose compared to lords' was the disappearance of the Roman state's coercive capacity. The labor compact changed, with workers recognizing fewer duties to landowners. This was incentive-compatible because it became too costly for landowners to enforce traditional obligations. Widely dispersed own-

8 Peter J. Boettke and Rosolino A. Candela, "Productive Specialization, Peaceful Cooperation and the Problem of the Predatory State: Lessons from Comparative Historical Political Economy," *Public Choice* 182, no. 3–4 (2020): 331–52.

9 Ennio E. Piano, "State Capacity and Public Choice: A Critical Survey," *Public Choice* 178, no. 1–2 (2019): 289–309.

10 Vincent J. Geloso and Alexander W. Salter, "State Capacity and Economic Development: Causal Mechanism or Correlative Filter?" *Journal of Economic Behavior & Organization* 170 (2020): 372–85.

11 Buchanan, *Limits of Liberty*.

ership and control of resources, by the fourteenth or fifteenth century, guaranteed security and (relatively) limited dues to feudal magnates. Economic power created the foundation for political power, which when exercised by the peasantry limited the reach of elites. Though peasants lacked formal representation in local parliaments and other assemblies of the time, this was a real check on power nonetheless.

The free cities and their commercial guilds provided another check on predation. Burghers frequently had chartered rights and liberties that made them independent of the feudal hierarchy. And as commercial centers specializing in the creation of wealth, cities often wielded significant formal and informal political power. This also constrained nascent states, in the late Middle Ages and early modernity, from engaging in excessive predation. Traditional elites—kings, noblemen, even bishops who exercised temporal authority—could not trample on the cities without killing the goose that laid the golden egg.

The mechanism suggested by Belloc is one of economic power restraining political power. Remember his summary of medieval Europe's de facto constitution: "The serf, secure in his position, and burdened only with regular dues, which were but a fraction of his produce; the freeholder, a man independent save for money dues, which were more of a tax than a rent; the guild, in which well-divided capital worked cooperatively for craft production, for transport and for commerce. . . . All, or most—the normal family—should own. And on ownership the freedom of the state should repose."[12] There are several works on the historical construction of state capacity that can be extended by incorporating Belloc's insights. For example, David Stasavage argues that representative government arose in Western Europe, and nowhere else, because of its de facto balance of power.[13] Andrew Young and I characterize this balance of power as a constitutional constraint on predation, which sowed the seeds of future good governance.[14] Young also writes persuasively about the importance of the

12 Belloc, *Servile State*, 79–80.

13 David Stasavage, "Representation and Consent: Why They Arose in Europe and Not Elsewhere," *Annual Review of Political Science* 19 (2016): 145–62.

14 Alexander W. Salter and Andrew T. Young, "Polycentric Sovereignty: The Medieval Constitution, Governance Quality, and the Wealth of Nations," *Social Science Quarterly* 100, no. 4 (June 2019): 1241–53; Salter and Young, "Medieval Representative Assemblies: Collective Action and Antecedents of Limit Government," *Constitutional Political Economy* 29 (2018): 171–92; see also Salter, "Rights to the Realm: Reconsidering Western Political Development," *American Political Science Review* 109, no. 4 (November 2015): 725–34.

free cities as a check on predation and a source of liberty, which created the background conditions for protective and productive governance.[15] What these works, along with Belloc's, have in common is their insistence on some prepolitical, or at least constitutional, restraints on the way power can be wielded.[16] This suggests state capacity was itself subject to constraints that shaped its growth, development, and use. While most social scientists think causality runs from politics to economics, Belloc provides the tools to construct an argument in terms of causality running from economics to politics.

The contemporary aspect has to do with state capacity as it is currently used. Here both Belloc and Chesterton have definite opinions. While passages from their writings may suggest a kind of conservative libertarianism, we can see this is a misreading considering the overall content of their works. Belloc and Chesterton are not opposed to the state per se. In fact, when kept within its proper bounds, both Belloc and Chesterton insist the state is good and necessary. It is not enough for the state to maintain a laissez-faire approach to economic matters. Belloc insists that a strong central authority must create and maintain the distributive state. Without the central government actively exercising these oversight powers, the distributist state may erode into one of the forms (private-dominated or public-dominated) of the servile state. Especially in *Essay*, Belloc is eloquent about the importance of using state power to protect the weak from the strong. He is also optimistic about state ownership and operation of certain industries, as well as public policy that tilts the playing field in favor of small, independent proprietors.

Chesterton makes similar claims, especially in *Outline*. While he is hesitant to make the state a prime mover in the quest for widely distributed property, he nonetheless affirms certain targeted measures that can improve the feasibility and durability of distributism. Especially the proposals from page 79 show his desire for a state that is limited yet vigorous in its pursuits. That Chesterton fears an expansive, omnicompetent state is clear from his remarks in *What's Wrong*, which emphasize pro-

15 Andrew T. Young, "How the City Air Made Us Free: The Self-Governing Medieval City and the Bourgeoisie Revaluation," *Journal of Private Enterprise* 32, no. 4 (2017): 31–47.

16 In economics, a constitution is a set of rules for making rules. It is a "meta-constraint" on politics. See James M. Buchanan, "The Constitution of Economic Policy," *American Economic Review* 77, no. 3 (1987): 243–50.

tecting the family from the state's grasp, especially in education and child-rearing.

The key, then, is a circumscribed state with a specific mandate to advance the common good. Provided the state remains within its legitimate bounds, state capacity and human flourishing are complementary. Currently, this perspective on state capacity is perhaps best represented in the school of political-economic thought known as ordoliberalism. Arising in Germany during the Weimar era and coming into fruition following the Second World War, ordoliberalism is a variant of liberalism that combines certain liberal tenets, such as respect for markets and limited government, with active state "police powers" so that the state may serve as a referee of the political-economic game.[17] For ordoliberals, human well-being requires the state to monitor and regulate economic outcomes, in order to preserve competitive markets against the specter of oligopoly or monopoly. This is compatible with distributists' concern with the concentrating tendencies of unchecked market activity.

There are some tensions, however. Belloc and Chesterton, as well as many others with distributist sympathies, would probably prefer more expansive state support for families, cooperatives, and similar groups than ordoliberals do. And distributists would be comfortable with restrictions on certain kinds of economic activity that ordoliberalism would have a harder time justifying. Nevertheless, there are significant overlaps between the concerns of distributists and ordoliberals. Both recognize the importance of state capacity, wielded competently, in the service of individual and social flourishing.

ECONOMIC FREEDOM, POLITICAL FREEDOM, AND INEQUALITY

The second literature that distributist insights complement is the empirical literature on economic freedom, political freedom, and inequality. First, we will consider the relationship between economic freedom and inequality.

17 Werner Bonefeld, "Freedom and the Strong State: On German Ordoliberalism," *New Political Economy* 17, no. 5 (2012): 633–56; Viktor J. Vanberg, "The Freiburg School: Walter Eucken and Ordoliberalism," Freiburger Diskussionspapiere zur Ordnungsökonomik, No. 04/11, Institut für Allgemeine Wirtschaftsforschung, Abteilung für Wirtschaftspolitik, AlbertLudwigs-Universität Freiburg, Freiburg, 2004; see also the academic journal *ORDO* for current theoretical and historical debates.

Economic Freedom and Inequality

The Economic Freedom of the World (EFW) index was first published by James Gwartney, Walter Block, and Robert Lawson in 1996,[18] and the index has been updated each year since. As of this writing, the most recent version is authored by James Gwartney, Joshua Hall, Robert Lawson, and Ryan Murphy.[19] The index gives countries an overall score from 1 to 10 based on a composite of rankings in five areas: size of government, legal system and security of property rights, sound money, freedom of international trade, and regulation. Each of these in turn has many subcomponents. To consider just a few, size of government includes government consumption, transfer payments, and top marginal tax rates; legal system and property rights includes judicial independence and contract enforcement; sound money includes growth of the money supply and the inflation rate; freedom of international trade includes tariffs, export compliance regulations, and international capital mobility; and regulation includes a host of restrictions on trade in the areas of financial markets, labor markets, and general business operations.[20]

Right away, we can see some similarities and differences between the view of economic freedom embodied in EFW and that subscribed to by distributists: "The EFW index places the concept of economic freedom within the classical liberal tradition that emphasizes the importance of private property, rule of law, free trade, sound money, and a limited role for government."[21] It thus entails a broadly libertarian approach to economic freedom, one that prioritizes negative liberty: freedom *from*. For Chesterton and Belloc, economic freedom is more expansive. It includes positive liberty: freedom *to*. Positive liberty is best achieved through widely dispersed property, according to distributists, but if anything, public policy to achieve and maintain such a distribution would count against freedom on the EFW view. This is not to say negative liberty is unimportant to Chesterton and

18 James Gwartney, Robert Lawson, and Walter Block, *Economic Freedom of the World: 1975–1995* (Vancouver, B.C.: Fraser Institute, 2016), https://www.fraserinstitute.org/sites/default/files/EconomicFreedomoftheWorld1975–1995.pdf.

19 James Gwartney, Robert Lawson, Joshua Hall, and Ryan Murphy, *Economic Freedom of the World: 2021 Annual Report* (Vancouver: Fraser Institute, 2021), https://www.fraserinstitute.org/sites/default/files/economic-freedom-of-the-world-2021.pdf.

20 For a full list, see https://www.fraserinstitute.org/economic-freedom/approach.

21 Joshua C. Hall and Robert A. Lawson, "Economic Freedom of the World: An Accounting of the Literature," *Contemporary Economic Policy* 32, no. 1 (January 2014): 1–19, at 1.

Belloc. For all distributists, freedom for persons, families, and local communities from the grasping tendencies of large, impersonal corporate bodies, both private and public, is a necessary component of economic freedom, but necessity does not imply sufficiency.

To see where distributism fits in, consider a recent review of the literature on economic freedom by Joshua Hall and Robert Lawson.[22] Of the more than 400 empirical papers that use EFW, Hall and Lawson look at the subset that uses economic freedom as an independent variable in statistical analyses. This means EFW explains either a "good" or "bad" outcome (itself the dependent variable). In nearly 200 studies, greater economic freedom corresponds to "good" outcomes, such as higher living standards, more than two-thirds of the time (134 out of 198 articles). Only in about 4 percent of studies (8 out of 198) does greater EFW correspond to "bad" outcomes. Although infrequent, one of these bad outcomes is sufficiently important to distributists to merit separate discussion: economic inequality.[23]

Virtually every principles-of-economics textbook will discuss the tradeoff between efficiency and equity. The legal and political rules that promote robust economic growth may lead to disparities in the accumulation of wealth, but attempts to equalize wealth through tax-and-transfer schemes weaken the incentives for creating wealth. Many economists do not view inequality as prima facie bad. Inequality can increase if the poor are getting richer, so long as the rich are getting richer even faster. Absolute living standards are more important: whether everyone has sufficient resources to lead decent lives. It is less clear why the gap should be specifically concerning.

But this is where distributism makes a crucial point: the gap itself may cause problems. First, we need to clarify the concept of equality. According to Chesterton and Belloc, equality of outcomes is not a goal of distributism. Such outcomes are neither necessary nor sufficient to promote an independence-centered view of freedom. Instead, what matters is a relatively equal distribution of property (productive assets). The possession of such assets by households is what prevents them from being dictated to by their counterparties in the market. Independence also contributes to the diffusion of power, and hence a free state. Nevertheless, income also matters, if for no other reason than income can be used to purchase productive assets. From a distributist perspective, greater income inequality resulting from greater

22 Hall and Lawson, "Economic Freedom of the World."

23 Hall and Lawson, "Economic Freedom of the World," 8.

economic freedom is not disqualifying, but it is still concerning and needs to be explored further.

Three of the eight bad results from economic freedom that Hall and Lawson outlined are inequality related. A more recent metastudy by Daniel Bennett and Boris Nikolaev surveys eight papers.[24] The results from this small literature are decidedly mixed. In the authors' words, "These ambiguous findings leave policymakers, development agencies and other reformers with little empirical guidance on the potential distributional effects of enacting institutional or policy reforms that either enhance or reduce economic freedom."[25] As yet, there is no consensus on whether economic freedom tends to make societies more unequal.

We should also consider the opposite relationship: the effects of inequality on economic freedom. Lawson recognizes this relationship's importance. In a 2019 paper titled "The Consequences and Causes of Economic Freedom," he writes, "If inequality is in fact detrimental to economic freedom, and if government-driven income redistribution reduces inequality, it could be the case that income redistribution, which is per se contrary to economic freedom, could indirectly contribute to greater economic freedom by reducing inequality. I'd hesitate to draw this conclusion at this point based on the limited evidence available, but this is certainly an area for further research."[26]

In another recent work, Lawson, along with Ryan Murphy and Benjamin Powell, explored the literature on the effects of inequality on economic freedom, which is also quite small. They found two papers that estimated how income inequality affects economic freedom and one paper that estimated how *wealth* inequality—of much more obvious concern for the distributists—affects economic freedom. In all cases, increased inequality was associated with lower economic freedom, although the wealth-inequality paper found this effect was present only in nondemocratic countries. The authors conclude there are possible indirect channels by which economic equality can bolster economic freedom.[27]

24 Daniel L. Bennett and Boris Nikolaev, "On the Ambiguous Economic Freedom-Inequality Relationship," *Empirical Economics* 53 (2017): 717–54. While the set of papers discussed by Hall and Lawson (2014) and Bennett and Nikolaev (2017) partly overlap, they are not the same.

25 Bennett and Nikolaev, "On the Ambiguous Economic Freedom-Inequality Relationship," 718.

26 Robert A. Lawson, "The Consequences and Causes of Economic Freedom," *Journal of Private Enterprise* 32, no. 3 (2019): 1–10, at 7–8.

27 Robert A. Lawson, Ryan H. Murphy, and Benjamin Powell, "The Determinants of Economic Freedom: A Survey," *Contemporary Economic Policy* 38, no. 4 (2020): 622–42, at 12–13.

The link between freedom and equality is a high-stakes research area to which distributist-influenced scholars can contribute. Because this literature is both young and small, the marginal contribution will likely have a large effect in steering the literature's course. Distributists' conception of equality and freedom can inform the construction and testing of hypotheses about the constituent parts of inequality. For example, distributists can focus on the variance explained by inequality in income-generating assets. This magnitude is potentially important for discussions about the causes and consequences of economic freedom.

The relationship between equality and freedom is too significant a research question to remain underexplored for long. Sooner or later, researchers will publish many more papers. If scholars informed by Belloc and Chesterton make contributions as this literature grows, we will learn more than we otherwise would have.

Economic Freedom and Political Freedom

Now we consider the subset of the literature that explores the relationship between economic freedom and political freedom. In these studies, political freedom is usually captured by the Polity IV index, which ranks countries based on a twenty-one-point scale ranging from −10 (hereditary absolute monarchy) to +10 (consolidated democracy).[28] This index is extensively used by economists and political scientists. Because distributists admire free and self-governing states, they have an obvious interest in the relationship between democracy and political freedom. Once again, however, distributists think differently about democracy than most scholars. While indices of political freedom are commensurate with various *procedural* components of democracy, such as universal-franchise voting and fair elections, distributists would place more emphasis on *structural* components. For example, distributists would insist not just on democracy but subsidiary-respecting democracy: keeping political activity at the most local level possible. Distributists would also place a high value on protections for the dignity of the human person, including barriers between the household and the state. This somewhat matches the distinction in the economic-freedom literature between democracy and *liberalism*. As Lawson, Murphy, and Powell note, "It should be mentioned that all the measures of democracy distinguish

28 Center for Systemic Peace, "The Polity Project: About Polity," https://www.systemicpeace.org/polityproject.html.

unfettered, majoritarian democracy with limited, constitutional democracy. These measures of democracy favor the limited, constitutional variety that includes important checks on majorities and protections for minority rights."[29] Checks on the democratic process, to the extent they are checks on the political process in general, are important in protecting freedom.

The relationship between economic freedom and democracy is somewhat noisy. Nevertheless, there is a pattern: "A slim majority of the papers found democracy to be positively linked with either the level of economic freedom or the degree of liberalization. Importantly, no papers found a negative relationship between democracy and economic freedom."[30] However, focusing specifically on political liberalism, the authors find much stronger results. Lawson, Murphy, and Powell report, "The overwhelming empirical finding . . . is that liberal political regimes, as variously measured, are positively associated with economic freedom."[31]

Thus, if political freedom is a composite of liberalism and democracy, there is support for the hypothesis of F. A. Hayek, Milton Friedman, and other classical-liberal scholars that economic freedom and political freedom mutually support each other.[32] Lawson summarizes this literature and provides a cautionary warning to those who have little patience for the democratic process:

> Those of us who favor economic freedom need *not* fear democracy or political freedom. Yes, democracy has its problems as identified by public choice scholars, many of whom have been associated with this association or are in the room today. But it is a gross error to conclude from our study of public choice that autocratic regimes are the answer. There has been a tendency for *some—some* I say, not all, or even most, but *some*—classical liberals to apologize for or brush away the brutality of countries like Chile or to advocate for the so-called Singapore model because those autocratic regimes have encouraged economic freedom.
>
> I am here to tell you that (1) this is wrong and (2) it won't work. First, shutting down people who disagree with you is flat out wrong, even if

29 Lawson, Murphy, and Powell, "Determinants," 9.

30 Lawson, Murphy, and Powell, "Determinants," 9.

31 Lawson, Murphy, and Powell, "Determinants," 10.

32 Cf. Robert A. Lawson and J. R. Clark. "Examining the Hayek–Friedman Hypothesis on Economic and Political Freedom," *Journal of Economic Behavior & Organization* 74, no. 3 (June 2010): 230–39.

> those voices are advocating socialism, fascism, or some other tyranny. Freedom of speech, assembly, and political participation is a required component of *any* classical liberal vision for a free society. *Socialists* may have no problem sacrificing human rights to the almighty pedestal of central planning, but we classical liberals are supposed to be better than them. Second, how many autocrats, except perhaps Pinochet or Lee Kwan Yew, have ushered in economic freedom for their countries? Exactly. For every Pinochet, there are dozens of tin-pot dictators who have ruined their nations. Any sober empirical analysis tells us that autocracies are the enemy not only of civil liberties but also of the economic freedom that we cherish so much, and that is the basis for our prosperity.[33]

Distributists will find much to applaud here. In addition to recognizing that political freedom and economic freedom usually buttress each other, Lawson argues there is a moral imperative to maintain political structures that are consensual and protective of individual rights.[34] Distributists would be more likely to speak in terms of human dignity than individual rights. They would also differ over which activities should be protected. Nevertheless, as with the link between economic freedom and inequality, those influenced by Chesterton and Belloc can contribute to the conversation on economic freedom and political freedom. Chesterton especially is eloquent on the importance of liberalism and democracy, as we saw earlier, and his remarks can serve as an obvious springboard for forming and testing hypotheses.

JUSTICE IN EXCHANGE

The final area is normative economics, specifically justice in exchange. Because economics focuses on what is, rather than what ought to be, questions of justice are usually outside its purview. However, there is not a complete separation. Many economists discuss normative issues in their works, and as citizens contributing to the democratic process, economists are often outspoken critics of perceived injustices. Yet it is widely believed that while economists can be normative, economics cannot be. There may be such a

33 Lawson, "Consequences and Causes," 7.

34 Also worth noting, given the distributists' aversion to socialism, are Lawson's remarks concerning the abuses of that system: "Our *democratic* socialist friends who promise political liberalism and civil liberties while controlling economic resources are selling snake oil. The data tell us that you can get and keep political and civil freedom only if you maintain some semblance of a market economy, and if you move toward *real* socialism, you will inevitably move toward political repression if not outright tyranny" (Lawson, "Consequences and Causes," 8).

thing as normative economics, but it is no longer economics per se; it is ethics informed by the economic way of thinking.

Whatever the ultimate status of the positive-normative distinction—whether it should be treated as epistemological, ontological, a mere disciplinary convention, or jettisoned altogether—this perspective is widespread among economists, who sometimes wander into normative territory without realizing it. Economists permit themselves to conduct analyses of welfare (preference satisfaction) but often fail to recognize questions of welfare can trespass on normative grounds when involving public policy.

When economists discuss welfare, the concept they use is almost always efficiency. The strictest conception of efficiency is Pareto efficiency. A situation is Pareto efficient if one person cannot be made better off without making another worse off. Correspondingly, a change is called a Pareto improvement if at least one individual is better off and nobody worse off. Pareto improvements are feasible in the models economists construct, but in the real world, this criterion is so restrictive as to be almost useless: For any change, somebody, somewhere, will be made worse off. For practical purposes, most economists work with the concept of Kaldor-Hicks efficiency: maximization of the dollar value of society's resources. It is straightforward to show that if all mutually beneficial exchanges have been made, the result will be Kaldor-Hicks efficient (hereafter "efficient"). Otherwise, additional trades would occur until the gains from trade were exhausted. Provided economists use efficiency as a descriptive engine of analysis, it is unobjectionable. Big problems arise, however, when economists use efficiency as prescriptive goal of public policy. Reducing welfare to self-perceived preference satisfaction leaves out an entire range of normative phenomena related to economic life, and perhaps the most important is the question of economic justice.

Distributists are well positioned to contribute to debates about economic justice, and Catholic social teaching offers reasonably clear criteria for determining justice in exchange. While these principles require interpretation to apply to particular situations, they nonetheless provide a coherent starting point. In fact, distributism begins with a concrete evaluative criterion: the widespread availability of productive property. How distributists proceed from this starting point depends on what issues they place in the analytical foreground vs. the analytical background. Should the focus be analyzing justice in exchange within the Catholic moral tradition? Or should the focus be using insights from Catholic social teaching to advance a conception of justice in exchange with broader appeal? Neither of these approaches is a priori correct. Almost certainly both are useful. Nevertheless, we must distinguish between them because they delineate different lines of scholarship. An example of each follows.

The Catholic Intellectual Tradition in the Analytical Foreground

Mary Hirschfeld's *Aquinas and the Market* is the most noteworthy recent attempt to expand the territory of normative economics.[35] Hirschfeld, a convert to Catholicism, earned PhDs in both economics and theology. As the title suggests, she seeks to correct economists' restricted approach to welfare by drawing upon St. Thomas Aquinas, one of the Catholic Church's greatest minds. In her book, she critiques economists' orthodox rational-choice model, especially the way that model treats the concept of ends (goals). Like the standard model, the Thomistic approach to value and choice is teleological, but unlike rational choice, ends are objective, not subjective. The ultimate end is the beatific vision: communion with the divine. The intermediate ends are those habits of character, which the Aristotelian ethical tradition calls virtues, that guide the reasoning agent toward his ultimate end. While many non-Catholics would approve a reformulation of economics in the context of theistic virtue ethics, this system's rootedness in Thomism places it in approaches to normative economics, with Catholic teaching in the analytical foreground.

Hirschfeld justifies her project by arguing, correctly, that "economics itself cannot provide a framework that orders economic flourishing to the higher ends economic flourishing should serve."[36] She uses Aquinas to show how this ordering of ends can and should be accomplished. A passage from chapter 3 usefully summarizes the similarities and differences between rational-choice teleology and Thomistic teleology: "Like economists, Aquinas believes that humans act for an end. Thomas calls that end happiness, while economists call it utility, but insofar as both Aquinas and economists believe that all human action is teleological, Aquinas's economics does not

35 Mary L. Hirschfeld, *Aquinas and the Market: Toward a Humane Economy* (Cambridge, Mass.: Harvard University Press, 2018). Portions of this subsection are derived from my review of Hirschfeld's book: Alexander W. Salter, "Book Review: *Aquinas and the Market: Toward a Humane Economy* by Mary Hirschfeld," *Christian Libertarian Review* 3 (2020): R6–R16.

36 Hirschfeld, *Aquinas and the Market: Toward a Humane Economy*, 3.

simply talk past modern-day economists. That said, Aquinas's understanding of that end differs substantially from the one envisioned by economists. In particular, Aquinas's conception of happiness is centered on the notion of perfection of our beings."[37]

The key is that, for Aquinas and those working within his system, "human choice is not about efficiently getting what we want so much as it is about learning how to want what is genuinely good."[38] This paradigm applies to economic matters as well. Preference satisfaction through consumption cannot be the relevant welfare criterion in light of the universal destination of economic goods: "Material goods, are, indeed, good. But they are purely instrumental. It is not enough to be wealthy. Happiness requires that we deploy our wealth toward the worthy end of realizing our nature as fully as possible in lives ordered to God."[39] Even more explicitly, from the fifth chapter, "The artificial economy—money, prices, profits, and markets—has a proper role in a humane economy. But for that to work, participants in the market need to act out of Aquinas's basic principles. Natural wealth is desirable insofar as it meets genuine needs; instrumental goods are properly ordered to the ends they are meant to serve; and as social creatures we have an interest in making sure our exchanges are just."[40]

Hirschfeld's arguments in chapter 6 about justice in exchange are forceful. Aquinas endorses the institution of private property, and not just as a concession to fallen human nature. Interestingly, in the Thomistic system, private property can be used to cultivate virtue. Aquinas also anticipates modern economic arguments for the coordinative benefits of an economic order founded on private property.[41] However, private property rights extend only to productive activities and *partial* allocation of the resulting income stream. Because everyone, especially the poor, has a right to the fruits of production, familiar privileges of, for example, residual claimancy are permissible only if they conform to the common good. In turn, the common good requires economic justice, a distribution of resources that confers an acceptable standard of living to all, reflecting their moral status as persons: "The key here is that proper decision making involves looking

37 Hirschfeld, *Aquinas and the Market: Toward a Humane Economy*, 68.

38 Hirschfeld, *Aquinas and the Market: Toward a Humane Economy*, 84

39 Hirschfeld, *Aquinas and the Market: Toward a Humane Economy*, 97.

40 Hirschfeld, *Aquinas and the Market: Toward a Humane Economy*, 138.

41 See p. 165 for a particularly Hayekian passage.

at goods and services in a larger context, asking what role they play in constructing the shape of our lives."[42] Justice in exchange features prominently in the discussion of just prices and just wages: "To pay a just price for a shirt, say, requires that one pay enough so that the weavers can earn a just wage. But what is a just wage? Surely, the just wage is what is sufficient to maintain the weaver at an appropriate standard of living. To the extent that our own income is the result of paying prices that are insufficient to maintain producers at an appropriate standard of living, and to the extent that we hire workers directly at less than a just wage, we violate the principles of economic justice."[43]

Hirschfeld titles the final chapter of her book "Toward a Humane Economy: A Pragmatic Approach." The chapter is really about a humane *economics* rather than a humane economy. Although Hirschfeld's work is impressive for its theistic treatment of value, choice, and exchange, it does not say much about concrete reforms. This is precisely where distributism is strongest. Within the Catholic intellectual tradition, there is a smooth gradient from Aquinas's humane economics, as interpreted by Hirschfeld, to a humane economy, as interpreted by Belloc and Chesterton. Economists themselves sometimes distinguish between the science of economics and the art of political economy. Employing this distinction, within a Catholic worldview, we can classify Hirschfeld as practicing the science of economics and the distributists as practicing the art of political economy. Hirschfeld investigates means, ends, and human flourishing, but she lacks an institutional landscape for realizing the values she highlights; the distributists work directly in the service of the institutional landscape, but often leave the underlying choice framework implicit, if not underdeveloped. In other words, they complement each other. We are left with a stimulating conclusion: these are each one-half of a research program, one that can flower when brought together.

Generalized Exchange in the Analytical Foreground

The second approach places exchange as such in the analytical foreground, with a focus on the formal qualities of an exchange that render it just. While compatible with the Catholic intellectual tradition, an exchange-centered approach proceeds without explicit reference to it. One example is Michael

42 Hirschfeld, *Aquinas and the Market: Toward a Humane Economy*, 177–78.

43 Hirschfeld, *Aquinas and the Market: Toward a Humane Economy*, 188.

Munger's idea of "euvoluntary," or truly voluntary, exchange.[44] Munger builds on a common moral intuition: for an exchange to be just, it must be "well and truly" voluntary.[45] This requires more than the absence of coercion or fraud. We must explicitly consider the parties' relative bargaining power. The results of the exchange matter as well, especially when there is an extensive division of labor. In such circumstances, social justice, which includes "the distribution of the benefits or economic surplus created by market institutions," may render exchanges that appear morally acceptable ex ante illicit ex post.[46] Munger elaborates on an argument made famous by John Stuart Mill, concerning the separability of production and distribution, to ground the idea of distributive injustices arising despite the lack of legal or commutative injustices. This argument focuses on:

> the revenues resulting from exchanges that made both parties better off, and that were undertaken under conditions in which property rights were private and exclusive. But after a number of exchanges have been made, and some traders have accumulated large surpluses, those private property rights are somehow transfigured into collectively defined common property. Simply put, that which was yours is now ours. And the reason is that if we were to allow private property to remain private, we would have to accept an inequitable distribution of goods, even though there was nothing unjust about any one of the exchanges that led to that distribution.[47]

However, Munger distinguishes his argument from typical social-justice arguments from, for example, the Rawlsian type. Instead, he introduces the idea of euvoluntary exchange and contends that (a) all euvoluntary exchanges are just, and (b) the social results of all euvoluntary exchanges are just. An exchange is euvoluntary, in Munger's framework, if it meets the following five requirements:

1. The conventional ownership of items, services, or currency by both parties;

44 Michael C. Munger, "Euvoluntary or Not, Exchange Is Just," *Social Philosophy and Policy* 28, no. 2 (July 2011): 192–211. For a formalization and extension, see Ricardo Andrés Guzmán and Michael C. Munger, "A Theory of Just Market Exchange," *Journal of Value Inquiry* 54 (2020): 1–28. See also Ricardo Andrés Guzmán and Michael C. Munger, "Euvoluntariness and Just Market Exchange: Moral Dilemmas from Locke's *Venditio*," *Public Choice* 158, no. 1/2 (2014): 39–49.

45 Munger, "Euvoluntary," 192.

46 Munger, "Euvoluntary," 192.

47 Munger, "Euvoluntary," 193.

2. The conventional capacity to transfer and assign this ownership to the other party;
3. The absence of regret, for both parties, after the exchange, in the sense that both receive value at least as great as was anticipated at the time when they agreed to the exchange;
4. Neither party is coerced, in the sense of being forced to exchange by threat ("If you don't trade, I will shoot you!"); and
5. Neither party is coerced in the alternative sense of being harmed by failing to exchange ("If I don't trade, I will starve!").[48]

Requirements (1), (2), and (4) are standard in most models of exchange used by economists. Requirement (3) is often recognized as a possibility by economists, who nonetheless argue that voluntary exchanges must be mutually beneficial ex ante, and that trial-and-error processes within markets mitigate the effects of violations to (3) ex post. Requirement (5), while present implicitly in many economic models—the model of monopoly is an obvious example—has received little explicit normative attention by economists, except as a cause of inefficiency. In other words, economists frequently explore the consequences of violations to (5) but rarely discuss transgressions of (5) as it relates to justice.

Munger goes on to illustrate euvoluntary exchange through several examples, including the familiar case of a parched wanderer in the desert, middlemen (merchants) in general, a highly entertaining case involving a shrewd priest in a World War II prisoner of war camp, and North Carolina following a hurricane. In some of these cases, the exchanges are euvoluntary; in others, they are not. In addition to defending the justice of euvoluntary exchange, Munger argues that "even exchanges that are not euvoluntary are generally welfare improving, and they improve the welfare of the least well off most of all."[49] Thus, even when exchanges are not euvoluntary, preventing them from happening (for example, proscribing them by law) makes things even worse. This is a familiar claim to economists, who are often baffled at the outrage among noneconomists when they defend such positions publicly. While this additional claim is interesting, what concerns us here is euvoluntary exchange itself. There are many

48 Munger, "Euvoluntary," 195. Munger also mentions there ought not be any uncompensated externalities. Guzmán and Munger, "Euvoluntariness," 41, list this as a separate requirement, bringing the total up to six. Cf. Guzmán and Munger, "Theory," 54n1.

49 Munger, "Euvoluntary," 211.

similarities between Munger's idea of justice in exchange and distributists' idea of justice in exchange.

One of the things distributism lacks is a foundation in concrete exchange activities. Distributists have said much about the institutional prerequisites of a free society, in terms of economic independence and political liberty. They have said comparatively little about the interactions among households, businesses, civic organizations, and government that take place within those institutions. Catholic teachings on distributive justice provide some guidance, especially on just prices, but since exchange activity can help *discover* the requirements of justice, there needs to be some analysis of exchange, in and of itself, that serves as a standard. For example, it is straightforward to assert that the level of wages must be sufficient to maintain a worker's livelihood, commensurate with his dignity as a bearer of the image of God, but how do we apply this principle to specific labor contracts? How high is high enough? How does this change when we consider the possibilities of non-wage compensation? What must contracts contain to promote productive and independent households, and by extension a free state? By itself, discussing the requirements of just exchange limits us to a high degree of abstraction, which makes putting principles into practice difficult.

Continuing the trend of "complements, not substitutes," this way of looking at justice in exchange should not be augmented by analyses of exchange that treat its constitutive features. The five requirements for euvoluntary exchange offer intriguing possibilities. Especially important is requirement (5). Transgressions of (5) are not quite the same thing as transgressions of economic independence, as distributists understand it, but there is substantial overlap. As Munger puts it, disparities in the "'Best Alternative to a Negotiated Agreement,' or BATNA for short," are *power* disparities.[50] If such disparities are widespread, then exchanges will likely violate the requirements of justice, as well as failing to uphold dignity and freedom. In fact, they may even reduce dignity and freedom. Munger's framework helps us classify exchanges, both ex ante and ex post, and permits a greater degree of analytical rigor than social justice alone.

Hence, the requirements for euvoluntariness serve as an evaluative criterion, at the level of individual exchanges, for those building on Belloc's and Chesterton's work. Both the narrow, intended acts of exchange and the broader, unintended results of exchange can be studied through the euvol-

50 Munger, "Euvoluntary," 196.

untary lens. We can explore whether specific exchanges satisfy the requirements for euvoluntary exchange. We can also see how well euvoluntary exchange works as a "filter" for promoting freedom-enhancing exchanges, while discouraging freedom-eroding exchanges. In fact, these two aspects of euvoluntary exchange also suggest a criterion for evaluating distributist proposals for institutional change: whether such changes make it more likely the modal exchange is euvoluntary.

To be clear, I am not claiming euvoluntary exchange can do all the "work" concerning economic justice hoped for by distributists and their fellow travelers. Those influenced by Catholic social teaching will probably be suspicious of Munger's claims that euvoluntariness is sufficient for justice in exchange. Even if it is not sufficient, however, it may still be necessary.[51] But if not, it is still a useful idea for analyzing concrete exchanges, given broader concerns about justice and freedom. Mainstream economics has a well-developed toolkit that builds from individual exchanges to entire networks of exchange. Distributist economics needs a similar toolkit for its own purposes.

CONCLUSION

Each of the above research programs—state capacity, economic and political freedom, and justice in exchange—is a significant scholarly enterprise. The debates taking place in these literatures will set the bounds of social-scientific and humanistic inquiry for years to come. They are not peripheral. The areas to which distributist-influenced scholars can contribute pose important questions. This survey is not exhaustive. Distributists can surely make a meaningful contribution to other literatures as well, but these three are full of low-hanging fruit.

Admittedly, discussing potential areas for contributions is rather abstract. While a necessary part of advancing a research program, it is still only one part. It would be incredibly helpful to have an example of a scholar who took both the humanistic concerns of distributists and the social-scientific rigor of economists and combined them. As it turns out, we have such an example. The next two chapters explore the thought of Wilhelm

51 Clearly, not all euvoluntary exchanges are just exchanges according to Catholic social teaching. Various forms of surrogate parenthood, for example, plausibly satisfy the euvoluntary conditions but are explicitly ruled out by the Catholic Church. However, the other possibility—that all just exchanges according to Catholic social teaching are euvoluntary—is worth considering.

Röpke, who, while not a Catholic, extensively studied Catholic social thought and used its teachings in his political-economic writings. Chapter 8 focuses on Röpke's conservative social philosophy and chapter 9 on his liberal political economy. While Röpke's conservatism in social matters did not always sit comfortably with his liberalism in political-economic matters, they meshed well enough to be quite fruitful. With Röpke as our exemplar, we can see how to put Belloc's and Chesterton's ideas to work.

Chapter 8

Röpke's Political Economy: *The Social Crisis of Our Time* and *A Humane Economy*

So far, we explored the social context for distributist thought within Catholic social teaching, went through classic works of distributism to glean their lessons for social philosophy, and surveyed contemporary academic literatures in which distributist insights can make fruitful contributions. These avenues suggest a way of doing political economy and social philosophy that respects the dignity of the human person, the balance between liberty and order, and the relationship between economic independence and political freedom. In addition to these guidelines, it would be quite helpful if we had a concrete example of how to practice this kind of humane social science.

Thankfully, we have such an example in Wilhelm Röpke, a German economist who was one of the intellectual godfathers of the postwar German *Wirtschaftswunder* (economic miracle)and committed both to rigorous scientific economics and Christian-humanist moral philosophy.[1] Although a Lutheran, Röpke was familiar with Catholic social teaching, often praising its principles in his writings. He also consciously drew on Chesterton and Belloc in his broader social-philosophic work on the building blocks of a free, humane, and bountiful economic order. Röpke was also one of the key figures in the development and spread of ordoliberalism, which we discussed briefly in the last chapter.

Röpke was born on October 10, 1899, in the small town of Schwarmstedt. Like many economists of his generation, he was radicalized by the horrors of World War I, seeking answers to society's problems in socialism. He devoted himself to economics to learn how such devastation might be staved off in the future, but like the Nobel laureate F. A. Hayek, when Röpke

1 Röpke's name is sometimes Anglicized as "Roepke." In these two chapters, I write "Röpke," even when quoting scholars who use the other spelling.

encountered the works of Ludwig von Mises, his views underwent a seismic shift towards economic and political liberalism. Röpke tempered his enthusiasm for markets and democracy, however, with an unshakable belief that man's commitments to the permanent things—beyond property rights, supply and demand, and competition—not only preceded economic arrangements but also made those arrangements possible. Röpke's positive analyses and normative loyalties made him one of the twentieth century's fiercest critics of totalitarianism. He had to flee Germany to avoid arrest by the Nazis, taking academic positions in Turkey, then Switzerland, where he spent the rest of his life. During and after the war, his writings defended Western civilization from all kinds of tyranny, especially socialism. He also achieved notable academic success, making important contributions to monetary economics, macroeconomics, and international economics.

Röpke was a (classical) liberal in politics, a subjectivist and marginalist in economics, and a Christian humanist in arts and letters. This is precisely the synthesis that can show us how to build on distributist insights through the application of price theory—to borrow a phrase from Deirdre McCloskey, "how to be human, though an economist."[2] This chapter and the one that follows survey key aspects of Röpke's thought, demonstrating how to achieve this balancing act. This chapter focuses on his social philosophy, showing he was a fellow traveler with the distributists and an advocate of Catholic social teaching's principles. The next chapter is devoted to his introductory price theory text, confirming his uncompromising fidelity to the economic way of thinking. We need both pillars to carry forward the distributist project, and Röpke shows us how to construct them.

Some words of caution and context before proceeding. First, these chapters are not original contributions to Röpke's place in the history of economic thought, nor his economic and political movements. I limit myself to making the case that Röpke was working within the distributist tradition, while simultaneously practicing orthodox microeconomics. This necessarily means I exclude much relevant material in order to keep the chapters to a manageable length. To my knowledge, however, I have not omitted anything that would contradict my characterization of Röpke. For those seeking to learn more about Röpke, several recent studies do a fine job of reconstructing, contextualizing, and even critiquing him. Samuel Gregg has written a

2 Cf. Deirdre McCloskey, *How to Be Human, though an Economist* (Ann Arbor: University of Michigan Press, 2000).

thorough analysis of Röpke's intellectual contributions.[3] Patricia Commun and Stefan Kolev have edited an anthology of scholarly contributions focused on Röpke.[4] And Daniel Hugger has edited a volume of Röpke's writings that were selected to give the reader an overview of Röpke's politics and economics.[5] Although Röpke is fairly obscure outside of conservative and libertarian circles, these new works show promise for a revival, which hopefully gets him the recognition he deserves.

Second, we are about to treat some polarizing themes. The nature of Röpke's balancing act tends to anger both economists who are skeptical of social philosophy, and social philosophers (especially those in the Catholic intellectual tradition) who are skeptical of economics. Röpke acknowledged as much. I beg the reader's patience, asking that Röpke be evaluated as a model of sound and humane economics in the context of both chapters, rather than one abstracted from the other. In fact, if I have written these chapters correctly, they should irritate those economists and social philosophers who believe they have nothing to learn from each other. Röpke is the archetype of the kind of thinker we need: the economist who plies his trade *within* the Western tradition's quest for the "good society," rather than independent of it or opposed to it.

THE PROBLEM OF PROLETARIANIZATION

Contextualizing the Crisis

The clearest indication that Röpke was a fellow traveler of the distributists is his preoccupation with *proletarianization*. Röpke explores this problem in depth in his 1942 volume, *The Social Crisis of Our Time*.[6] In this book, Röpke combines his training as an economist with a broader social-philosophical outlook. He is especially concerned by increased centralization and bureaucratization of social institutions, both private and public. Röpke worries these trends hollow out civil society, which he regards as necessary to check predatory behavior by businesses and the state, as well as to provide an independent social avenue for human flourishing.

3 Samuel Gregg, *Wilhelm Röpke's Political Economy* (Cheltenham: Edward Elgar, 2010).

4 Patricia Commun and Stefan Kolev, eds., *Wilhelm Röpke (1899–1966): A Liberal Political Economist and Conservative Social Philosopher* (Cham, Switzerland: Springer International, 2018).

5 Daniel J. Hugger, *The Humane Economist: A Wilhelm Röpke Reader* (Grand Rapids, Mich.: Acton Institute, 2019).

6 Wilhelm Röpke, *The Social Crisis of Our Time* (Rutgers, N.J.: Transaction Publishers, [1942] 1992).

The foreword and introduction to the 1992 edition certainly suggest Röpke's approach to economics is more humanistic in its outlook than his contemporaries.' The foreword is written by Russell Kirk, the godfather of postwar American conservatism. Kirk, a staunch Burkean traditionalist, "regarded with some suspicion many practitioners of the Dismal Science"[7] but is glad to exempt Röpke. Praising Röpke's "humane imagination,"[8] Kirk insists that "Edmund Burke, despite his general condemnation of economists . . . would have relished Röpke's company."[9] The heart of Röpke's political economy was the search for a humane alternative to capitalism and socialism—not the unimaginative compromise of the welfare state but a genuine political-economic revolution that retained the virtues of liberal democracy and market economy while eschewing their vices. Röpke's political economy was "humanized by being related to moral and intellectual ends, humanized by being reduced to human scale. Röpke proposed to abolish the proletariat, not by reducing everyone to proletarian status . . . but by restoring property, function, and dignity to the mass of folk."[10]

The introduction to the 1992 edition was written by William F. Campbell, who highlights the importance of Christian humanism, especially Catholic social teaching, to Röpke's work: "Although a Protestant, Röpke was a Protestant in the tradition of Hugo Grotius that flowed from the Erasmian tradition. As a Christian humanist in the best sense of the word, he was very sympathetic to Catholic traditions. In particular, he labored at the reasoned application of the traditional Catholic principle of subsidiarity more than any other economist in this century."[11] In applying these principles, Röpke had much in common with "the English Distributist movement of Chesterton and Belloc. The latter were explicitly acknowledged by Röpke."[12] He applied his skills as an economist and social philosopher to explore, understand, and reform the "constitution" of Western countries, where "constitution" is interpreted broadly to include "manners, mores, and customs" in addition to formal statutes and other kinds of positive law.[13]

7 Russell Kirk, foreword, in Röpke, *Social Crisis*, vii.

8 Kirk, foreword, in *Social Crisis*, viii.

9 Kirk, foreword, in *Social Crisis*, ix.

10 Kirk, foreword, in *Social Crisis*, ix–x.

11 William F. Campbell, "Introduction to the Transaction Edition," in Röpke, *Social Crisis*, xiii–xiv.

12 Campbell, "Introduction," in *Social Crisis*, xvi.

13 Campbell, "Introduction," in *Social Crisis*, xxiv.

Proletarianization: The Problem in Brief

Now we can turn to Röpke's analysis of proletarianization. Röpke's first task is to convince the reader that, despite the scientific and technological wonders of modern life, there is a sickness plaguing the nations of the West. The "unique mechanical and quantitative achievements of a technical civilization do not disembarrass us of the eternal problems of an ordered society and an existence compatible with human dignity," Röpke insists.[14] Writing during World War II, the problems he raises concerning the breakdown of peaceful intercourse between nations, as well as the social tensions within nations, were understandably more concerning for his audience than for us, but as Röpke notes, the questions he tackles are perennial. They demand careful study today just as they did eighty years ago. For this reason, Röpke grounds his analysis in the universalist axiom that "there are fundamental truths on which all men are agreed and that there are courses of action corresponding to them which are therefore, so to speak, 'natural.' When not abandoning themselves to the ecstasy of mass intoxication, people know after all very well what is healthy and what is unhealthy, what is strong and what decadent, what is just and what unjust, what is legitimate and what against the law, what is keeping with the nature of man and what is not."[15]

In Röpke's view, the chief failing of modern social and political thought is its rejection of these axioms. This explains the rise of totalitarianism in some countries and the withering of liberalism into mass democracy combined with managerial technocracy in others. Röpke is not so doctrinaire as to regard these as equally bad, but he refuses to condone the latter as a defense against the former. His concern is providing the intellectual foundations for the restoration of a healthy society. Such a society, "firmly resting on its own foundation, possesses a genuine 'structure' with many intermediate stages; it exhibits a necessarily 'hierarchical' composition (i.e., determined by the social importance of certain functions, services and leadership qualities), whereas each individual has the good fortune of knowing his position" in the various communities "such as the neighborhood, the family, the parish, the Church, the occupation," which are the social grounds for human flourishing.[16]

14 Röpke, *Social Crisis*, 2.

15 Röpke, *Social Crisis*, 4.

16 Röpke, *Social Crisis*, 10.

Instead of a balanced social order that provides a natural home to men and their aspirations, Western societies have unfortunately stumbled into a "colossal and over-complicated apparatus for catering for the masses, that orgy of technology and organization, mammoth industries, infinite division of labor, bloated cities and industrial areas, the speed and instability of economic life, that materialist and rationalist life without tradition . . . the undermining of everything permanent and rooted, the subjugation of the whole globe by a mechanical, positivist civilization."[17] This is the source of "proletarianization," which Röpke defines as "economic and social dependence, a rootless, tenemented life, where men are strangers to nature, and overwhelmed by the dreariness of work."[18] By no means the result of capitalism alone, Röpke points to "certain political and social measures taken by the state, which are responsible for proletarianization having become the fate of the masses, a fate which threatens the life of our society more than anything else and condemns millions to an existence which prevents the positive development of their faculties either as human beings or citizens."[19] Similar to Belloc and Chesterton, Röpke worries proletarianization is caused by, and increasingly contributes to, "giant enterprises and concentrations of property [which] have made a large part of the population dependent, urbanized cogs in the industrial-commercial hierarchy, recipients of wages and salaries, thus bringing about that socio-economic collectivization with which we are now acquainted."[20]

Proletarianization creates a large population that is unable and unwilling to maintain a pluralistic society with many sources of authority. Such countervailing authorities help citizens develop their potentials and practice virtue. They are crucial for resisting abuses of power—a kind of social checks-and-balances system that is political in a broader, Aristotelian sense. Röpke argues proletarianization is a failure both of politics and economics, which are, in turn, an interdependent network of social orders that, while conceptually distinct, largely overlap. Politically, "centralization and bureaucracy have mechanized the state at the expense of an organic vertical structure based on federalism or communal self-government, and have thus repeated in the narrower sphere of constitutional and administrative problems the levelling process of spiritual collectivization characterizing society

17 Röpke, *Social Crisis*, 13–14.

18 Röpke, *Social Crisis*, 14.

19 Röpke, *Social Crisis*, 14.

20 Röpke, *Social Crisis*, 15.

as a whole."[21] Economically, he indicts the system's "instability; its lack of social justice; the growing opportunities for monopolistic enrichment and the blackmailing policies of special interest; the faulty functioning of many individual markets; proletarianization, commercialization and concentration of power, excesses of speculation and destruction of capital; the insensate and unnatural way of life imposed on men against which they finally rebel, driven by a vague feeling of discontent and lured by nebulous goals."[22]

Proletarianization can be resisted, and society reinvigorated, only by "an economic policy which is in one sense conservative and radical," Röpke concludes.[23] It is "conservative in insisting on the preservation of continuity in cultural and economic development, making the defense of the basic values and principles of a free personality its highest, immutable aim," and "radical in its diagnosis of the disintegration of our 'liberal' social and economic system . . . its criticism of the errors of liberal philosophy and practice . . . lack of respect for moribund institutions, privileges, ideologies, and dogmas, and . . . in its unorthodox choice of the means which today seem appropriate for the attainment of the permanent goal of every culture based on the freedom of the individual."[24] By "unorthodox choice of the means," Röpke means creative institutional craftsmanship to prevent monopoly capitalism and tyrannical socialism, both of which crush human liberty. As a "conservative liberal," Röpke follows in the footsteps of Burke, Tocqueville, and Acton. His liberalism affirms "an individualist culture, a delicate balance between liberty and constraint, which man needs, and a society delivered from the original sin of violence and exploitation, a non-collectivist, non-feudal and non-mediaeval society."[25] Röpke's vision is a restored burgher's republic, grounded in "bourgeois virtue,"[26] which organically reconciles liberty and progress on the one hand, and order and equality on the other.[27]

21 Röpke, *Social Crisis*, 17.

22 Röpke, *Social Crisis*, 18–19.

23 Röpke, *Social Crisis*, 21.

24 Röpke, *Social Crisis*, 21–22. Here Röpke means "individualist" in a similar manner to other Christian humanists when they use the word "personalist."

25 Röpke, *Social Crisis*, 22.

26 Cf. Deirdre McCloskey, *Bourgeois Virtues: Ethics for an Age of Commerce* (Chicago: University of Chicago Press, 2006).

27 The bourgeoisie played an important role in the rise of Röpke's kind of liberalism, embodied in "vigorous, organically integrated democracies" that achieved liberty for the many through "stages of a gradual growth," rather than through revolution, as in the tragic cases of France and Russia. Röpke, *Social Crisis*, 44–45.

Röpke devotes significant space to exploring where nineteenth-century liberalism went wrong and finding the ultimate source of proletarianization. Much of this material repeats themes from Belloc and Chesterton, so I will not go into it in detail. Instead, I note that Röpke's analysis of proletarianization explicitly builds on Belloc and Chesterton. Röpke warns the reader that

> the industrial proletariat is merely the particularly conspicuous and best known expression of a far more general process of 'proletarianization.' The latter term applies . . . whenever big business, concentration of capital and a predominant market economy (at the cost of self-sufficiency) have resulted in a large part of the population's becoming dependent, urbanized receivers of indirect incomes (wages and salaries), members of the industrial-commercial hierarchy, and wherever that economic and social collectivization has set in. . . . It is also characteristic of such a proletarized world that it can no longer think in anything but in terms of money and income.[28]

In this passage, Röpke cites Chesterton's *Outline* and Belloc's *Essay* in support of his own arguments.[29] Clearly Röpke is not only carrying forward distributist concerns; he consciously situates his work in their tradition as well.

Proscribing Proletarianization

Röpke spends most of his efforts in *Social Crisis* analyzing where liberalism went wrong and explaining why neither pure (laissez-faire) capitalism nor socialism is the answer. There are prescriptive elements as well. Although not as developed as in his later works, *Social Crisis* does contain an outline of the good society, constituted to balance order and liberty. He also makes specific proposals for, for example, agricultural and industrial policy. I will not engage these issues as I did for Chesterton and Belloc. I limit myself to exploring the broad themes of his reforms. Since this is a book about distributism, I survey Röpke's proposals from *Social Crisis* to provide additional evidence that he and the distributists had the same broad goals. The similarity lies in ends, not in means, as will become increasingly clear in the next chapter.

Röpke reminds the reader of the dangers of collectivization, which is characterized by "abolition of freedom and of the sphere of private personality, extreme mechanization, rigid hierarchies and proletarization, [and]

28 Röpke, *Social Crisis*, 145.

29 Röpke, *Social Crisis*, 175.

the kneading of society into a dough-like lump," with the result that "human dignity, freedom and justice have completely vanished," and only poverty remains.[30] Socialism is the chief cause of this misery, but he does not embrace laissez-faire as the solution. Instead, Röpke affirms a conception of economic freedom very much like that of the distributists, but freedom is not a sufficient condition for social health:

> Economic freedom as an essential form of personal liberty and as a premise of everything that follows belongs undeniably to the total picture of a society which is diametrically opposed to collectivism. While this social order is necessarily based on economic freedom, other factors are also essential. In order to recognize the true antithesis of a collectivist society we must look far beyond economic freedom. We shall find it in a society in which the greatest possible number of people leads a life based on private property and a self-chosen occupation, a life that gives them inward and, as much as possible, outward independence, which enables them to be really free and to consider economic liberty as a matter of course.[31]

Thus for Röpke, economic freedom is not solely a negative restraint on interference. It is also a positive condition for independent action. This perspective on economic freedom, with its dual negative-positive aspects, fits neatly with Belloc's and Chesterton's perspectives. As another example, consider his views on capital ownership: "The misery of 'capitalism,' we must point out to the socialists, is not due to some men owning capital, but rather to others not owning any, and thus being proletarians."[32]

In addition to widespread property ownership, Röpke pays special attention to the importance of competition in economic affairs. Competition is the great equalizer, preventing excessive accumulations of economic power, which can be wielded to acquire political power. In turn, political power can entrench economic power, creating a vicious circle of rent-seeking. Röpke's definition of economic freedom requires robust competition in the marketplace. Competition "is indeed the *conditio sine qua non* of any recovery of our sick society."[33] Widely dispersed property ownership, which promotes self-sufficiency, along with competition, are

30 Röpke, *Social Crisis*, 176.

31 Röpke, *Social Crisis*, 177–78.

32 Röpke, *Social Crisis*, 178.

33 Röpke, *Social Crisis*, 180.

the pillars of Röpke's economic order, but we must not ask from competition more that it can deliver. Distancing himself from those who argue competition is a *sufficient* guarantee of social well-being, Röpke claims only that competition "is a means of establishing order and exercising control in the narrow sphere of a market economy based on the division of labor, but not a principle on which a whole society can be built."[34] To protect the competitive order and prevent a race to the bottom, "there should be a strong state, aloof from the hungry hordes of vested interests, a high standard of business ethics, an undegenerated community of people ready to co-operate with each other, who have a natural attachment to, and a firm place in society."[35]

How do these views influence Röpke's thinking on economic policy? Here, Röpke makes clear the state's role is not to interfere piecemeal in economic life but to set up the "rules of the game" such that the predictable outcome of the market process is the maintenance of both order and liberty. Constant tinkering by the public authorities cannot help but push society toward collectivism. Instead, "it will always be in our interest to realize our economic aims by attempting changes in the framework of the economic system, but not by interfering with the actual mechanism of the market economy itself which is characterized by the price mechanism and competition."[36] Röpke distinguishes between market-compatible and market-incompatible interventions by the state. The former do not impede the pricing process. Instead, they address the underlying governance of commerce. The latter, on the other hand, do impede the pricing process, artificially modifying the terms of trade, diminishing the price system's ability to convey information about opportunity cost. This is made worse by political elites picking winners and losers in the marketplace. On these definitions, Röpke believes there is a wide latitude for market-compatible interventions to, for example, cushion the losses of business owners in an economic sector that becomes unviable (without artificially propping up the industry and impeding necessary economic adjustments), redistributing income, fighting monopolies, and even "manag[ing] individual enterprises or even whole branches of production" so "long as the state entrepreneur respects . . . [the basic laws of market economy] and as long as it is not a

34 Röpke, *Social Crisis*, 181.

35 Röpke, *Social Crisis*, 181.

36 Röpke, *Social Crisis*, 184.

case of general nationalization which completely eliminates the market economy."[37]

These ideas are a natural segue to Röpke's theory of the state. Ideally, the state is strong enough to resist capture by special interests, as well as competent enough to implement corrective public policy. "A strong state," Röpke insists, "is by no means one that meddles in everything and tries to monopolize all functions. On the contrary, not busyness but independence from group interests and the inflexible will to exercise its authority and preserve its dignity as a representative of the community, mark the really strong state, whereas the state that acts as a maid of all work, finally degenerates into a miserable weakling, and falls victim to the vested interests."[38] Ultimately, the state should be "an energetic umpire whose task it is neither to take part in the game nor to prescribe their movements to the players, who is, rather, completely impartial and incorruptible and sees to it that the rules of the game and of sportsmanship are strictly observed."[39]

To achieve these goals, Röpke encourage social philosophers to maintain "a radical spirit which keeps the great general aim of a free, just, de-collectivized, de-centralized and de-proletarized society before our eyes and encourages us to undertake, where necessary, even incisive operations."[40] But Röpke is careful to distinguish between the positive and normative dimensions of his restorative project. A social "scientist who recommends political and economic measures is bound by certain limits which he cannot overstep without entering the field of the subjective, and therefore debatable, opinions."[41] When moving from questions of ends to questions of means, "the greater becomes the degree of subjectivity and, therefore, the greater the number of points on which agreement can no longer be presupposed."[42] Röpke should be read not as surrendering to the (supposed) fact-value distinction but instead locating the proper place of social science in achieving what is, ultimately, an ethical endeavor. This is not diffidence but prudence.

The final chapter of *Social Crisis* considers how to alter the rules of the economic game to promote humane living. Röpke considers agriculture,

37 Röpke, *Social Crisis*, 190.

38 Röpke, *Social Crisis*, 192.

39 Röpke, *Social Crisis*, 192.

40 Röpke, *Social Crisis*, 199.

41 Röpke, *Social Crisis*, 200.

42 Röpke, *Social Crisis*, 200.

artisans and small merchants, large-scale industry, social policy, antimonopoly policy, and international relations. Again, I am not interested in the specific policies Röpke had in mind. Instead, I focus on how Röpke thought about these issues, because Röpke's way of thinking connects his work to that of the distributists. Select quotes suffice to convey Röpke's positions.

For agriculture, Röpke's main concern is preserving independent peasant proprietors, which really means promoting the productive family unit: "It is an essential characteristic of peasant agriculture that the size of each farm does not exceed the working capacity of one family . . . as a rule it is the property of the farmer, thus embodying tradition and the succession of generations; it is embedded in the social organization of the family and the kinship group," so that agriculture "counter-balances the industrial and urban aspects of our civilization with tradition and conservatism, economic independence and self-sufficiency, many-sided activity and development, proximity to nature, moderation and tranquility, a natural and full existence near the sources of life, and a humble integration into the chain of birth and death."[43]

For artisans and small traders, Röpke reminds us of the "great and supremely important goal, namely, to promote and strengthen all forms of living and working which have not yet succumbed to collectivization and proletarization," and hence the desirability of commercial laws that create room for small, independent enterprises to thrive.[44] Röpke acknowledges such laws would make goods and services more expensive than otherwise, but he insists that "consumers who can at all afford it should not shrink from the sacrifice of a few cents in order to carry out an economic policy of their own and support artisans to the best of their ability for the good of the community," so long as they can "find in the artisan himself a willing partner to this scheme, ready to give his best."[45] This is a restatement of Belloc's "liberty externality," an uncompensated benefit of widespread property and capital ownership.

Röpke's ideas for large-scale industry are similar. He wants to deproletarianize industry, even if this creates economic costs, including reduced industrial profitability. The sacrifice "as regards immediate and measurable profitableness and technical practicability . . . will be repaid in a wider, social sense and may in the long run even redound to the advantage of enterprise

43 Röpke, *Social Crisis*, 202–3.

44 Röpke, *Social Crisis*, 213.

45 Röpke, *Social Crisis*, 217.

itself. If we take into consideration the sociological consequences of proletarization, we are . . . entitled to the conclusion that in certain circumstances the mechanical organization of industrial plants which permits the cheapest form of production on the basis of measurable costs, *may in the end prove to be the most expensive for society as a whole*."[46]

Röpke's thoughts on social policy contain the fewest positive proposals. He is most sure of what will *not* work. This section contains a vignette that explicitly connects him to the Christian humanist tradition. First Röpke castigates modern welfare policy because it ignores "the fact that the root of the evil is to be found not in material causes but in proletarization, that . . . this type of social policy has only too often sought to solve matters by social legislation which necessitated a more and more comprehensive and growing welfare bureaucracy. . . . The result of such a 'progressive' reform of social policy is the further proletarization of the country."[47] Röpke then recounts his experience trying to convince a welfare bureaucrat to reorient social policy toward ordered liberty, rather than mere "incomes policy," which shuffles around purchasing power without solving any real problems. The bureaucrat, in some astonishment, asked, "'Why, you are a Catholic, are you?'" Röpke replied that "one did not have to be a Catholic in order to see things this way."[48] Even more explicitly, Röpke argues the "task is really to attack the source of the evil and to do away with the proletariat itself—to achieve what the Papal Encyclical *Quadragesima Anno* (1931) has termed the *Redemptio Proletariorum*."[49]

As for antimonopoly and other procompetitive policies, Röpke writes, "In economic life, too, the saying holds good that liberty without restraint is license, and if we desire a free market the framework of conditions, rules and institutions must be all the stronger and more inflexible. Laissez-faire—yes, but within a framework laid down by a permanent and clear-sighted market police in the widest sense of the word."[50] The goal of such policy is to promote the public interest by curbing market power: "If we identify the 'public interest' with that of the consuming community it is clear that monopoly violates this interest. It leads to an allocation of productive forces

46 Röpke, *Social Crisis*, 221, emphasis added.

47 Röpke, *Social Crisis*, 223.

48 Röpke, *Social Crisis*, 224.

49 Röpke, *Social Crisis*, 225.

50 Röpke, *Social Crisis*, 228.

other than that corresponding to the preferences of the population with regard to what and how much of everything wanted shall be produced."[51] Röpke reminds the reader that, more often than not, monopolies come from the state picking favorites, rather than the natural operation of markets: "We must remember that in the great majority of cases it was the state itself which through its legislative, administrative and judicial activities first created the conditions favorable to the formation of monopolies. There are in fact not many monopolies in the world which would exist without privileges having been consciously or unconsciously granted by the state, or without some sort of legislative or administrative measure, legal decision or financial policy having been responsible for it," and thus the first imperative of the state in this area is to do no harm.[52] Nevertheless, according to Röpke, monopolies can occasionally arise out of market competition, in which case the "general principle should be the destruction of monopolies instead of mere monopoly control which is politically dangerous and mostly illusionary."[53]

Internationally, Röpke wants to reconstruct a peaceful and cooperative order along classical-liberal lines, similar to the nineteenth century. The foundations of this new order must be strong enough to resist the siren calls of nationalism and statism. This is not just an economic task, but a political and moral one as well. A humane international order "cannot extend further than the sphere of political, social and moral integration which guarantees a minimum of law, order, security, and dependable ethics."[54] Although not generally a fan of the Middle Ages, Röpke acknowledges that "however much we may find fault with them in other respects, [they] possessed to a very high degree an international order which lost none of its effects because it was essentially of a moral-theological nature and its denominational limitations confided it to Christendom."[55] Conserving the virtues bequeathed by the Middle Ages while diminishing the vices (frequent armed conflicts, widespread bondage and servitude, etc.) should be the liberal's first task. To sustain itself, the international order must be multilateral. This is especially important for the division of labor across national boundaries: "Only when

51 Röpke, *Social Crisis*, 229.

52 Röpke, *Social Crisis*, 230.

53 Röpke, *Social Crisis*, 234.

54 Röpke, *Social Crisis*, 238.

55 Röpke, *Social Crisis*, 238.

it is multilateral is the world economic order, just as any national economy, a market, price and payments union, and only then can it also be a production union."[56] According to Röpke, the best way forward is "a return to a liberal and multilateral form of world trade with tolerable tariffs, most-favored-nations clauses, the policy of the open door, the gold standard, and the elimination of closed compulsory blocks (with their machinery of exchange controls and clearing arrangements)."[57]

HUMANIZING THE ECONOMY

Escaping Enmassment

If Röpke's *Social Crisis* is primarily a diagnosis, his *Humane Economy* is the accompanying treatment.[58] Röpke explains how free markets and limited government contribute to the common good. Economists will probably find *Humane Economy* easier reading than *Social Crisis*, but there is still plenty in this volume that will make them uneasy, so long as their moral imagination is limited to efficiency. As Röpke notes in the introduction to the English translation:

> One group of critics will reject the book *en bloc* because it is in flat contradiction with their more or less collectivist and centrist ideas. Another will tell me that in this book . . . they really appreciate only what is to be found in the world of supply and demand—the world of property—and not what lies beyond. These are the inveterate rationalists, the hard-boiled economists, the prosaic utilitarians. . . . Third, there will be those who, on the contrary, blame me for being a hard-headed economist myself and who will find something worth praising only in that part of the book which deals with things beyond supply and demand. These are the pure moralists and romantics. . . . Finally there may be a fourth group of readers who take a favorable view of the book as a whole and who regard it as one of the virtues to have incurred the disapproval of the other three groups.[59]

56 Röpke, *Social Crisis*, 241.

57 Röpke, *Social Crisis*, 242.

58 Wilhelm Röpke, *A Humane Economy: The Social Framework of the Free Market* (Wilmington, Del.: ISI Books, [1960] 1998). On page 1 of the 1998 edition, Röpke explicitly situates *Humane Economy* as a follow-up and revisiting of the themes he first explored in *Social Crisis*, along with two other works he wrote during the Second World War.

59 Röpke, *Humane Economy*, xii.

Röpke continues down the path blazed by the distributists. In his introduction, Dermot Quinn asserts that *Humane Economy* "draws on Chesterton, Belloc, and the English distributist tradition" in many of its arguments.[60] Quinn continues, "Both Röpke and the distributists held that private property widely diffused was the principal foundation of political freedom, the surest defense against the self-aggrandizing state. . . . Ownership at once presupposes individual rights and promotes them. Röpke saw it as the cornerstone of the humane economy; Chesterton saw it as the outline of sanity; Belloc saw its absence as characteristic of a servile state. . . . Property broadly understood represented a 'particular philosophy of life, . . . a particular social and moral universe.'"[61] Quinn recognizes Röpke's emphasis on property derives from his concerns with resisting proletarianization.

Röpke begins by laying out his ideological sympathies more explicitly than in *Social Crisis*. It was not difficult to discern Röpke's conservative liberalism in the earlier work, but in *Humane Economy*, there is no room for doubt: "If it is liberal to entrust economic order, not to planning, coercion, and penalties, but to the spontaneous and free co-operation of the people through the market, price, and competition, and at the same time to regard property as the pillar of this free order, then I speak as a liberal."[62] Yet at the same time, "in those levels where each man's social philosophy is rooted," Röpke wonders, "I am not at all sure that I do not belong to the conservative rather than the liberal camp, in so far as I dissociate myself from . . . utilitarianism, progressivism, secularism, rationalism, optimism, and what Eric Voegelin aptly calls 'immanentism' or 'social gnosticism.'"[63] In Röpke's social philosophy, man is "the likeness of God," and it "is an appalling sin to reduce man to a means . . . and that each man's soul is something unique, irreplaceable, priceless, in comparison with which all other things are as naught."[64] Röpke links this belief to his advocacy for markets: "It is for the same reasons that I champion an economic order ruled by free prices and markets . . . this is the only economic order com-

60 Dermot Quinn, introduction, in Röpke, *Humane Economy*, xvii.

61 Quinn, introduction, *Humane Economy*, xviii.

62 Röpke, *Humane Economy*, 3.

63 Röpke, *Humane Economy*, 3–4. The nonelided version of the passage makes clear Röpke views these "isms," while not necessarily inherent in liberalism, as hangers-on of a distressingly high frequency.

64 Röpke, *Humane Economy*, 5.

patible with human freedom, with a state and society which safeguard freedom, and with the rule of law."[65] The threat to this order, the "all-pervading problem," lies in the centralization and bureaucratization of social life: "concentration of economic and social power beside and under the state; concentration of decision and responsibility, which thereby become more and more anonymous, unchallengeable, and inscrutable; and concentration of people in organizations, towns and industrial centers, and firms and factories."[66] The inevitable result is the destruction of "the middle class properly so called, that is, an independent class possessed of small or moderate property and income, a sense of responsibility, and those civic virtues without which a free and well-ordered society cannot, in the long run, survive."[67] Economic reforms, by themselves, will not solve this: "Market economy, price mechanism, and competition are fine, but they are not enough."[68] The end goal is not simply economic laissez-faire but a society in which "wealth would be widely dispersed; people's lives would have solid foundations; genuine communities, from the family upward, would form a background of moral support for the individual; there would be counterweights to competition and the mechanical operation of prices; people would have roots and not be adrift in life without anchor; there would be a broad belt of an independent middle class, a healthy balance between town and country, industry and agriculture."[69] The conditions under which such a society can be recovered and preserved occupy Röpke's attention for the remainder of *Humane Economy*.

Röpke's views on social problems have evolved since *Social Crisis*, although it would be wrong to view *Humane Economy* as a break with his earlier writings. There is, in fact, significant continuity. Röpke now focuses on the problem of the "mass society" and "enmassment."[70] Building on the work of Spanish philosopher and social critic Jose Ortega y Gasset, Röpke acknowledges that this idea has become something of a fad, too quickly and carelessly employed. Nevertheless, Röpke insists the problem is real, stating

65 Röpke, *Humane Economy*, 5.

66 Röpke, *Humane Economy*, 32.

67 Röpke, *Humane Economy*, 32.

68 Röpke, *Humane Economy*, 35.

69 Röpke, *Humane Economy*, 35.

70 Röpke never uses the term "enmassment," but many times, he uses variations such as "mass man," "mass state," etc. I use "enmassment" to represent what is common across these terms.

that it "is the crucial issue for the moral, spiritual, political, economic, and social future of the world into which we are born."[71]

The mass society is not the same as the proletarianized society, although they are closely related.[72] Proletarianization results from economic and political transformations that make it difficult for ordinary men to own capital. With that comes the erosion of independence and freedom. Enmassment, in Röpke's framework, is broader. It means a change in the scale in human relationships, both in private and public, which leaves individuals without any kind of spiritual anchor. Rules and procedures crowd out personal relationships. Furthermore, the impersonal does not merely replace the personal. It grows alarmingly beyond its proper bounds, suffocating individuality. As a result, "the world is too much with us."[73] Röpke laments the "sheer oppressive quantity . . . surrounding us everywhere; masses of people who are all more or less the same—or who are at least assimilated in appearance and behavior; overwhelming quantities of man-made things, everywhere, the traces of people, their organizations, their claims."[74] The inevitable result is that "all poetry and dignity, and with them the very spice of life and its human content, go out of life."[75]

Röpke acknowledges the immense productive capabilities unleashed by modern capitalism. As an economist, he appreciates the consequences of rising living standards, but he despises the Pollyannaish view that atrophied social relationships are merely benign adaptations to new economic and political realities. Something *real* is being lost, even if most economists do not acknowledge it.[76] Even if restricted to subjective welfare, Röpke thinks an argument can be made that not all is for the better: "Is it not, we may modestly ask, part of the standard of living that people should feel well and happy and should not lack what Burke calls the 'unbought graces of

71 Röpke, *Humane Economy*, 38.

72 On p. 56, Röpke writes that "urbanization, industrialization, and proletarianization (in a well-defined sense) are only the special aspects of" the rise of mass society. This suggests Röpke has come to view proletarianization as part of a larger malady, which is enmassment.

73 The title of a Wordsworth sonnet.

74 Röpke, *Humane Economy*, 39.

75 Röpke, *Humane Economy*, 41.

76 Röpke laments the "modern technical and pseudo-scientific pragmatism and utilitarianism and their total inability to grasp that the achievements of the natural sciences, important and formative though they are, cannot change man's nature as primarily a spiritual and moral being" (Röpke, *Humane Economy*, 63).

life'—nature, privacy, beauty, dignity, birds and woods and fields and flowers, repose and true leisure, as distinct from that break in the rush which is called 'spare time' and has to be filled by some hectic activity?"[77]

An important but neglected feature of the "good society" is balance between liberty and order, which includes a balance between the personal and the social. Mass society exhibits "a shift of the center of gravity towards collectivity and away from the individual, at rest within himself and holding his own as an integral personality. The equilibrium between individual and society, their relation of constant tension and genuine antimony, is disturbed in favor of society."[78] Röpke worries that the individual is "losing his own features, soul, intrinsic worth and personality because and in so far as he is immersed in the 'mass,' and the latter is 'mass' because and in so far as it consists of such 'depersonalized' individuals." These passages are important because they demonstrate Röpke's argument against mass society is not merely aesthetic. Instead, his concern is for human flourishing: persons developing their talents toward the end of a well-lived life. Human flourishing is best promoted when the personal and impersonal forces in society are balanced, but this balance is precarious. Once disturbed, there is no automatic process to restore the equilibrium.

Röpke gives a concrete illustration of enmassment in his analysis of democracy. Rather than viewing democracy as an unalloyed good, he insists that it can contribute to mass society and thus destroy the conditions for humane living. Röpke contrasts "liberal democracy of the Anglo-Saxon and Swiss kind" with "the Jacobin brand of democracy," insisting that "the latter has increasingly become the dominating force of democracy in our times precisely because it is appropriate to mass society."[79] The former kind of democracy, as the result of historical development rather than revolutionary fervor, is better suited to preserving the social and political traditions that exist anterior to the state and can constrain its excesses: "Anglo-Saxon and Swiss democracy are rooted in historical soil that is centuries older than universal suffrage; they grew up in an age when the ancient elements of freedom, whether of classical, Christian, or Germanic origin, were still a live reality and when the area of rights and obligations was firmly circumscribed by a society whose fabric and structure were the very opposite of

77 Röpke, *Humane Economy*, 49.

78 Röpke, *Humane Economy*, 52–53.

79 Röpke, *Humane Economy*, 66.

modern mass society."[80] In other words, liberal democracy in the Anglo-Saxon and Swiss traditions is compatible with humane living because it respects limits on its own scope of action. These limits ensure other social spaces, especially the all-important institutions of civil society, have room to grow. Jacobin democracy, "typical of a spirit which is not content to accept what is but must forever reopen every question," respects no limits, and thus "is precisely the mark of mass society and mass man."[81]

Concluding his discussion of mass society, Röpke acknowledges that critics may accuse him of romanticism. Since Röpke is very much a practitioner of economic science—as he demonstrates in the subsequent section, and even more convincingly in the next chapter—such accusations miss the point. Of his social vision, Röpke admits "it certainly is romantic, if by that term we understand resistance to the destruction of dignity and poetry and the 'unbought graces of life.'"[82] Waxing Chestertonian, Röpke declares, "If this is romanticism, we profess it unreservedly and proudly. . . . We do not want to set the clock back; we want to set it right."[83] Furthermore, Röpke wishes to save economics from those economists who, because they are specialists in the analysis of means, dismiss out of hand any debate over ends. Quoting the passage of Burke's *Revolutions* that disparages "sophisters, oeconomists, and calculators," Röpke rhetorically asks:

> Shall we not prove to Burke that he has done the "oeconomists" an injustice? Shall we not dissociate ourselves from the sophisters and calculators? Of what avail is any amount of well-being if, at the same time, we steadily render the world more vulgar, uglier, noisier, and drearier and if men lose the moral and spiritual foundations of their existence? Man simply does not live by radio, automobiles, and refrigerators alone, but by the whole unpurchaseable world beyond the market and turnover figures, the world of dignity, beauty, poetry, grace, chivalry, love, and friendship, the world of community, variety of life, freedom, and fullness of personality. Circumstances which debar man from such a life or make it difficult for him stand irrevocably convicted, for they destroy the essence of his nature.[84]

80 Röpke, *Humane Economy*, 68.

81 Röpke, *Humane Economy*, 69.

82 Röpke, *Humane Economy*, 88.

83 Röpke, *Humane Economy*, 88.

84 Röpke, *Humane Economy*, 89.

Markets and the Common Good

But how can such lofty goals be reconciled with the extensive division of labor in a market economy? Overcoming these tensions is Röpke's main task in *Humane Economy*. Röpke scorns the claims, frequently made by those hostile to economics and commerce, that the market is the primary cause of mass society, but he does recognize that unless governed by an appropriate set of background institutions, markets can contribute to enmassment. Röpke wants to convey the belief that "the sphere of the market, of competition, of the system where supply and demand move prices and thereby govern production, may be regarded and defended only as part of a wider general order encompassing ethics, law, the natural conditions of life and happiness, the state, politics, and power."[85] In other words, well-governed markets are necessary for a humane economy, but are not sufficient.

"The market economy rests not on one pillar but on two," Röpke reminds us. "It presupposes not only the principle of free prices and competition but also the institution of private ownership, in the true sense of legally safeguarded freedom to dispose of one's property, including freedom of testation."[86] Ownership is a particularly important prerequisite because it affords "protection of the individual sphere from political power."[87] Competition is both "an institution for stimulating effort" and "a device for regulating and ordering the economic process."[88] It is "the incomparable strength of the market economy that it alone can take advantage of the dual nature of competition, which is genuine and fully effective only when it is whole . . . but this prerogative stands and falls by private ownership of the means of production."[89] Proponents of economic collectivization err when they assert these functions of the market can be "instrumentalized," and thus performed by some other set of institutions than ownership and competition. This is an illusion. Only the market economy, resting on both genuine ownership and competition, can deliver the goods. The question is how to humanize it.

Röpke then discusses the "fact that the market economy is a form of economic order belonging to a particular philosophy of life and to a

85 Röpke, *Humane Economy*, 90–91.

86 Röpke, *Humane Economy*, 94.

87 Röpke, *Humane Economy*, 94.

88 Röpke, *Humane Economy*, 95.

89 Röpke, *Humane Economy*, 97.

particular social and moral universe."[90] He contends "that the market economy has a bourgeois foundation." The normative commitments inherent in such a society—including but not limited to "individual effort and responsibility, absolute norms and values," and "independence based on ownership"—contribute to strong and dynamic communities. The "bourgeois order" is "the opposite of the proletarianized society . . . and also the opposite of the mass society as discussed in the preceding chapter. Independence, ownership, individual reserves, saving, the sense of responsibility, rational planning of one's own life—all that is alien, if not repulsive, to proletarianized mass society. Yet precisely that is the condition of society which cherishes its liberty."[91] Even more clearly, it is "private ownership which principally distinguishes a non-proletarian form of life from a proletarian one."[92] Thus, a society robust against proletarianization requires markets.

"To this end," Röpke continues, "we need a combination of supreme moral sensibility and economic knowledge. Economically ignorant moralism is as objectionable as morally callous economism. Ethics and economics are two equally difficult subjects, and while the former needs discerning and expert reason, the latter cannot do without humane values."[93] Integrating economics and ethics is required to refute the error that there is "no necessary connection between political and spiritual freedom on the one hand and economic freedom on the other."[94] On the contrary, all these freedoms are inexorably linked. Therefore, negative freedom, although important, is insufficient for a nonproletarianized economy and polity. Again, what is required is a delicate balancing act: "Romanticizing and moralistic contempt of the economy, including the contempt of the impulses which move the market economy and the institutions which support it, must be as far from our minds as economism, materialism, and utilitarianism."[95]

The ethical foundations of a market economy require not only a dedication to the "bourgeois virtues"[96] but also the recognition that "we move on an intermediate plane. It is not the summit of heroes and saints, of simon-

90 Röpke, *Humane Economy*, 98.
91 Röpke, *Humane Economy*, 99.
92 Röpke, *Humane Economy*, 103.
93 Röpke, *Humane Economy*, 104.
94 Röpke, *Humane Economy*, 105.
95 Röpke, *Humane Economy*, 107.
96 Cf. McCloskey, *Bourgeois Virtues*.

pure altruism, selfless dedication, and contemplative calm, but neither is it the lowlands of open or concealed struggle in which force and cunning determine the victor and the vanquished."[97] The world of commerce, "in which we do business, bargain, calculate, speculate, compare bids, and explore markets ethically corresponds by and large to that middle level at which the whole of everyday life goes on."[98] This is fundamentally a conservative, antiutopian insight. As before, Röpke counsels not timidity but prudence in what we ask of commercial society. These insights are the result of hard-won philosophical advancements, especially "eighteenth-century social and moral philosophy, which is the source of our own discipline of political economy," which has "liberated the crafts and commercial activities . . . from the stigma of the feudal era and to have obtained for them the ethical position to which they are entitled and which we now take for granted."[99]

But it would be a grave error to think Röpke believes markets contain within themselves the means of social pacification and advancement. Röpke is no *doux commerce* optimist. His position is that markets can cope with human foibles, but only if they build on prior ethical traditions and practices. Morals and markets must work together. Society cannot progress to an advanced division of labor without certain "ethical reserves" that sustain the increasing prevalence of commercial bonds. "The market, competition, and the play of supply and demand do not create these ethical reserves; they presuppose them and consume them. These reserves must come from outside the market, and no textbook on economics can replace them."[100] "Self-discipline, a sense of justice, honesty, fairness, chivalry, moderation, public spirit, respect for human dignity, [and] firm ethical norms" must first exist. "Family, church, genuine communities, and tradition" must nourish them.[101]

Imparting these truths is part of the "tasks and responsibilities falling to the academic representatives of economics,"[102] and thus, while it is appropriate to clarify which kinds of statements are descriptive and which prescriptive, economists do their profession and their society an injustice when they exclude the latter from their discourse. Already in Röpke's time, the

97 Röpke, *Humane Economy*, 116.

98 Röpke, *Humane Economy*, 117.

99 Röpke, *Humane Economy*, 119.

100 Röpke, *Humane Economy*, 125.

101 Röpke, *Humane Economy*, 125.

102 Röpke, *Humane Economy*, 149.

increasing specialization—one might call it siloing—of economists had pushed the profession in the direction of technocracy. While many "seem to think that the principal function of economics is to prepare the domination of society by 'specialists' in economics, statistics, and planning," Röpke contends this is both unscientific and inhumane.[103] Economics is properly an "anti-ideological, anti-utopian, disillusioning science. It could render society the invaluable service of lowering the temperature of political passions, counteracting mass myths, and making life difficult for demagogues, financial wizards, and economic magicians."[104] Economists cannot retreat "into the ivory tower of scientific neutrality. Least of all can social scientists be spared a decision at the cross-roads of our civilization; we must not only be able to read the signs, but we must know which way to point and lead: the road to freedom, humanity, and unswerving truth or the road to serfdom, violation of human nature, and falsehood. To evade this decision would be just as much *trahison des clercs* as to sacrifice the dignity of our science, which is truth, to the political and social passions of our time."[105]

To preserve civilization, social scientists once again must embrace the challenges of decentralized self-governance, resisting false lures of efficiency and expediency. Advocates of "federalism and local government" are the natural "friends of the peasantry, the crafts, and middle classes, and the small firm and of widely dispersed private property and the lovers of nature and of the human scale in all things" and must counterbalance "the advocates of large-scale industry, technical and organizational rationality, huge associations, and giant cities."[106] The mass society is one where there are few or no social barriers between the individual and corporate-political behemoths. The humane society is one where there are many such barriers. Furthermore, advocates of human-scale relationships must appeal to ultimate values. Refusing to step beyond the bounds of social science in making an argument for the good society is at best misguided, and at worst cowardly. A decentralist "must in all circumstances be a convinced universalist; he must keep his eye on a larger community which is all the more genuine for being structured and articulated. His center is God, and this is why he refuses to accept human centers instead, that is, precisely that which con-

103 Röpke, *Humane Economy*, 149.

104 Röpke, *Humane Economy*, 150.

105 Röpke, *Humane Economy*, 150.

106 Röpke, *Humane Economy*, 229.

sistent centrism, in the form of collectivism, intends to present him with."[107] As opposed to centrism, which yields enmassment and proletarianization, decentralism affords the social space for genuine political and economic liberty. Röpke worries about "whether genuine democracy and a free market economy are, in the long run, compatible with a state of affairs in which the crushing majority of the population consists of dependent wage and salary earners."[108] The only alternative for believers in democracy (meaning self-governance, not plebiscites) and markets (meaning consent and competition, not capitalistic oligarchy) is multiple independent centers of social decision making.

In conclusion, all roads Röpke walks in *Humane Economy* start from, and lead to, a single point: the institutional foundations of human flourishing. While sometimes he meanders, he always arrives at his destination. His arguments about economics and politics, enmassment and independence, centralization and decentralization, are summarized admirably by Dermot Quinn:

> Free markets are preferable to tyranny not because they enrich us but because they moralize us. They connect us to authentic human communities, allowing us to be self-reliant yet also honorably dependent on the effort of others. And precisely for that reason, to make a *cult* of the market is to detach it from its own moral imperatives. Markets do not generate moral norms; they presume them. Moreover, they offer the freedom of self-discipline, not unanchored greed. Besides, for all their excellence, markets are not everything. The vital things, Röpke realized, are those beyond supply and demand, beyond the world of property, beyond the calculator's reach. Such is the point and paradox of the book. A humane economy is only, in the end, a shadowy reflection of the divine one.[109]

107 Röpke, *Humane Economy*, 233.

108 Röpke, *Humane Economy*, 240.

109 Quinn, introduction, xx.

Chapter 9

Röpke's Political Economy: *The Economics of the Free Society*

Having surveyed Röpke's social philosophy, we now turn to his economics. Röpke's writings on the former drew upon the latter. As we will see, the reverse is also true in his economics text, *The Economics of the Free Society*.[1] Nevertheless, the emphasis has changed: What was in the background in his social-philosophic writings is in the foreground in his economics text, as is appropriate.

Röpke wrote his book, the first edition of which was published in 1937, because he perceived "the pedagogical need of a coherent description of the whole of the economic process. Such a description should be scrupulously scientific. But it should also be adapted to the understanding, interests, and experience of a people of average education."[2] Röpke intended this to be an introductory text. This is an important point. In economics, the introductory text has a special place in the hierarchy of knowledge. Unlike many other disciplines, where scientific advancement makes it necessary for introductory texts to be frequently modified, an introductory economics text—if it is a good text—presents what is universal and unchanging in economics: the *economic way of thinking*. Because economics as a discipline is defined by *how* it studies things, rather than *what* it studies, additional expertise in economics adds refinement and sophistication to the mechanisms covered in an introductory text but does not supplant them. Hence, the introductory economics text is an author's summing up of the most general and vital points of economics. It reflects the author's view on what everyone needs to know. Precisely because of its

1 Wilhelm Röpke, *The Economics of the Free Society*, translated by Patrick M. Boarman (Chicago: Henry Regnery, [1961] 1963).

2 Röpke, *Economics*, vi. The version referenced in this chapter is translated from the ninth German edition, which was published in 1961.

breadth and ease of accessibility, the introductory text can fulfill this ecumenical function, which is my purpose for using *The Economics of the Free Society* as the key to Röpke's economics.

Röpke's economics falls within what Peter Boettke calls the "mainline" of economic thought,[3] which is not necessarily the same as the mainstream. "Mainline," in this typology, "is defined by a set of positive propositions about social order that were held in common from Adam Smith onward, but mainstream economics is a sociological concept related to what is currently fashionable among the scientific elite of the profession."[4] Mainline economics embraces the rationality postulate—defined broadly as purposive human action—as an engine for doing social science, but it also recognizes that rationality is filtered through social institutions, from which govern the incentives and information individuals confront. This emphasis on institutional analysis points to three tenets about "the nature of human action and the role of institutions . . . (1) there are limits to the benevolence that individuals can rely on and therefore they face cognitive and epistemic limits as they negotiate the social world, but (2) formal and informal institutions guide and direct human activity, and so (3) social cooperation is possible without central direction."[5] Röpke's concern in his text with the "rules of the game" governing economic and political life demonstrates he is institutionally focused. His statements about how those rules generate predictable outcomes cannot be comprehended without the rationality postulate. Röpke is unquestionably operating within the Smithian economics tradition, which calls into question the claims that this tradition is incompatible with Catholic social teaching, or in the search for a humane social order more generally.

As with the previous chapter on Röpke's social-philosophy books, this chapter is not an exhaustive survey of his *The Economics of the Free Society*. I omit entirely the material on macroeconomics and business cycles, and most of the material on money and banking. When I elaborate on specific points associated with a given chapter, I do not explore all he has to say within that chapter. One such case is his questionable and, at times, quasi-

3 Peter J. Boettke, *Living Economics: Yesterday, Today, and Tomorrow* (Oakland, Calif.: Independent Institute, 2012); Peter J. Boettke, Stefanie Haeffele-Balch, and Virgil Henry Storr, eds., *Mainline Economics: Six Nobel Lectures in the Tradition of Adam Smith* (Arlington, Va.: Mercatus Center, 2016); and Matthew D. Mitchell and Peter J. Boettke, *Applied Mainline Economics: Bridging the Gap between Theory and Policy* (Arlington, Va.: Mercatus Center, 2017).

4 Boettke, *Living Economics*, xvii.

5 Boettke, Haeffele-Balch, and Storr, *Mainline Economics*, 4.

Malthusian views on population growth in the chapter dedicated to the division of labor. My selections are focused on showing how Röpke's economics, at its core, comprises the orthodox principles stressed by economists in the marginalist-subjectivist tradition, which are carried forward today by scholars in the mainline.

THE MARVEL OF THE MARKET

Philosophy begins in wonder. Economics, too, begins in wonder, although its object is a constituent of being rather than being as such. That object is the commercial world and the regularity therein. Despite its variety and complexity, we immediately notice the degree to which economic activity, which is comprised of the actions of millions of persons, families, and organizations pursuing their own affairs, is *orderly*. The plans of producers tend to coincide with the desires of consumers. For Röpke, as for virtually all economists, this is a remarkable thing. Calling attention to it is the proper introduction to economic science. Economic complexity, especially the division of labor, "presupposes . . . a harmonious coordination of the divided elements of the economic process."[6] Two questions arise: "Who in the countries of the free world is charged with this coordination? What would happen if no one were in charge?"[7]

Röpke's answer is, "Nobody. No dictator rules the economy, deciding who shall perform the needed work and prescribing what goods and how much of each shall be produced and brought to market."[8] The "extraordinarily complex mechanism" of the market-based economic system "functions without conscious central control by any agency whatever."[9] In contrast to anarchy in politics, "anarchy in economics, strangely, produces an opposite result: an orderly cosmos. Our economic system may be anarchic, but it is not chaotic."[10] This is why economic science exists: "Honesty compels the admission that the existence of ordered anarchy is cause for astonishment, that it is something which urgently requires explanation."[11] Coordination in

6 Röpke, *Economics*, 2–3.

7 Röpke, *Economics*, 3.

8 Röpke, *Economics*, 3.

9 Röpke, *Economics*, 4, emphasis removed.

10 Röpke, *Economics*, 4. Here "anarchic" means "without hierarchical control," not "without rules and order." The market economy is clearly governed, but not by political fiat.

11 Röpke, *Economics*, 4.

absence of command requires something else to do the coordinating. Economics is the discipline that identifies the coordination mechanisms.

At the same time, Röpke warns against tacitly mechanizing the economy. The "economic system is not an objective mechanical thing which functions whether we will or no, but a process to which we all contribute in the totality of our reflections and our decisions. At bottom, it is the millions upon millions of subjective elements taking place in the mind of each individual which forms the substrata of economic phenomena."[12] We must ascertain how decisions are made and then how the resulting choices feed into the market, interacting with the choices of countless others.

When choosing, the first thing we must reckon with is scarcity: our wants are unlimited, but our capacity to satisfy them is not. We must economize: "Our whole life is made up of decisions which seek to establish a satisfactory balance between our unlimited wants and the limited means at hand to satisfy them. To say that economic goods are limited in quantity is simply to say that the existing stock of such goods are unable to satisfy the total subjective demand for them."[13] By "subjective demand," Röpke merely refers to the principle that, for a (positive) theory of value, goods are desired for their ability to satisfy some want. For the purposes of explaining economic behavior, value does not inhere in goods. Value is a relationship between goods and a mind capable of ascertaining how those goods can be used to achieve some goal. This is the concept of utility, ubiquitously employed in economics. Utility is specific and contextual: "not a general utility based on the degree of the good's vital importance, but the specific, concrete utility of a definite quantity of the good."[14] From this follows the all-important principle of marginal utility: "With increasing satisfaction of a want, the utility (satisfaction or enjoyment) furnished by each successive dose diminishes. Moreover, take away any one of a number of identical units and the loss of utility or satisfaction will be the same as if any other had been taken away. It follows that the minimum utility of the last dose or increment determines the utility of every other unit of the supply and therefore the utility of the whole supply. . . . We call the utility of this last dose *final* or *marginal utility*."[15]

12 Röpke, *Economics*, 7.

13 Röpke, *Economics*, 8.

14 Röpke, *Economics*, 8.

15 Röpke, *Economics*, 9.

Combining the brute fact of scarcity with the formal choice architecture of marginal utility leads to a powerful interpretive framework for understanding consumer behavior: "It is certain that we shall arrange our purchases in such a fashion that the satisfaction procured by the last increment of one commodity will be approximately equal to that afforded by the last increment of any other commodity. This is the abstract explanation of what is, in reality, a very simple process, something we do at every hour of the day without waiting on the proper formula."[16] Röpke asserts this *equimarginal principle* is something we all do, even if we do not realize we are doing it. We do not need to know economics for economics to describe our behavior. Whether aware of it or not, our "whole life is made up of an immense number of similar decisions serving to balance continuously means with wants. Choice, limitation, equalization of marginal utilities—these are the concepts to which we must repeatedly return. They determine how we use our incomes, how we direct our businesses, how we organize production, how we divide up our time between work and leisure, and even between sleep and wakefulness."[17]

COST AND PRODUCTION

Scarcity is a basic feature of reality. It is universal. But how societies cope with scarcity depends on their (contingent) political and economic institutions. Different economic systems have different schemes for producing and distributing goods. Röpke focuses on three possible methods: First, "the ethically negative method of using violence and/or fraud." Second, "the ethically positive one of altruism." Third, the "ethically neutral method by which, in virtue of a contractual reciprocity between the parties to the exchange, an increase of one's well-being is achieved by means of an increase in the well-being in others."[18] This last method, which Röpke refers to as the "business principle," is the primary way we deal with scarcity in market economies.

While the business principle is ethically neutral, it is not ethically vacuous. It relies on a specific set of internalized norms among producers and consumers. Röpke declares, "Only the powerful influences of religion, morality, and law appear able to induce us to adhere scrupulously to the

16 Röpke, *Economics*, 13.

17 Röpke, *Economics*, 13–14.

18 Röpke, *Economics*, 21–22, emphasis removed.

third method."[19] Furthermore, a businessman "who adheres unbendingly to the principle of exact reciprocity in exchange does not, by so doing, remain completely neutral in an ethical sense."[20] Reciprocity in the market requires dedication, integrity, and honesty; these moral reserves, to echo a point from *Humane Economy*, must come from somewhere other than the market. Röpke's concluding remarks on the business principle are worth quoting at length:

> "Business" is a product of civilization and it cannot exist for long in the absence of a specific constellation of conditions, chiefly moral, which support our civilization. The economic ingredient in the constellation is, as we shall see, free competition. But free competition cannot function unless there is a general acceptance of such norms of conduct as willingness to abide by the rules of the game and to respect the rights of others, to maintain professional integrity and professional pride, and to avoid deceit, corruption, and the manipulation of the power of the state for personal selfish ends.[21]

Having presented the business principle, Röpke goes deeper into the choice calculus of producers by discussing the nature of costs. As it turns out, the same economizing logic Röpke traced in his discussion of consumption applies to production as well. Production "changes nothing with respect to the need for practicing economy in the use of means, but that it simply results of the transfer of the problem to a higher level (or levels)."[22] Employing the factors of production in the service of a business plan requires forsaking the use of those inputs for some other plan; cost and choice are inseparable for producers as well as for consumers: "The costs of production, in sum, owe their existence and their amount to the competition of alternative uses for the factors of production. They stand for utilities which escape us at some other point in the national economy."[23] The relative costs of the factors of production are determined by "the intensity of competition among these alternative uses . . . of the aforementioned factors of production."[24] In sum, "the problem of costs is nothing other than the prob-

19 Röpke, *Economics*, 21–22.

20 Röpke, *Economics*, 22.

21 Röpke, *Economics*, 24–25.

22 Röpke, *Economics*, 25.

23 Röpke, *Economics*, 26, note and emphasis removed.

24 Röpke, *Economics*, 27.

lem of deciding whether the productive forces of a country will be better employed in one direction than in another."[25]

Now Röpke discusses production and allocation schemes in various economic systems. Each of these schemes involves a specific mechanism for bringing the supply of a good into equilibrium with the demand for it. The simplest is the system of the queue: first come, first served. However, "This system is so unsatisfactory and so little able to guarantee that the most urgent needs of the community itself will be met that the recourse to it is had only in exceptional cases."[26]

Next comes the rationing system: "Goods are supplied gratis, but equilibrium is obtained by a systematic distribution of the available goods (rationing). It is such a mechanism which would operate in a pure Communist economy."[27] Aside from small and specific cases, such as the allocation of field rations to soldiers, this system also is highly unsatisfactory.

Next is the mixed system, in which "prices are introduced" but do not fully ration resources; some command mechanism is also present.[28] This system almost always relies on legally controlled prices. Experience with such systems in World War II showed their defects: "When prices were prevented from rising to the point where supply and demand exactly balanced, a part of demand necessarily remained unsatisfied."[29] But this frustrated demand does not disappear; it is merely redirected into surreptitious and frequently unsavory directions: "Black markets, under-the-counter deals, illegal currency transactions—a thousand years' experience has shown that these things accompany price control as shadows do the light."[30] Unfortunately, how we wish this system to work does not affect how it actually works. The system's pitfalls remain, whatever the intentions of its advocates: "Keeping the prices of commodities as low as possible for reasons of social justice discourages their production precisely in the degree to which the price-controlled goods are essential."[31]

25 Röpke, *Economics*, 28, emphasis removed.

26 Röpke, *Economics*, 28.

27 Röpke, *Economics*, 29.

28 Röpke, *Economics*, 29.

29 Röpke, *Economics*, 30.

30 Röpke, *Economics*, 31.

31 Röpke, *Economics*, 32.

Then there is the price system, whose "principal characteristic is that equilibrium (choice and limitation) is attained by leaving prices free to adapt themselves to the market situation, so that there is neither an excess of unsatisfied demand nor an excess of unabsorbed supply (equilibrium price)."[32] This system has two principal virtues: Because consumers bear the costs of consumption, it is consumers who drive the production process. Producer supply tracks consumer demand. Second, because price is tied to cost, producers organize the nation's productive resources in a way that results in higher-valued wants being satisfied first. Röpke does not praise the price system unreservedly, however. He explicitly adds the caveat, "Even if the price system functioned ideally, the factors of production would be employed in the 'best possible' manner only in relation to the existing (and unequal) distribution of income. No one will seriously pretend that our present distribution of income is the best possible."[33] Economists "should not make the mistake of equating the explanation of the price system with a glorification of it, for this would be to fall into the error of the classical school which derived from such explanation premature conclusions with respect to economic policy (laissez-faire liberalism)."[34] Nevertheless, based on a positive evaluation of how it works, "we must conclude that the price system, in spite of all its imperfections and in spite of those situations in which it is inapplicable, remains the most natural method of solving the problem of economic equilibrium."[35]

Röpke concludes with the special case of "collective economy," for those cases where demand for the good is expressed jointly, and it is impossible "to distinguish the specific utility accruing to individuals from the satisfaction thereof. Some familiar examples are . . . the armed forces, for a police force, for protection against epidemics, for street lights."[36] Here Röpke outlines public-goods theory, which involves goods that are nonrivalrous (Alice consuming more does not reduce the amount available for Bob) and nonexcludable (Alice and Bob both enjoy the full benefits of the good, even if they do not pay for it). Röpke thinks many so-called collective goods can be adequately provided by the price system: "Bridges and roads, for exam-

32 Röpke, *Economics*, 33.

33 Röpke, *Economics*, 34.

34 Röpke, *Economics*, 34.

35 Röpke, *Economics*, 34.

36 Röpke, *Economics*, 35.

ple, are, as a general rule, paid for on a collective basis out of taxes, although there is no reason why the price system would not work equally well in such cases. For proof, we need only recall the practice, common enough in former times and now revived in some countries, of charging tolls for the use of highways and bridges."[37] Despite the abuse of the concept, genuine collective goods exist, and it "is the business of the state to satisfy these collective demands."[38]

THE DIVISION OF LABOR: PROMISES AND PERILS

Studying alternative systems for allocating resources helps us appreciate the uniqueness of markets. Röpke stresses the "extreme specialization of labor, or what we call the division of labor."[39] In economies with an extensive division of labor, "the modern producer personally consumes only a fraction, if anything, of his specialized output."[40] The benefit of specialization is high productivity: Ordinary workers in a modern market economy have consumptive opportunities that dwarf those of kings from centuries past.

What makes this system work? How is the division of labor coordinated? With workers choosing their specialties according to their self-perceived comparative advantage, something must make the whole economic process coherent. Röpke begins with "the whole series of rights and liberties associated with" the independent production choices of an economy's myriad producers: "private ownership of the means of production, right of inheritance, freedom of contract, freedom to choose one's occupation, and many others."[41] These institutions are the building blocks on which the complex economic edifice rests. Another particularly important institution is money, which enables indirect exchange. Money, "as a medium of exchange and a common denominator of the values of all goods, does away at one stroke with the difficulties of exchange in kind [barter]."[42]

Private property and money are both required for the market mechanism—resource allocation guided by relative prices—to function. "Thanks to the continuous exchange of goods against money and to the social

37 Röpke, *Economics*, 35.

38 Röpke, *Economics*, 35.

39 Röpke, *Economics*, 41.

40 Röpke, *Economics*, 41.

41 Röpke, *Economics*, 45, note omitted.

42 Röpke, *Economics*, 46.

division of labor upon which such exchange is contingent, prices are formed without which there can be no rational economic calculation . . . we shall find that no economy, however rudimentary, has been able to function without calculation in prices and money."[43]

Röpke emphasizes the institutions underlying markets are just as much a political matter as an economic one. The state must "establish a disciplined and stable monetary system so that money will enjoy general confidence and unite the disparate operations of the division of labor in a single payment community."[44] More generally, "the great risks implicit in an extreme dependence of all individuals in society upon each other are tolerable in the long run only where an efficiently administered legal system and unwritten but generally accepted code of minimum moral precepts assure to the participants in the division of labor that they will be able to carry on their activities in an atmosphere of mutual confidence and security."[45] Ultimately "a significant division of labor" is downstream from "the prerequisites of a monetary system, a legal system, and an appropriate moral system," and cannot exist without them.[46] Röpke discusses the institutions that make this possible, including at the international level, where there is no world-state to provide the framework. He writes favorably about internalized norms of fair play among nations, as well as the international gold standard, in the old liberal world order. Absent state command, these were invaluable for achieving a global division of labor.

Röpke goes on to discuss the limitations and dangers of the division of labor. "It is well known," Röpke begins, "that too intensive a division of labor can result in the atrophy of certain of our vital functions."[47] He worries that the "highly specialized man is robbed of the chance to experience the fulness of his own personality; he becomes stunted." As the division of labor proceeds, it "leads increasingly to mechanization, to monotonous uniformity, to social and spiritual centralization, to the assembly-line production of human beings, to depersonalization, to collectivization—in a word, to complete meaninglessness which may one day generate a terrible revolt of

43 Röpke, *Economics*, 47.

44 Röpke, *Economics*, 48.

45 Röpke, *Economics*, 48.

46 Röpke, *Economics*, 49.

47 Röpke, *Economics*, 63. Adam Smith, the great theorist of the division of labor, believed as much, too.

the masses thus victimized."[48] This passage reads like Belloc and Chesterton. However, Röpke immediately follows with a more cautious assessment: "But lest we exaggerate these evils, it is well to remember that we are speaking here only of dangers and tendencies. It is not true that specialized work is always more monotonous than non-specialized work, particularly since the progress of technology (automation) has made it possible to turn over to the machine, in large part, precisely those motions which are most monotonous."[49] Good management, creative plant organization, and instilling in workers "the professional pride of craftsmanship" can go a long way toward softening the division of labor's harsher aspects.[50]

The division of labor may also create hazardous political incentives:

> Thanks to the division of labor, each one of us in our role as producers is desirous of keeping our goods and services rare, and therefore as expensive as possible in relation to other goods. By the same token, in our role of consumer, each of us is desirous of having abundance and cheapness prevail in all categories of goods other than those which we ourselves happen to produce. But since the consumer's interest is spread over innumerable goods, the judgment of each man in economic matters is determined more by his position as producer than by his position as consumer.[51]

Hence, there is a "latent disharmony between consumer and producer" that requires "effective and continuous competition" to redress.[52] The state must ensure robust competition within the market and resist all attempts by special interest groups to capture the machinery of public policy to advance their material ends, contrary to the requirements of the common good.

The division of labor, for Röpke, is a double-edged sword. On the one hand, it greatly increases productivity, contributing to the material well-being of millions. On the other hand, it sometimes makes economies more fragile, since the "greater the refinement of the division of labor, the less the economic system is able to resist internal and external disturbances" that arise from changes in sustainable patterns of specialization

48 Röpke, *Economics*, 63–64.

49 Röpke, *Economics*, 64.

50 Röpke, *Economics*, 64.

51 Röpke, *Economics*, 68.

52 Röpke, *Economics*, 69, emphasis removed.

and trade.[53] But we cannot undo specialization: "The die is cast. For the growth of productivity which accomplished the extensive and intensive development of the division of labor is now claimed as a birthright by the new millions of individuals who owe their very existence to it."[54] As a result, we "cannot go back, we cannot cause a contraction in the division of labor without putting in peril the lives of numberless millions of human beings and thereby the very existence of our social order."[55] Only one possibility remains: curbing the excesses of the division of labor in the service of an economic order that is robust, efficient, and humane.

PRICES MAKE THE WORLD GO 'ROUND

Now we come to the heart of the matter. What coordinates the extensive division of labor in market economies? How do the institutions of property and money combine to bring order to commercial affairs? These are the most important questions for the economic theory of markets, frequently called "price theory," for reasons that will soon become clear.

A market price "at a given moment is determined by supply and demand."[56] Supply and demand function operate as a negative feedback loop: "When there is a disparity between supply and demand, the price rises or falls until, under the counterinfluence of price, supply and demand are brought into equilibrium."[57] Equilibrium is reached when price clears the market, that is, when supply and demand are brought into balance, meaning there is neither a surplus nor shortage of goods. Along with virtually all economists, Röpke regards the free fluctuation of prices on the market in response to changes in supply and demand as essential for a well-ordered economy. When the pricing process is attenuated by law, as during the First and Second World Wars, the result "was that the regulatory function of free formation of prices was arrested, provoking the now familiar chain reaction in which the unsatisfied segments of demand produced first the queue and finally rationing."[58] The takeaway is clear: "The mechanism of price forma-

53 Röpke, *Economics*, 71; cf. Arnold Kling, *Specialization and Trade: A Re-introduction to Economics* (Washington, D.C.: Cato Institute, 2016).

54 Röpke, *Economics*, 71.

55 Röpke, *Economics*, 71.

56 Röpke, *Economics*, 142.

57 Röpke, *Economics*, 143.

58 Röpke, *Economics*, 144.

tion is such a vital cog in the greater mechanism of our economic system that it cannot be tampered with without forcing us to enter upon a path which ends in socialism pure and simple."[59] To be clear, Röpke is not arguing that price controls lead to full socialism. Instead, he contends "that interferences with the price mechanism lead to ever more drastic and extensive interferences culminating in the completely planned economy of socialism."[60] The road leads somewhere we do not wish to go, but we do not have to walk it. However far along we have gone, we can still turn back. Ultimately, "the formation of prices is the regulator of our economic system and that it cannot be tampered with without requiring, in the end, a reconstruction of the entire economic system."[61] In terms of resource allocation, free price formation and administrative-executive fiat are contradictory principles. One must give way to the other.

For producers, prices are an input into profit-and-loss calculations. Producers use these calculations to ascertain whether they are satisfying consumer demand: "If prices were insufficient to cover costs, producers would incur losses which would no longer permit them to maintain production to the previous extent; supply, in such cases, diminishes, causing prices to rise until they have once again attained the level of costs."[62] Producers with a cost advantage enjoy "extra profit which results from the gap between the market price and their low costs of production (producers' rent)."[63] This is the market telling producers they are adding value to society's scarce resources, from the perspective of consumers. Profit thus plays both an incentive-aligning and information-generating role: It not only entices producers to seek it but also serves as a signal of desirable production choices. In a market economy, however, so long as it is competitive, profits are hard to find and even harder to keep. Competition among firms "gnaws away night and day at producers' rents to the exceeding displeasure of the producers who strive by every available means to curb competition, including the (unfortunately) easy matter of getting the state to lend them a sympathetic ear."[64]

59 Röpke, *Economics*, 144.

60 Röpke, *Economics*, 145.

61 Röpke, *Economics*, 146.

62 Röpke, *Economics*, 150.

63 Röpke, *Economics*, 150. In economics, "rent" means the difference between what a factor of production earns and the minimum required to keep that factor employed. Competition typically dissipates rents.

64 Röpke, *Economics*, 151.

Thus, "there is a powerful force which . . . pushes prices down to the level of costs, namely, the increased supply which results from the competition among the producers to sell at the higher price."[65] However, Röpke also notes that this force is not irresistible: "The more ineffective this force becomes, the closer we approach to *monopoly*."[66] Monopoly, according to Röpke, is a wrench in the gears of the market process. Its distinguishing feature "is that it (or they) can freely determine the amount of supply; and where supply is sufficiently curtailed, prices can be held above the level of costs."[67] Economists refer to the ability of a firm to charge prices in excess of cost *market power*. The presence of market power is what makes markets uncompetitive.

Upon closer examination, it appears that all markets, at least at some times, contain firms with market power. Does this mean capitalism inevitably results in monopolies? By no means. Röpke informs us "the fact that free competition does not really exist in the chemically pure state, and that many prices contain a certain monopolistic element, must not lead us to conclude that our economic system rests, at bottom, no longer on competition but on monopoly. Such a conclusion would be quite wrong."[68] While sometimes monopoly is the result of market forces, as in the case of natural monopoly, monopoly is oftentimes a creature of the state:[69] "Indeed, it is astonishing how, in every case, competition sooner or later triumphs over monopoly, if only it is given the chance. To say that 'competitive capitalism' is necessarily 'monopoly capitalism' is simply untrue. The truth is, there is hardly a monopoly worth the name at whose birth, in one way or another, the state has not acted as midwife."[70] The churning of real-world markets renders market power incredibly difficult to maintain, so long as other firms are free to enter an industry and compete with the would-be monopolist. However, the state frequently creates barriers to entry, which ensures monopoly rents. "There would probably be few monopolies in the world

65 Röpke, *Economics*, 153.

66 Röpke, *Economics*, 153, emphasis in original.

67 Röpke, *Economics*, 153.

68 Röpke, *Economics*, 157.

69 A natural monopoly exists when the fixed costs of production are so large that average costs continue to fall as production increases. As a result, a single firm can more efficiently service the whole market than several smaller firms. A classic example is utilities, such as power and water companies.

70 Röpke, *Economics*, 159.

today," Röpke continues, "if the state, for numerous reasons, had not intervened with all the weight of its authority, its juridical prestige, and its more or less monopoly-favoring economic policy . . . against the natural tendency towards competition."[71] Economic profits are $20 bills on the sidewalk. Firms will not pass them by unless something prevents them from reaching down and taking them. Unfortunately, that "something" is frequently misguided public policy.

Whatever its sources, monopoly is a valid cause for concern. Monopoly power is morally suspect, because it severs the link between effort and reward typical in markets. Monopoly power also distorts the pricing process, weakening the coordinative function of markets. As Röpke puts it, "consensus may be said to exist on the point that monopoly is basically undesirable because it involves the exercise of a degree of power in the economic and social life of the community which, even where the power is not consciously abused, appears incompatible with the ideals of freedom and justice and in addition creates the danger of disturbances of economic equilibrium and a lessening of productivity."[72] Monopoly is just as much a political as an economic problem: "Monopolists dispose of a degree of power over their markets and over the economy which a well-ordered, purposeful economic system based on a just relationship between performance and reward cannot tolerate."[73] The best protection against monopoly, both preventative and curative, is competition. Röpke reminds us that so long as there exists "a situation of continuous striving for the favor of the consumers, the concept of monopoly is correspondingly narrowed and limited to those cases in which this striving with its temporary positions of power is eliminated and replaced by a situation of permanently protected positions of power in the market."[74]

For Röpke, maintaining competitive markets is a just and necessary function of the state. He firmly insists that "the outmoded old-liberal view that the desirable situation of free competition is self-perpetuating so long as the state refrains from economic interventions of any kind has been shown to be a fateful error."[75] Thus, "the governments of the free nations of the world cannot avoid the obligation of making the restraint and reduction

71 Röpke, *Economics*, 159, emphasis removed.

72 Röpke, *Economics*, 161.

73 Röpke, *Economics*, 162.

74 Röpke, *Economics*, 163.

75 Röpke, *Economics*, 164.

of monopoly the object of a specific antimonopoly policy."[76] As an example, Röpke discusses anticartel policy. Cartels form when "a number of producers have joined together for the express purpose of eliminating competition among themselves. . . . In this case, freedom of contract is uniquely and illegitimately misused to restrict contractual freedom and hence economic freedom in general."[77] The state acts rightly when it refuses to grant legitimacy to agreements formed in restraint of trade. Lawful authority should uphold the principle that contract and consent cannot be used to undermine the freedom that they presuppose.

Röpke concludes by discussing international trade and international price formation. Immediately, he denigrates autarky as a feasible or desirable goal: "For a highly developed country, self-sufficiency remains a dream and . . . not even a pleasant dream—all the less pleasant the larger, the richer, and the more powerful a country is and wishes to remain."[78] But economists have not had much success, whether today or in Röpke's time, in convincing the public. A perennial problem "is the astonishing inability of most people to comprehend any matters relating to international trade—a purblindness such as they manifest towards no other aspect of economic life."[79] The key to understanding the economics of international trade is, strictly speaking, there *is no* economics of international trade. External trade, "exactly as internal trade . . . rests on the division of labor and on the exchange of goods resulting from this division of labor."[80] That participants in international trade "belong to different payment communities does not any more change its underlying character than the fact that they possess different passports and different residences."[81] The most persistent popular belief about international trade, that imports are somehow "bad" and exports "good," is fallacious. Imports are the goal; exports are the means of achieving that goal: "The less must a country export to pay for its imports, i.e., the higher are export prices in comparison to import prices, the greater is that country's gain from the international division of labor."[82]

76 Röpke, *Economics*, 165.

77 Röpke, *Economics*, 165.

78 Röpke, *Economics*, 168.

79 Röpke, *Economics*, 170.

80 Röpke, *Economics*, 170.

81 Röpke, *Economics*, 170.

82 Röpke, *Economics*, 171.

Does it follow that states always and everywhere must embrace unilateral free trade? "Should all countries then proceed to pension off their customs officials?" Not so fast, Röpke says. "Although worse things could befall mankind, our preceding reflections have had no such radical objective in view. Foreign trade, in fact, encompasses a number of problems which are extremely difficult to solve and which may justify some degree of state regulation. But these problems are quite other than what they are usually thought to be."[83] One such problem arises from the division of labor itself. Röpke worries that in some cases, "for the increase in productivity which we owe to the division of labor we must pay a price in the form of possible economic, social, and cultural disadvantages. The further the division of labor is pushed, the more proper it becomes to ask the question whether this price is not too high."[84] Röpke soundly rejects the fashionable belief among intellectuals that economics is nothing more than ideological cover for laissez-faire, at home and abroad: "Economics does not teach that every intervention of the state is an evil; it teaches only that it is necessary to weigh carefully the facts in the given case, and thereby proves itself to be the indispensable instrument of a far-sighted and genuinely national policy."[85]

THE DISTRIBUTION OF INCOME, OR HOW NOT TO ACHIEVE SOCIAL JUSTICE

Now Röpke directly engages the area of economics where economists most frequently receive pushback: the distribution of income: "The contrast between rich and poor, between the hovel and the palace, between the haves and the have-nots—this is the great question which for thousands of years has agitated the minds and hearts of men."[86] How does the economic way of thinking help us understand distribution?

For Röpke, the place to start is the same as with other questions: supply and demand. Price theory analyzes the distribution of income in terms of factor payments: "The principal categories which we establish for a theory of functional income distribution are wages, rent, interest and profits,

83 Röpke, *Economics*, 172.

84 Röpke, *Economics*, 172.

85 Röpke, *Economics*, 172.

86 Röpke, *Economics*, 184.

corresponding to the factors of production labor, land, capital, and entrepreneurship."[87] Thus, factor payments depend on the prices for the factors of production: "Hence, the explanation of the functional distribution of income involves the application of the general principles of price theory."[88] The laws of supply and demand govern the distribution of income, via the familiar pricing process: "That wages in one country stand at such and such a level, that rents, interest, and profits are of such and such an amount—this is hardly to be ascribed to chance. Rather, these situations are the result of specific economic data. Every attempt to alter such data by force will produce disorder in the economic system which, in turn, will engender still greater counter-forces."[89] Röpke believes much of the indignation regarding unjust distributions of income (and by implication the distribution of wealth), while well-intentioned, is ultimately misguided: "But instead of trying to acquire the facile reputation of a 'social-minded' man by vague demands for a 'just wage,' by railing against 'interest slavery' and 'profiteering,' by emotional outpourings over 'gluttonous landlords,' and real estate 'speculators,' and instead of shoving aside as 'liberalistic' the objections of those who understand something of these matters, one would serve his country better by applying himself to an unprejudiced study of the complex interrelationships of the economy."[90]

As an example, Röpke considers attempts to implement a just wage policy, increasing the returns to labor by forcibly reducing the returns to capital. While possible, Röpke notes that price theory predicts a host of unintended consequences, which many would regard as worse than the initial problem: "Among the principal disturbances of such a wage policy would be a critical reduction of the economy's supply of capital and a slowing down of investment activity with its consequent effects on employment opportunities."[91]

Yet prudential policy, aimed at small adjustments, may be both possible and benign in its secondary consequences. There are, in fact, "circumstances under which wage increases may be absorbed without damage to the

87 Röpke, *Economics*, 185. In economics, "land" refers to all natural resources, i.e., the unproduced factors of production other than labor.

88 Röpke, *Economics*, 185.

89 Röpke, *Economics*, 186.

90 Röpke, *Economics*, 186.

91 Röpke, *Economics*, 187.

national economy. We ought also never forget that there is always a degree of 'play' between the moving parts of our economic mechanism, making it possible to apply corrective measures without provoking countermovements."[92] Röpke counsels using price theory to discover when such situations are possible. Prudent policy regarding the distribution of wealth involves more than just economic knowledge, but economic knowledge is necessary for the policy's prudence.

Price formation for capital and land (interest and rent) follows the same process as for labor (wages), but Röpke emphasizes the final factor payment, entrepreneurs' profit, functions differently. Profit accruing to entrepreneurs "is distinguished from the previously considered types of income in that it represents merely a differential gain and not the market-determined price accruing from the sale of a 'service' as it is usually understood."[93] Entrepreneurship, in Röpke's framework, is functionally associated with bearing risk and uncertainty. The entrepreneur creatively rearranges the factors of production to satisfy hitherto-unmet consumer demand, earning profit only when such endeavors are successful. Entrepreneurship, which drives the market process, is thus a special kind of arbitrage.[94] Profit performs an important role in a market economy: "We must not forget that the *possibility* of the entrepreneur making profits as a reward for efficient service is no less necessary to the functioning of our economic system than the possibility of his suffering losses as punishment for being inefficient."[95] Furthermore, the market system contains within itself a means of dissipating profit: "It is to be noted that competition furnishes us with a very efficacious means of eliminating entrepreneur's profits in cases where they are only a nonfunctional source of enrichment and of reserving such profits for those who perform useful services."[96] It is one of the great virtues of market systems, as opposed to economic systems that rely on command and control, that entrepreneurs themselves take on the risks associated with innovations in production and reap rewards (or punishments) proportionate to the benefits (or harms) they create for consumers.

92 Röpke, *Economics*, 188.

93 Röpke, *Economics*, 190.

94 Cf. Frank Knight, *Risk, Uncertainty, and Profit* (New York, 1921); Ludwig von Mises, *Human Action: A Treatise on Economics* (Auburn, Ala.: Ludwig von Mises Institute, [1949] 2008, 286–92); Israel Kirzner, *Competition and Entrepreneurship* (Chicago: University of Chicago Press, 1973).

95 Ropke, *Economics*, 191.

96 Röpke, *Economics*, 191.

Röpke wants to introduce nuance into distributional debates. Price theory provides the required tools, but his goal is not to eliminate such debates. Sometimes, the distribution of income *should* change. Employing an analogy to democratic politics, Röpke notes that "the 'capitalistic' economic process can be compared to a continuing plebiscite in which each piece of currency represents a ballot."[97] The objection, of course, is that "the ballots are in truth very unequally distributed."[98] It is true that market systems give consumers what they want, "But since what counts are only those wants which are backed up by money, we have not the right to regard the outcome of the consumers' plebiscite as a complete and satisfying one."[99] Röpke regards it as "thoroughly possible, and even necessary, to bring about changes in distribution so long as such action does not result in the destruction of the high achievements of our economic system in the realm of production."[100]

Röpke is particularly concerned with intelligent policies for increasing wages. These policies require careful price-theoretic reasoning. The goal is to increase the productivity of labor, because "everything which increases the productivity of labor, increases wages."[101] This suggests a strong link between wage levels and broad-based economic growth: "It turns out that the functional distribution of income is the more prejudicial to wage income the poorer—i.e., the more unproductive, the more 'proletarian,' and capital-poor—a country is."[102] A policy for "raising the national level of wages" should be primarily focused on growth, rather than redistribution:[103] "Such a policy will consist of the following: increasing capital wealth (by means, if need be, of capital imports and a rational organization of credit), allocation of the factors of production to their most productive uses, intelligent participation in the international division of labor, exploitation of technological and organizational progress, restrained increases in population, a reasonable economic policy in all fields, peace, security, confidence and order—such are the bases of national prosperity."[104] As a result of rising

97 Röpke, *Economics*, 197.

98 Röpke, *Economics*, 197, emphasis removed.

99 Röpke, *Economics*, 197.

100 Röpke, *Economics*, 198.

101 Röpke, *Economics*, 198.

102 Röpke, *Economics*, 199.

103 Röpke, *Economics*, 199.

104 Röpke, *Economics*, 199–200. Many economists would question Röpke's analysis of population growth, as well as find it morally suspect.

wages, the working classes will find it easier to save and thus access capital markets for wealth preservation and growth. This will enable workers to acquire property and other income-generating assets: "The consequence will be a 'de-proletarianization' which ought to be close to the hearts of those who need no propertyless masses for the fulfilment of their political ambitions."[105] Finally, Röpke reminds us that "antimonopoly policy is . . . always good income policy," hearkening back to his insights on industrial organization from the previous chapter.[106]

Röpke ends his discussion of the distribution of income with a careful endorsement of "extra-economic correction of the distribution of income."[107] The state can use its taxing and spending powers to alter the distribution of income at the margin. Many introductory economics textbooks speak favorably of this "first bake the pie, then slice it up" approach, which relies on the analytic separability of production and distribution. Of course, production and distribution are not really different processes; one cannot alter the latter without changing incentives for the former. Nevertheless, this approach is more efficient than popular proposals that have no regard for price theory. Röpke notes "a considerable portion of public finances is devoted to such rectification, supplemented by the efforts of private welfare groups. Obviously, there are certain limits which may not be overstepped if paralyzing effects on the process of production are to be avoided. It is, of course, clear that the state can go much further in employing such corrective measures the smaller are its expenditures for other purposes."[108]

THINKING IN SYSTEMS: VISTAS OF POLITICAL ECONOMY

Röpke concludes his text with a discussion of comparative economic systems. The essential task for the student of comparative systems is to comprehend "the real nature of the economic structure" and ascertain "ways by which it can be freed of its imperfections and degeneracies, and its power to function increased instead of diminished. Only when this step has been taken are we at liberty to choose between our economic system and a more or less collectivistic one, for only then will we have full awareness of all we would give

105 Röpke, *Economics*, 200.

106 Röpke, *Economics*, 200.

107 Röpke, *Economics*, 200, emphasis removed.

108 Röpke, *Economics*, 200.

up, and all that we would receive, in choosing the one over the other."[109] We cannot make an intelligent choice over economic systems if we do not know how they work. Röpke laments that "the same people who untiringly attack the rationalist, mechanical, and artificial character of our economic system with its industrialization, its proletarianization, and urbanization, seek salvation in planned economy and centralized organization, i.e., in an economic structure which will be still more rationalist, still more mechanical, and still more artificial than the existing one."[110] Price theory must be brought to bear on these questions if we want actual results to match intended results.

Market economies are governed by the pricing process. Wages, interest, rent, and profit are especially important in guiding production plans and bringing them into harmony with consumption plans. Collectivist economic systems, in which there is neither private property nor money, must find some alternative mechanism for coordinating economic activity. But is there any such mechanism in collectivist systems that can function as effectively as the price system? Röpke believes the "probability of its being able to do so is remote."[111]

Yet Röpke sees many troubling aspects in the economic systems of the Western nations. Especially pernicious are the ways public policy weakens the profit-and-loss system by privatizing profits while socializing losses.[112] Without the "assurance that deficient performance will find its inexorable punishment in the losses and finally in the bankruptcy proceedings" that punish firms for squandering resources, the economic system becomes skewed.[113] Markets work only when profits *and losses* govern production, but because the latter are politically unpopular, corporations frequently pervert the political process by forcing taxpayers to underwrite their poor decisions. To prevent this, governments must be restless promoters of competition and resist the influence of corporate power over politics. This requires "a strong state—impartial and powerful—standing above the melee of economic interests, quite the contrary to the widely held opinion that 'capitalism' can thrive only where there is a weak government."[114]

109 Röpke, *Economics*, 232.

110 Röpke, *Economics*, 233.

111 Röpke, *Economics*, 234.

112 Röpke, *Economics*, 236.

113 Röpke, *Economics*, 236.

114 Röpke, *Economics*, 236.

The collective or planned economy, as an alternative to capitalism, certainly has no problem with "a strong state," but should we prefer it? Röpke answers decisively in the negative. First, Röpke explains the difference between market and collective economies: "Whereas the market economy is founded on the complicated interplay of the decisions freely made by all groups entering the market, the collectivist planned economy aims at replacing this spontaneous process by commands from above, and at turning over to a group of government officials the responsibility for decisions respecting the use to be made of the economy's productive resources."[115] Röpke even prefers the appellation "economy of the bureaucrats or command economy" for these systems.[116] The difference in incentives between market and command economies cannot be overstated: "The uncorrupted market economy is the functioning planned economy of those whose business it is; the collectivist economy is the non-functioning planned economy of those whose business it is not."[117] Equally problematic is the lack of an information-generating mechanism akin to the market price system. How can rational economic calculation proceed without prices to act as signals of relative resource scarcities? The "enormous, insurmountable difficulties which such a system would have to struggle with" stem from pervasive incentive and information problems.

The above problems explain why command economies, most notably the communist powers of Röpke's time, were unable to match the Western nations in terms of production, especially of consumers' goods, which most directly affect living standards. There is, however, one virtue—if we may call it that—of communism: it is extraordinarily effective at marshaling resources in the service of specific political goals. Röpke warns, "We must avoid overestimating Communism as an economic system serving mankind. But it is equally incumbent on us not to underestimate it as a system of the most extreme concentration of economic power in the service of politics—in the service of a politics whose ultimate goal to destroy and enslave the free world can be ignored only by the hopelessly blind among us."[118]

Given the grave defects of command economies, we seem to have little choice but to shore up the deficiencies of market economies: "We find that

115 Röpke, *Economics*, 240.

116 Röpke, *Economics*, 240.

117 Röpke, *Economics*, 240.

118 Röpke, *Economics*, 246.

this system is composed of a complicated network of contractual relationships which, however, join together to produce an ordered whole—thanks to the mechanism of the market. It is a combination of freedom and order, representing what is probably the highest level to which these two ideals can simultaneously attain."[119] While at a foundational level the system is sound, Röpke also believes it "needs a complete 'overhaul,' if we wish to arrest the process of degeneration before it ends in an intolerable degree of unproductivity and—what is worse—corruption and injustice. . . . The job cannot be done by merely adopting a negative approach and abstaining from action, i.e., by a return to simple 'laissez-faire' methods."[120] Röpke identifies four problems that require attention: "1) the problem of order; 2) the social problem; 3) the political problem of the distribution of power; and 4) the moral-vital problem, as we may describe it in brief."[121]

Röpke believes a well-ordered economy "results in the right things being produced in the right proportions at the right time in the right place and with the right methods of production."[122] The choice of an economic system is necessarily discrete:

> It cannot be too strongly emphasized that as far as the task of ordering economic life is concerned, we have only this exclusive choice between a market economy and a command economy. We cannot take refuge in some third alternative, in cooperatives, trade unions, in undertakings patterned after the much-cited but much-misunderstood Tennessee Valley Authority, corporatism, industry council plans, vocational orders, or any other form of 'ersatz' socialism. We must choose between price and state command, between the market or the authorities, between economic freedom or bureaucracy. . . . He who chooses the market economy must, however, also choose: free formation of prices, competition, risk of loss and chance for gain, individual responsibility, free enterprise, private property.[123]

Röpke clearly believes in markets, but "the market economy, of itself, will furnish only a solution only to the problem of order."[124] To solve the

119 Röpke, *Economics*, 250.

120 Röpke, *Economics*, 251.

121 Röpke, *Economics*, 253.

122 Röpke, *Economics*, 253.

123 Röpke, *Economics*, 254.

124 Röpke, *Economics*, 255.

other three problems, we need to be imaginative. Röpke looks for a solution founded on markets (in turn founded on private property and money) while also going beyond "the old worn-out road of 'capitalism.'"[125] Solving the second problem, the social problem, means finding ways "to provide security and protection to the weak by a certain correction of the distribution obtaining under the market economy."[126] Solving the third problem, the political problem, requires (in part) creating conditions "in which no economic and consequently no political power groups can long prosper."[127]

Last is the moral-vital problem. Röpke insists that, in addition to the aforementioned issues, "it is at least as important to ask what the effects of such a system are on the moral and spiritual condition of man—on those intangibles which constitute the real meaning of his existence and the foundation of his happiness. How does this system affect man in his capacity as a person called to revere the Most High, as neighbor and citizen impelled toward community with his fellowmen, as member of a family and as a worker?"[128] Röpke believes it is not only legitimate but necessary for economists to consider the relationship of economic systems to the good life. Unfortunately, "in our time this kind of life is most gravely menaced by mechanization, depersonalization, proletarianization, breaking up of the family, the growth of a mass society, and other items on the debit side of our urban-mechanical civilization."[129] These are grave problems, but they are not the market's problems to solve. The market "makes no pretense of providing solutions to the problems described above. It merely supplies the framework within which we must seek the answers to these last and most fundamental questions."[130] Röpke does not offer any specific policy proposals, but he looks favorably on "the favoring of the ownership of small and medium-sized properties, independent farming, the decentralization of industrial areas, the restoration of dignity and meaning of work, the reanimation of professional pride and professional ethics, [and] the promotion of communal solidarity."[131] Knowing Röpke, it is probable he has in

125 Röpke, *Economics*, 254.

126 Röpke, *Economics*, 255.

127 Röpke, *Economics*, 255.

128 Röpke, *Economics*, 255–56.

129 Röpke, *Economics*, 256.

130 Röpke, *Economics*, 256.

131 Röpke, *Economics*, 257.

mind many approaches that rely on neither market nor state but rather the all-important institutions of civil society.

Röpke's final paragraph is worth quoting in full. It concisely summarizes his views on economics, social philosophy, and the relationship between them:

> But whatever specific form the economic policy of the future will take, it will stand no chance of success if it is not shaped by experts thoroughly acquainted with the structure and mechanism of our economic system and if it is not executed with the understanding, the support and the cooperation of the broad masses of the population who know what is at stake. To bring this to pass is the great practical task of the science of human behavior which we call economics. Economics can successfully accomplish this task only if it is not itself sucked into the vortex of the contemporary crisis of civilization, and if it does not finally fall victim to the uncomprehending attacks to which it is exposed at present. It is reported that Napoleon once took umbrage at the obstinate behavior of one of his officials and reprimanded him for it. The honest servant replied: Sire, one can support oneself only on that which offers resistance. The same may be said of the science of economics.[132]

REFLECTING ON RÖPKE

What can we learn from Röpke's perspective on social philosophy and economics? Two conclusions are indisputable. First, in social philosophy, he shares many of Chesterton's and Belloc's views regarding the nature of the good society. It is fair to characterize him as a fellow traveler of the distributists, although not a distributist himself. Second, in economics, his approach to analyzing markets and politics is decidedly price-theoretic. This is not to say Röpke's *The Economics of the Free Society* is a standard introductory text. It clearly is not. His book contains many digressions and elaborations that touch on moral and political philosophy, which was uncommon even in Röpke's time. But he is clear where the price theory ends and where these other fields begin. Furthermore, rigorous price theory is the means for achieving a humane social order. While Röpke says upholding the common good requires more than price theory, he also regards price theory as indispensable to the common good.

132 Röpke, *Economics*, 257–58.

For those who want to understand, renew, and maintain a humane social order, Röpke offers a model of how to do economics and social philosophy. Previous chapters focused on the *what*: areas within contemporary economics and political economy to which distributists (and fellow travelers) can contribute. The two chapters on Röpke focus on the *how*: they show a powerful mind at work, one that takes both price theory and Catholic social teaching seriously. Röpke's career is an "existence proof": his scholarship demonstrates it is possible to be a good citizen by doing good economics. His Christian humanism bolsters his social science, and vice versa.

Distributists have nothing to fear from price theory, Röpke teaches us, but they have a good deal to fear from ignoring it.

Chapter 10

Conclusion: Frontiers of Distributism

DISTRIBUTISM, CATHOLIC SOCIAL TEACHING, AND THE ROLE OF ECONOMICS

It is traditional in a concluding chapter to recapitulate, but multiple summaries of my arguments appeared in previous chapters. Furthermore, the chapters on Röpke serve as a capstone for harmonizing the rigor of economic science with the humanism of political-economic art. We know the ground we covered. The road ahead is what matters.

This book is one way of understanding common-good capitalism, which in turn is one way of understanding the economic and political implications of Catholic social teaching. The conversation around these issues must continue. An important question is whether this book's perspective is sufficiently radical. The introduction set a high tone, but was the analysis of distributism according to economic science and political-economic art sufficiently innovative? Readers skeptical of economics may think I have merely smuggled in the discipline's orthodoxies through the back door. In ascribing scientific status to economics, with independent standards for judging distributism's proposals, have I assumed that which was to be proved?

I hope it is unsurprising that I accept the facts but deny the charge. If there is no science of economics—if price theory, the study of purposive human action in commerce, is a mirage—then the distinction between science and art vanishes. For those who think the distinction was a self-serving cover to protect a degraded moral philosophy, cutting out the diseased tissue may be just what the doctor ordered. For Mary Hirschfeld, whose recent book *Aquinas and the Market* is required reading for anyone interested in this controversy, it *is* just what the doctor ordered.[1] Economics is sick, but the Angelic Doctor has the cure.

1 Mary Hirschfeld, *Aquinas and the Market: Toward a Humane Economy* (Cambridge, Mass.: Harvard University Press, 2018).

Building on Aquinas, Hirschfeld calls for a reconstitution of economics. The goal is bolstering the teleological aspect of human decision making with an explicit commitment to axiological realism. The following quote captures what Hirschfeld thinks, on Thomistic grounds, is wrong with economics:

> On Aquinas's own account, we would expect much human behavior to be well described by the sort of constrained optimization economists describe—because humans very often if not mostly act out of the lower form of reason that we share with animals and that does look like a series of optimization problems. The problem with the economic approach is that it identifies such decision making as rational. And with that comes a normative implication that permeates economic science, and indeed the public square. To wit, insofar as we think of the pursuit of happiness as an exercise in constrained maximization, it seems natural to focus one's attention on loosening those restraints. Economic growth and technological progress are embedded as ultimate goods, because they allow us to reach more desirable bundles of goods. Collectively, we seem to think that what it would take to have better paintings is more paint.[2]

I quoted Hirschfeld approvingly in earlier chapters. I admire her book, which should occupy a place of honor in future discussions of economics and the common good. However, I view her project as a contribution to political economy rather than a reconstruction of economics. Hirschfeld is surely correct that economists often abuse the positive-normative distinction, which results in them venturing into (bad) ethical discourse without realizing it. Economists identify as scientists, yet much of what they do is not scientific. This does not mean, however, that we need to theologize economics. As Catherine Pakaluk, an economist at the Catholic University of America, writes in her review of *Aquinas and the Market*, Hirschfeld's "theological consideration of economic questions is fine as far as it goes.... But if we want to know how to actually move toward a humane economy, as Hirschfeld promises us, it will not do. We need better economics—not theology."[3]

"What is needed for a *humane* economics," Pakaluk continues, "is not theological economics, but a rediscovery of the call to understand the world through an economic science replete with wonder and admiration—some-

2 Hirschfeld, *Aquinas*, 117.

3 Catherine Ruth Pakaluk, "Whither Humane Economics? In Defense of Wonder and Admiration in Natural Science," *Public Discourse*, March 27, 2019, https://www.thepublicdiscourse.com/2019/03/50583/.

thing missing in contemporary economics as much as in the drab theology of many ethicists. Properly delineated, this is not a rejection of ethics in economics, but a recovery of the normative dimension of reality."[4] I wholeheartedly embrace Pakaluk's delineation. We do economics because the patterns of commerce fascinate our intellects, and because we want to bring markets and government into the right relation. Focusing on the second consideration, we could even say the science of economics is *for* the art of political economy. Good economics informs our broader conversations about the good society. Having these conversations and acting upon them is part of what it means to be human. Furthermore, the good society is *real*. It impels us to reflect and reform for higher reasons than intersubjective agreement. This is why the science-art distinction is necessary. Without apportioning to science and art their proper tasks, how can we fulfill our dual mandate to know for the sake of knowing, and know for the sake of improving?

What I call the science of economics, the rhetorician and cultural critic Richard Weaver would call the "objective approach" to social studies. The following thoughts of his are useful for thinking about the proper spheres of science and art: "It may be true that the objective kind of approach—the *Wertfrei* type of analysis—is useful in discovering and analyzing some lines of cause and effect which are parts of cultural structures. The suspension of the moral judgment is a posture regularly assumed by science in some phases of its investigation. But this is a matter of phase or stage. . . . The impulse to say, 'This is bad,' 'This is good,' and 'This is best' is finally an irresistible and a rightful one."[5]

We lose nothing by distinguishing the "lines of cause and effect" from the "irresistible and rightful" call of oughtness. The humane economist does not sunder reality by giving science and art their dues. The fruitfulness of future discussions depends on carefully selecting the right starting point.

A DISTRIBUTIST POLITICAL PARTY?

For distributists, political reform is a necessary component of the larger project to build a society that supports human flourishing. Politics is not among the most important things in life, yet politics matters greatly nonetheless, because it secures the conditions for pursuing higher goods. C. S.

4 Pakaluk, "Whither Humane Economics?" emphasis added.

5 Richard Weaver, *Visions of Order: The Cultural Crisis of Our Time* (Wilmington, Del.: ISI Books, [1964] 1995), 76–77.

Lewis, the famed author and Christian apologist, expressed this sentiment beautifully. As far as I am aware, he was not a distributist, but his stance toward government is one that distributists can heartily endorse:

> It is easy to think the State has a lot of different objects—military, political, economic and what not. But in a way things are much simpler than that. The State exists simply to promote and to protect the ordinary happiness of human beings in this life. A husband and wife chatting over a fire, a couple of friends having a game of darts in a pub, a man reading a book in his own room or digging in his own garden—that is what the State is there for. And unless they are helping to increase and prolong and protect such moments, all the laws, parliaments, armies, courts, police, economics, etc., are simply a waste of time.[6]

The key is how the state can "increase and prolong and protect" man's pursuit of the higher goods. Here politics is crucial. Freedom and solidarity reinforce each other. Understood in light of Catholic social teaching, collective action must create the framework for securing both liberty and the common good.

There is no one-size-fits-all formula for government. Political actors in different times and places will adopt different goals and strategies, depending on the specific social barriers to human dignity. One commonality, at least in democracies, is the necessity of building a public support base and organizing a winning coalition. Political parties are immensely helpful for these tasks. In the United States, a political party explicitly formulated on distributist principles has recently enjoyed some prominence. The American Solidarity Party (ASP), formed in 2011, "identifies itself as a Christian Democratic political party" influenced by "Catholic social teaching starting with the papal encyclical Rerum Novarum by Pope Leo XIII, and by the Neo-Calvinist worldview as heralded by the Dutch Prime Minister, Abraham Kuyper."[7] While third parties face enormous hurdles in U.S. politics, the association of some high-profile communitarian conservatives, such as Notre Dame's Patrick Deneen, with the party has brought ASP to the public's attention.

6 C. S. Lewis, *Mere Christianity*, in *The Complete C. S. Lewis Signature Classics* (New York: HarperCollins, 2002), 159.

7 "Christian Democracy," American Solidarity Party, accessed March 29, 2022, https://www.solidarity-party.org/blog/2017/10/26/christian-democracy.

ASP's platform is not shy about its debt to distributism. The "Economics" section of the platform proclaims, "The American Solidarity Party believes that political economy (economics) is a branch of political ethics, and therefore rejects models of economic behavior that undermine human dignity with greed and naked self-interest. We advocate for an economic system which focuses on creating a society of wide-spread ownership *(sometimes referred to as 'distributism')* rather than having the effect of degrading the human person as a cog in the machine."[8] Surveying this portion of the party platform can give us an idea of what distributist reforms would look like. Three areas in harmony with distributism deserve special attention. The first is the primacy of the family. The second is the importance of economic freedom through economic independence. The third is curtailing private power's outsized presence in the public square.[9]

The first tenet in ASP's platform asserts, "Our goal is to create conditions which allow single-income families to support themselves with dignity." Commerce is not an end in itself. Production and consumption are *for* something: the flourishing of the family, which remains the basic unit of society. "Industrial policy and economic incentives need to be re-ordered to place human dignity first and to recognize that the family is the basic unit of economic production. We are committed to policies that emphasize local production, family-owned businesses, and cooperative ownership structures," the platform continues.

All well and good, but what reforms follow from this? In terms of freedom through independence, ASP supports "mechanisms that allow workers to share in the ownership and management of their production, such as trade guilds, cooperatives, and employee stock ownership programs." Particularly intriguing is their plank for benefits reform: "Unemployment benefits need to include the option of allowing beneficiaries to take their benefits in the form of start-up capital to start or purchase businesses or create cooperative enterprises that help them to escape poverty on their own terms." There are also several less innovative policies, such as bolstering organized labor. "We support policies that encourage the formation and strengthening of labor unions," the platform asserts. "Efforts by private entities to use public power to prevent union activities or to

8 "Principles and Platform," American Solidarity Party, accessed March 29, 2022, https://www.solidarity-party.org/platform, emphasis added.

9 All subsequent quotes taken from the party-platform website.

retaliate against workers who organize for their rights ought to be resisted at every level."

ASP's platform is most concrete when it comes to the third category, the proposals for curbing the power of capital. At the most basic level, the platform suggests rethinking the universality of the corporate form itself: "We will work to restore the requirement that corporations must serve a public good in order to be granted the benefit of limited liability. We support the prohibition of corporate bylaws and the repeal of state legislation requiring shareholder profit to trump considerations such as employee wellbeing and environmental protection." The party also calls "for the repeal of corporate welfare policies, for shifting the tax system to target unearned income and reckless financiers, and for changing regulations to benefit small and locally-owned businesses rather than multinational corporations" and "taxes on land, capital gains, and financial transactions."

Also prominent, and notable given the policy discussions in Washington occurring as of this writing, is an appeal for antitrust enforcement: "The bloated, 'too big to fail,' multinational economic concerns which dominate the economic landscape need to be brought to heel and concerted antitrust action must be taken to break up the oligarchies that use their private power to corruptly influence public governance." In addition, ASP's platform echoes the traditional distributist concern with carefully monitoring natural monopolies. These productive enterprises "and the common inheritance of the natural world need to be closely managed and protected by the public and not surrendered for a pittance to private greed. . . . Policies that deliver citizens their fair share of our common wealth and inheritance of natural resources are to be encouraged in the form of a citizen's dividend and baby bonds."[10]

While the economic portion of the platform is the most relevant to distributism, policy planks from other sections also reflect these themes. In terms of health care, ASP supports "universal healthcare by diverse means, including single-payer initiatives, direct subsidization of provider networks, subsidized education for medical professionals willing to work in rural areas, support for cost-sharing programs and mutual aid societies, home care grants, simplified regulation, and the easing of restrictions on the importation of prescription drugs." In the "Family" section, we see calls for

10 Elsewhere, the platform goes into more detail: "Public resources must remain public, including transportation services, toll roads and bridges, community policing and parking enforcement, prisons, and energy and water utilities."

"workplace accommodations for parents, including paid parental leave, flexible scheduling, and affordable child care." These proposals, and many others not mentioned here, have the explicit goal of strengthening productive households.

Furthermore, these planks are not blanket endorsements of a larger federal government. "We believe that local governments are most competent to solve community-based problems," ASP asserts in a particularly distributist vein. And "in keeping with the principle of subsidiarity, there should be more autonomy of local governments from state governments wherever possible. There should be legal accountability of higher levels of government to lower levels." All forms of power, public and private, must stay within their proper bounds.

These remarks are not an endorsement of the American Solidarity Party. My goal is describing with charity a political program explicitly rooted in distributism and Catholic social thought, not defending it. That said, I do find ASP's Christian conception of the common good refreshing and would like to see it have a larger role in public discourse. Current political trends favor more communitarian forms of conservatism, which means debates about the common good will become increasingly frequent. Distributism deserves a seat at the table.[11] As a distributist political party, therefore, ASP merits our attention, despite (or perhaps because of) not maintaining a trendy policy shop or commissioning mountains of white papers.

NEITHER COMMERCE NOR POLITICS: DISTRIBUTISM AND CIVIL SOCIETY

My analysis of distributism focused on the boundaries between markets and politics. This is a natural consequence of using price theory to investigate distributism. Economic science focuses on the mechanisms of markets, which includes how various public policies affect these mechanisms. Political-economic art, although broader, also concerns the proper role of markets and states, but human flourishing requires more than simply drawing the line in the "right" place. Civil society, which comprises citizens' associational life in areas that do not fit neatly into politics or economics, matters at least as much.

11 Cf. Alexander William Salter, "'Common Good' Conservatism's Catholic Roots," *Wall Street Journal*, May 20, 2021.

As we saw, Belloc and Chesterton dedicated their efforts to showing why conventional ways of thinking about economics and politics were wrong. The problem was not merely the conclusions; it was the very orientation to social problems, which emphasized expediency over human dignity. By no means, however, did Belloc and Chesterton ignore civil society. Belloc's work is the more traditionally economic and political, but even he affirmed voluntary associations among merchants, artisans, and farmers. Such organizations exercise a communal-governance function yet are not commercial nor governmental. As for Chesterton, he clearly believes the most important things in life are beyond trading and governing. His devotion to the family and emphasis on formative education are the clearest examples. Most important of all is their loyalty to the church. Belloc's and Chesterton's vision of a rightly ordered society comes from Catholic social teaching. While they did not write programs for social renewal solely for Catholics, we cannot make sense of their project apart from the centrality of organized religion to personal and communal flourishing.

Civil society is a source of governance. We must not conflate *governance* with *government*. Rules and order come from many places. We must also not think about civil society in purely instrumental terms. It is too easy to reduce associational life to a supporting buttress for business and government, but civil society matters for its own sake. Human flourishing is both personal and communal. We participate in fraternal, educational, and religious institutions not because they make us better business executives or public servants but because they make us better *persons*.

This book paid comparatively little attention to civil society. That shortcoming was probably unavoidable, given the nature of my project: revisiting distributism in light of contemporary economics. The civil-society gap must be filled as the conversation unfolds. Fortunately, we have resources on which to draw.

The obvious place to start is the work of Elinor Ostrom, the 2009 Nobel laureate in economics, who won the prize "for her analysis of economic governance, especially the commons."[12] Her pioneering studies on common-pool-resource governance were part of a broader research agenda on the space between economics and politics. Indeed, the title of her Nobel address, "Beyond Markets and States," demonstrates her commitment to

12 Nobel Foundation, "Elinor Ostrom," https://www.nobelprize.org/prizes/economic-sciences/2009/ostrom/facts/.

exploring the rich varieties of communal life that cannot be reduced to the commerce-government dichotomy.[13] Ostrom describes her research as a challenge to this dichotomy:

> The market was seen as the optimal institution for the production and exchange of private goods. For nonprivate goods, on the other hand, one needed "the" government to impose rules and taxes to force self-interested individuals to contribute necessary resources and refrain from self-seeking activities. Without a hierarchical government to induce compliance, self-seeking citizens and officials would fail to generate efficient levels of public goods, such as peace and security, at multiple scales. A single governmental unit, for example, was strongly recommended to reduce the "chaotic" structure of metropolitan governance, increase efficiency, limit conflict among governmental units, and best serve a homogeneous view of the public. This dichotomous view of the world explained patterns of interaction and outcomes related to markets for the production and exchange of strictly private goods, but it has not adequately accounted for internal dynamics within private firms. Nor does it adequately deal with the wide diversity of institutional arrangements that humans craft to govern, provide, and manage public goods and common-pool resources.[14]

Ostrom conducted numerous empirical studies, including fieldwork and experiments. She also developed novel theories to better understand the rich diversity of governance institutions. Markets and states are not absent, yet neither are they the main source of orderly conduct. Human beings simply do not live by siloing themselves in this way. As Ostrom concludes, we need to move beyond top-down policy frameworks designed "to force (or nudge) entirely self-interested individuals to achieve better outcomes." As an alternative, "a core goal of public policy should be to facilitate the development of institutions that bring out the best in humans. We need to ask how diverse polycentric institutions help or hinder the innovativeness, learning, adapting, trustworthiness, levels of cooperation of participant, and the achievement of more effective, equitable, and sustainable outcomes at multiple scales."[15] The word "polycentricity" appears in these references several times. This refers to the scale, scope, and structure of

13 Elinor Ostrom, "Beyond Markets and States: Polycentric Governance of Complex Economic Systems," *American Economic Review* 100, no. 3 (2010): 641–72.

14 Ostrom, "Beyond Markets," 642, citations omitted.

15 Ostrom, "Beyond Markets," 665, citations omitted.

governance institutions. Vincent Ostrom (Elinor's husband and frequent collaborator), Charles Tiebout, and Robert Warren give the classic definition:

> "Polycentric" connotes many centers of decision making that are formally independent of each other. Whether they actually function independently, or instead constitute an interdependent system of relations, is an empirical question in particular cases. To the extent that they take each other into account in competitive relationships, enter into various contractual and cooperative undertakings or have recourse to central mechanisms to resolve conflicts, the various political jurisdictions in a metropolitan area may function in a coherent manner with consistent and predictable patterns of interacting behavior. To the extent that this is so, they may be said to function as a "system."[16]

Ostrom, Tiebout, and Warren developed this concept in their studies of metropolitan government, but its applicability is much broader. It readily lends itself to the study of civil society. Especially for those who value the principle of subsidiarity from Catholic social teaching, as well as related ideas such as "sphere sovereignty" from Reformed political thought, polycentricity is an invaluable conceptual tool for understanding how institutional design affects human flourishing. As Paul Dragos Aligica, Peter Boettke, and Vlad Tarko write, "On its logical development toward the notion of polycentrism, the functional analysis of governance structures and their countervailing powers discussed above moves smoothly to the domain of the voluntary association and civil society . . . the focus needs to shift outside the confines of the state and its administrative-bureaucratic apparatus. More precisely, the focus needs to be in the domain of community, civil society, nongovernment and nonprofit forms of organization."[17]

I believe there is much fertile ground at the intersection of distributism and Ostrom's kind of institutional analysis. In fact, this is probably more

16 Vincent Ostrom, Charles Tiebout, and Robert Warren, "The Organization of Government in Metropolitan Areas: A Theoretical Inquiry," *American Political Science Review* 55, no. 4 (1961): 831–42.

17 Paul Dragos Aligica, Peter Boettke, and Vlad Tarko, *Public Governance and the Classical-Liberal Perspective: Political Economy Foundations* (New York: Oxford University Press, 2019), 65–66. As the title suggests, these authors are writing from a classically liberal point of view, which may make some advocates of Catholic social teaching uneasy. They have nothing to fear. The lessons Aligica, Boettke, and Tarko draw concerning civil society generalize across normative frameworks. Arguably, they become even more relevant from the perspective of communitarian personalism.

important than conventional discussions of markets, governments, and public policy. Regardless of the organizational forms of commerce and politics, the "quest for community" endures.[18] Without authentic community, characterized by a rich associational life, individuals reify the market, the state, or both. This crowds out the good life, as Belloc and Chesterton saw. It was also a central theme of Röpke's reconstructive project, which unambiguously drew on distributist insights. Human flourishing requires ordered liberty, and ordered liberty requires both a shelter from, and a check on, the market and the state. A society animated by distributist principles necessarily contains a robust network of associational organizations, which reflect and embody polycentricity.

In his classic work on the promises and perils of democracy, Vincent Ostrom writes, "The challenge that I believe everyone confronts everywhere is how to achieve greater self-governing capabilities in confronting problems and realizing opportunities in light of the diverse contexts in which people live."[19] Democratic citizens should reject "a system of command and control emanating from a single center of Supreme Authority within each State" and embrace "principles of self-responsibility in self-governing communities of relationships."[20] Belloc, Chesterton, and Röpke would wholly endorse these sentiments. The rights and duties of civic life, emphasized by Catholic social teaching and reflected in distributist principles, require "self-governing communities of relationships." Studying and engaging in civil society are central, not peripheral, to distributism.

FROM PROPERTY, LIBERTY

Belloc's and Chesterton's most important claim is that property creates liberty. This simple statement is rich with meaning. Understanding it requires a more expansive definition of property, and a more humanistic conception of liberty, than usually found in today's academic journals and public-intellectual periodicals. We are used to thinking liberty precedes property: Political institutions that protect human freedom create the necessary conditions for accumulating wealth. Distributists do not reject this line of causality but do insist something important is missing. It is true that political freedom promotes economic

18 Robert Nisbet, *The Quest for Community* (Wilmington, Del.: ISI Books, [1953] 2010).

19 Vincent Ostrom, *The Meaning of Democracy and the Vulnerability of Democracies: A Response to Toqueville's Challenge* (Ann Arbor: University of Michigan Press, 1997), 4.

20 Ostrom, *The Meaning of Democracy and the Vulnerability of Democracies*, 4.

freedom, but, distributists warn, political freedom itself arises only under a specific set of conditions. Those conditions are best described as the *propertied society*, constituted by widespread ownership. Property is both a means of sustenance and a refuge from the vicissitudes of the market.

More than twenty years ago, Richard Pipes, a leading historian of the Russian Revolution, published *Property and Freedom*.[21] Although he was probably unfamiliar with the distributists, or the works of distributist-influenced economists such as Röpke, his message in this important book echoes many distributist themes. The divergent political-economic trajectories of Western Europe and Russia captivated Pipes. Why did these other countries progress to liberty, democracy, and wealth, while Russia so many times in her history succumbed to tyranny and poverty? Pipes "became aware that one of the fundamental differences . . . lay in the weak development of property [in Russia]."[22] In exploring the nature of property and the institutions that govern its distribution, Pipes discovered a tradition that illuminated the social and moral dimensions of ownership. He explains, "Property is of two kinds, productive, i.e., the kind that can create more property (e.g., land, capital), and personal, which serves exclusively for use (e.g., housing, clothing, weapons, jewelry). Such is the customary usage. But more broadly, in the terminology of Western theory since the late Middle Ages, 'property' has come to encompass everything that properly belongs to a person (*suum* in Latin), including his life and liberty. *It is this broad definition of property or 'propriety,' . . . that provides the philosophical link between ownership and freedom*."[23]

Pipes discusses the "metamorphosis, revolutionary in its implications" of property, as an idea, in seventeenth-century England. Included in this new conception was the "'birthright' of Englishmen," which meant "such prerogatives as every human being, no matter how humble, enjoyed simply by virtue of being human. . . . Together with the notion of *suum*, it formed the basis of the modern concept of human rights, a concept unknown anywhere outside the range of Western civilization."[24] It is worth noting Pipes draws heavily on the protoliberal and liberal traditions in English political thought, which eventually reached fruition in America. Indeed, Pipes's own

21 Richard Pipes, *Property and Freedom* (New York: Alfred Knopf, 1999).

22 Pipes, *Property and Freedom*, xi.

23 Pipes, *Property and Freedom*, xv, emphasis added.

24 Pipes, *Property and Freedom*, 31.

perspective on the relationship between property and freedom is decidedly liberal. But this is not as important as the *framework* Pipes (re)discovers and embraces. He is surely correct that a morally expansive conception of property includes what persons are due in virtue of their humanity. This is why his study matters for distributism.

Well then: what are human persons due? Informed by Catholic social teaching, distributists would answer this question very differently than, say, Thomas Hobbes or John Locke. This is because Catholic social teaching affirms a specific anthropology, or understanding, of what it means to be human. We do not need to enter the ongoing (and seemingly interminable) debate about the anthropology of classical liberalism. It is enough to recognize Catholic social teaching has one, making the moral content of property much thicker.

Pipes's "philosophical link between ownership and freedom" helps us understand distributism's claim that property gives birth to liberty. Property "in both the narrow and broad senses of the word, provides the key to the emergence of political and legal institutions that guarantee liberty."[25] Belloc could have written this sentence. And while Belloc emphasizes different "political and legal institutions"—and fundamentally different ideas of property and liberty—his mode of reasoning fits with Pipes's. Furthermore, Pipes's belief that "there is an intimate connection between public guarantees of ownership and individual liberty: that while property in some form is possible without liberty, the contrary is inconceivable" is the very claim advanced by Chesterton in his broadsides against big business and big government.[26] Again, Chesterton argues for different ends, but we learn something important from the formal similarity of means.

There is an inescapable connection between ownership and freedom, the distributists argue, but unlike Pipes, the distributists affirm both negative and positive liberty: "Freedom does *not* include the so-called 'right' to public security and support (as implied in the slogan phrases 'freedom from want' and 'the right to housing') which infringe on the rights of others since it is they who have to pay for them," Pipes declares. "Such 'rights' are at best a moral claim, and at worst, if enforced by public authority, an unearned privilege."[27] This is the clearest indication that Pipes's conceptions

25 Pipes, *Property and Freedom*, xii.

26 Pipes, *Property and Freedom*, xii.

27 Pipes, *Property and Freedom*, xvi.

of liberty and property are classically liberal, if not outright libertarian. His implication that freedom is somehow divorceable from "a moral claim" would astound the distributists. They would also insist "the so-called 'right' to public security and support" is very real. Because freedom requires the means to live a dignified life, therefore, distributists support institutional safeguards for economic independence. The individual *and communal* requirements of liberty, understood within Catholic social teaching as a constituent element of human dignity and the common good, both deserve public defense.

Yet distributism is not a Catholic version of welfarism. Transfer payments and social programs, no matter how generous, are neither necessary nor sufficient to create a propertied society. Refreshingly, distributism has the power to change the terms of the conversation about distributive justice. While the Right and Left quibble at the margins, Belloc and Chesterton, as well as those influenced by them such as Röpke, push for genuine economic independence as the foundation for authentic community. The question is, how do we get there?

To answer this question, distributism needs nothing less than its own version of Pipes's project. Pipes does impressive historical and prescriptive work in his book, although I did not discuss the latter. Distributism likewise can benefit from both historical and prescriptive research projects. Historically, we need to discover what societies most closely embodied distributist principles, even (perhaps especially) if there was no conscious attempt to do so. Prescriptively, we need to ascertain what institutional reforms can achieve distributist goals. This latter task is more speculative and difficult. For example, we know a distributist society requires economic independence. Mere cash transfers cannot achieve this, so what can? If economic independence means protection against the vagaries of the market, this is a tall order. Extending the division of labor increases the interconnectedness of markets. Commercial intercourse spreads across the globe at an incredible pace and shows no signs of slowing down. What does economic independence mean, given these background conditions? If you can put a price on something, by definition the market touches it. You can always put a price on property based on its expected productivity, so how do we strike a balance between insulation and responsiveness? I do not have an answer, or even the beginnings of an answer, but I am confident a dedicated cohort of distributist-influenced scholars, public intellectuals, and elected officials can flesh out a version of distributism for the twenty-first century and beyond.

The division of labor can proceed in this way. For scholars, especially those with economics training, the imperative is working through the logic of means and ends to develop a new political-economic paradigm, which will be successful only if we keep to the strictures of economic science. As Röpke taught us, rigorous economics is a necessary component of humane political economy. We need hardnosed, price-theoretic analyses of various government and market reforms informed by distributist thought. We also need broader comparative-institutional studies to understand which "rules of the game" best promote distributist outcomes.

For policy experts and public intellectuals, the goal is ascertaining what reforms we need and what the likely consequences will be. Whereas economists, theologians, and others within the academy (or similar institutions) should treat distributism as an object of inquiry, intellectuals focused on policy and persuasion should treat distributism as an overarching context for specific proposals. Public policy is an obvious case, but not the only one. Ideas for businesses and civil society organizations matter at just as much, and oftentimes more. F. A. Hayek called intellectuals "secondhand dealers in ideas." He was not being condescending. They perform the essential task of making "their peculiar opinions of moment influence decisions" with the ultimate goal of "shaping public opinion."[28] The distributist vision of a propertied society requires convincing the public of its merits.

For elected officials and other public servants, there are three related tasks: building electoral coalitions, responsibly administering solutions, and working toward a constitutional order in which distributist reforms are sustainable. Scholars conceive and intellectuals persuade, but politicians must rally. Much of the distributist critique of inhumane political and economic institutions will be popular, and perhaps even populist. Elected officials must simultaneously cultivate public dissatisfaction with existing affairs while calming the predictable excesses of popular passions. Without great care, various outcome-egalitarian movements on both the Left and Right could absorb, and hence nullify, the distributist project. Alternatively, distributists' enthusiasm for economic justice sometimes presents temptations for political extremism.[29] Both atrophy and hypertrophy are unhealthy

28 F. A. Hayek, "The Intellectuals and Socialism," *University of Chicago Law Review* 16, no. 3 (1949), https://www.jstor.org/stable/1597903?origin=crossref&seq=1.

29 While today this is more common on the extreme left, historically, it was more common on the extreme right. For example, Belloc's and Chesterton's "passion for justice, democracy and liberty, and compassion for the poor" occasionally made them impatient with British politics.

conditions for the body politic. This is not to say distributist political leaders must compromise on core beliefs. Distributism *is* redistributive, in the true sense of the word. This means something very different than in mainstream public discussions about, for example, transfer payments and the social safety net. It is not about possessing, but *owning*.

Micah's prophecy is the rallying cry of distributism: "But they shall sit every man under his vine and under his fig tree, and none shall make them afraid; for the mouth of the LORD of hosts has spoken."[30] To achieve liberty, protect property. This is the essence of the distributist message. Catholic social teaching provides the motivation. Belloc and Chesterton made the first attempt, flawed in some ways and profound in others. Röpke, a fellow traveler, carried their work forward by harmonizing the science of economics with the art of political economy. Here the endeavor stands. There are many trends in the academy, the organs of public deliberation, and politics that bode ill for distributism, yet as Chesterton reminds us, "Ahab has not his kingdom so long as Naboth has his vineyard." Economics and politics at a human scale is always difficult, but never impossible. To achieve it, the conversation between distributism and price theory must continue.

Sometimes they wrote favorably about right-wing corporatism. Cf. Kevin L. Morris, "Fascism and British Catholic Writers 1924–1939: Part I," *New Blackfriars* 80, no. 935 (1999): 32–45, at 35. Contemporary distributists overwhelmingly affirm the importance of constitutional order for day-to-day politics, as well as the common good. The American Solidarity Party does so explicitly in the civil rights portion of its platform.

30 Mi 4:4 RSV.

Bibliography

Acemoglu, Daron, and James A. Robinson. *Why Nations Fail: The Origins of Power, Prosperity, and Poverty*. New York: Crown Publishing Group, 2012.

———. *The Narrow Corridor: States, Societies, and the Fate of Liberty*. New York: Penguin Press, 2019.

"Against the Dead Consensus." *First Things*, March 3, 2019. https://www.firstthings.com/web-exclusives/2019/03/against-the-dead-consensus.

Aligica, Paul Dragos, Peter Boettke, and Vlad Tarko. *Public Governance and the Classical-Liberal Perspective: Political Economy Foundations*. New York: Oxford University Press, 2019. https://doi.org/10.1093/oso/9780190267032.001.0001.

American Solidarity Party. "Christian Democracy." Accessed March 29, 2022. https://www.solidarity-party.org/blog/2017/10/26/christian-democracy.

———. "Principles and Platform." Accessed March 29, 2022. https://www.solidarity-party.org/platform.

Azariadis, Costas, and John Stachurski. "Poverty Traps." In *Handbook of Economic Growth*, edited by Philippe Aghion and Steven Durlauf, 295–384. Amsterdam: Elsevier, 2006.

Bauer, Peter Tamas. *From Subsistence to Exchange and Other Essays*. Princeton, N.J.: Princeton University Press, 2000. https://doi.org/10.1515/9781400824649.

Baumol, William J. "Contestable Markets: An Uprising in the Theory of Industry Structure." *American Economic Review* 72, no. 1 (1982): 1–15.

Baumol, William, John Panzar, and Robert Willig. *Contestable Markets and the Theory of Industry Structure*. New York: Harcourt Brace, 1988.

Becker, Gary. "A Theory of the Allocation of Time." *Economic Journal (London)* 75, no. 299 (1965): 493–517.

———. *A Treatise on the Family*. Cambridge, Mass.: Harvard University Press, 1981.

Belloc, Hilaire. *An Essay on the Restoration of Property*. Norfolk, Va.: IHS Press, 2009. First published in 1936.

———. *The Servile State*. Indianapolis, Ind.: Liberty Fund, 1977.

Berlin, Isaiah. "Two Concepts of Liberty." In Isaiah Berlin, *Four Essays on Liberty*. Oxford: Oxford University Press, 1969.

Besley, Timothy, and Torsten Persson. "The Origins of State Capacity: Property Rights, Taxation, and Politics." *American Economic Review* 99, no. 4 (2009): 1218–44.

———. "State Capacity, Conflict, and Development." *Econometrica* 78, no. 1 (January 2010): 1–34.

———. *Pillars of Prosperity: The Political Economics of Development Clusters*. Princeton, N.J.: Princeton University Press, 2011.

Boettke, Peter J. *Living Economics: Yesterday, Today, and Tomorrow*. Oakland, Calif.: Independent Institute, 2012.

Boettke, Peter J., and Rosolino A. Candela. "Price Theory as a Prophylactic against Popular Fallacies." *Journal of Institutional Economics* 13, no. 3 (2017): 725–52.

———. "Productive Specialization, Peaceful Cooperation and the Problem of the Predatory State: Lessons from Comparative Historical Political Economy." *Public Choice* 182, no. 3–4 (2020): 331–52.

Boettke, Peter J., Stefanie Haeffele-Balch, and Virgil Henry Storr, eds. *Mainline Economics: Six Nobel Lectures in the Tradition of Adam Smith*. Arlington, Va.: Mercatus Center, 2016.

Bonefeld, Werner. "Freedom and the Strong State: On German Ordoliberalism." *New Political Economy* 17, no. 5 (2012): 633–56.

Broadberry, Stephen, et al. *British Economic Growth, 1270–1870*. Cambridge: Cambridge University Press, 2015.

Browning, Martin, Pierre-Andre Chiappori, and Yoram Weiss. *Economics of the Family*. New York: Cambridge University Press, 2014.

Buchanan, James M. "The Thomas Jefferson Center for Studies in Political Economy." *University of Virginia Newsletter* 35, no. 2 (1958).

———. *The Limits of Liberty: Between Anarchy and Leviathan*. Chicago: University of Chicago Press, 1975.

———. "The Constitution of Economic Policy." *American Economic Review* 77, no. 3 (1987): 243–50.

———. *Economics: Between Predictive Science and Moral Philosophy*. College Station: Texas A&M Press, 1987.

Buchanan, James M., and Roger Congleton. *Politics by Principle, Not Interest: Towards Nondiscriminatory Democracy*. Cambridge: Cambridge University Press, 1998. https://doi.org/10.1017/CBO9780511664816.

Buchanan, James M., and Gordon Tullock. *The Calculus of Consent: Logical Foundations of Constitutional Democracy*. Ann Arbor: University of Michigan Press, 1962.

Callahan, Eugene, and Alexander William Salter. "Dead Ends and Living Currents: Distributism as a Progressive Research Program." *Christian Libertarian Review* 1 (2018): 118–39.

Campbell, William F. "Introduction to the Transaction Edition." In Wilhelm Röpke, *The Social Crisis of Our Time*. Rutgers: N.J.: Transaction Publishers, 1992. First published in 1942.

Catholic Church. *Catechism of the Catholic Church*.

Center for Systemic Peace. 2021. "The Polity Project: About Polity." Accessed March 29, 2022. https://www.systemicpeace.org/polityproject.html.

Chesterton, G. K. *Orthodoxy*. New York: John Lane, 1908.

———. *What's Wrong with the World*. New York: Dover Publications, 2007. First published in 1910.

———. *The Outline of Sanity*. Norfolk, Va.: IHS Press, 2001. First published in 1926.

Clark, John Bates. *The Distribution of Wealth: A Theory of Wages, Interests, and Profits*. London, New York: Macmillan, 1899.

Coase, Ronald. "The Nature of the Firm." *Economica* 4, no. 16 (1937): 386–405.

Commun, Patricia, and Stefan Kolev, eds. *Wilhelm Röpke (1899–1966): A Liberal Political Economist and Conservative Social Philosopher*. Cham, Switzerland: Springer International, 2018. https://doi.org/10.1007/978-3-319-68357-7.

DeLorme, Charles D., W. Scott Frame, and David R. Kamerschen. "Empirical Evidence on a Special-Interest-Group Perspective to Antitrust." *Public Choice* 92, no. 3–4 (1997): 317–35.

Deneen, Patrick. *Why Liberalism Failed*. New Haven, Conn.: Yale University Press, 2018.

DiLorenzo, Thomas J. "The Origins of Antitrust: An Interest-Group Perspective." *International Review of Law and Economics* 5, no. 1 (1985): 73–90.

Easterly, William. "Reliving the 1950s: The Big Push, Poverty Traps, and Takeoffs in Economic Development." *Journal of Economic Growth* 11, no. 4 (2006): 289–318. https://doi.org/10.1007/s10887-006-9006-7.

———. *The White Man's Burden: Why the West's Efforts to Aid the Rest Have Done So Much Ill and So Little Good*. New York: Penguin Press, 2006.

Epstein, S. "Craft Guilds, Apprenticeship, and Technological Change in Preindustrial Europe." *Journal of Economic History* 58, no. 3 (1998): 684–713.

Epstein, S., and Maarten Praak. *Guilds, Innovation, and the European Economy, 1400–1800*. Cambridge: Cambridge University Press, 2008.

Folsom, B. W. *The Myth of the Robber Barons: A New Look at the Rise of Big Business in America*. Herndon, Va.: Young America's Foundation, 1991.

Fraser Institute. "Approach." Accessed March 29, 2022. https://www.fraserinstitute.org/economic-freedom/approach.

Gaus, Gerald. *Political Concepts and Political Theories*. Boulder, Colo.: Westview Press, 2000.

Geloso, Vincent J. "Collusion and Combines in Canada, 1880–1890." *Scandinavian Economic History Review* 68, no. 1 (2020): 66–84.

Geloso, Vincent J., and Peter Lindert. "Relative Costs of Living, for Richer and Poorer, 1688–1914." *Cliometrica* 14, no. 3 (2020): 417–42.

Geloso, Vincent J., and Alexander W. Salter. "State Capacity and Economic Development: Causal Mechanism or Correlative Filter?" *Journal of Economic Behavior & Organization* 170 (2020): 372–85.

Gibbons, Robert. *Game Theory for Applied Economists*. Princeton, N.J.: Princeton University Press, 1992.

Green, T. H. "Liberal Legislation and Freedom of Contract." Various reprintings.

Gregg, Samuel. *Wilhelm Röpke's Political Economy*. Cheltenham: Edward Elgar, 2010. https://doi.org/10.4337/9781849803328.

Guzmán, Ricardo Andrés, and Michael C. Munger. "Euvoluntariness and Just Market Exchange: Moral Dilemmas from Locke's *Venditio*." *Public Choice* 158, no. 1/2 (2014): 39–49. https://doi.org/10.1007/s11127-013-0090-x.

———. "A Theory of Just Market Exchange." *Journal of Value Inquiry* 54, no. 1 (2020): 1–28.

Gwartney, James, Robert Lawson, and Walter Block. *Economic Freedom of the World: 1975–1995*. Vancouver: Fraser Institute, 2016. https://www.fraserinstitute.org/sites/default/files/EconomicFreedomoftheWorld1975-1995.pdf.

Gwartney, James, Robert Lawson, Joshua Hall, and Ryan Murphy. *Economic Freedom of the World: 2021 Annual Report*. Vancouver: Fraser Institute. https://www.fraserinstitute.org/sites/default/files/economic-freedom-of-the-world-2021.pdf.

Hall, Joshua C., and Robert A. Lawson. "Economic Freedom of the World: An Accounting of the Literature." *Contemporary Economic Policy* 32, no. 1 (January 2014): 1–19.

Hayek, F. A. *The Road to Serfdom*. Edited by Bruce Caldwell. Chicago: University of Chicago Press, 2007. First published in 1944. https://doi.org/10.7208/chicago/9780226320533.001.0001.

———. "The Intellectuals and Socialism." *University of Chicago Law Review* 16, no. 3 (1949). https://www.jstor.org/stable/1597903?origin=crossref&seq=1.

———. *The Constitution of Liberty*. Chicago: University of Chicago Press, 1960.

Hickson, Charles, and Earl Thompson. "A New Theory of Guilds and European Economic Development." *Explorations in Economic History* 28, no. 2 (1991): 127–67.

Hirschfeld, Mary L. *Aquinas and the Market: Toward a Humane Economy*. Cambridge, Mass.: Harvard University Press, 2018. https://doi.org/10.4159/9780674988620.

Hoffman, Philip, David S. Jacks, Patricia A. Levin, and Peter H. Lindert. "Real Inequality in Europe since 1500." *Journal of Economic History* 62, no. 2 (2002): 322–55.

Holcombe, Randall G. *Political Capitalism: How Economic and Political Power Is Made and Maintained*. Cambridge: Cambridge University Press, 2018. https://doi.org/10.1017/9781108637251.

Huberman, Michael, and Chris Minns. "The Times They Are Not Changin': Days and Hours of Work in Old and New Worlds, 1870–2000." *Explorations in Economic History* 44, no. 4 (2007): 538–67.

Hugger, Daniel J. *The Humane Economist: A Wilhelm Röpke Reader*. Grand Rapids, Mich.: Acton Institute, 2019.

Johnson, Noel D., and Mark Koyama. "States and Economic Growth: Capacity and Constraints." *Explorations in Economic History* 64 (April 2017): 1–20.

Keynes, John Neville. *The Scope and Method of Political Economy*. London: Macmillan, 1904.

Kirk, Russell. Foreword. In Wilhelm Röpke, *The Social Crisis of Our Time*. Rutgers, N.J.: Transaction Publishers, 1992. First published in 1942.

Kirzner, Israel. *Competition and Entrepreneurship*. Chicago: University of Chicago Press, 1973.

Kling, Arnold. *Specialization and Trade: A Re-introduction to Economics*. Washington, D.C.: Cato Institute, 2016.

Knight, Frank. *Risk, Uncertainty, and Profit*. New York: Houghton Mifflin Co., 1921.

Lawson, Robert A. "The Consequences and Causes of Economic Freedom." *Journal of Private Enterprise* 32, no. 3 (2019): 1–10.

Lawson, Robert A., and J. R. Clark. "Examining the Hayek–Friedman Hypothesis on Economic and Political Freedom." *Journal of Economic Behavior & Organization* 74, no. 3 (June 2010): 230–39.

Lawson, Robert A., Ryan H. Murphy, and Benjamin Powell. "The Determinants of Economic Freedom: A Survey." *Contemporary Economic Policy* 38, no. 4 (2020): 622–42.

Leeson, Peter T. "Economics Is Not Statistics (and Vice Versa)." *Journal of Institutional Economics* 16, no. 4 (2020): 423–25.

Leo XIII. *Rerum Novarum*. 1891. http://w2.vatican.va/content/leo-xiii/en/encyclicals/documents/hf_l-xiii_enc_15051891_rerum-novarum.html.

Lewis, C. S. "Mere Christianity." In *The Complete C. S. Lewis Signature Classics*. New York: HarperCollins, 2002.

Lindert, Peter, and Jeffrey Williamson. "English Workers' Living Standards during the Industrial Revolution: A New Look." *Economic History Review* 36, no. 1 (1983): 1–25.

Mankiw, N. Gregory. *Principles of Microeconomics*, 9th ed. Cengage Learning. https://www.cengage.com/c/principles-of-economics-9e-mankiw/9780357038314PF/.

McCloskey, Deirdre. *How to Be Human, though an Economist*. Ann Arbor: University of Michigan Press, 2000. https://doi.org/10.3998/mpub.11551.

———. *Bourgeois Virtues: Ethics for an Age of Commerce*. Chicago: University of Chicago Press, 2006. https://doi.org/10.7208/chicago/9780226556673.001.0001.

McGee, John S. "Predatory Price Cutting: The Standard Oil (N.J.) Case." *Journal of Law & Economics* 1 (1958): 137–69.

Médaille, John. "An Introduction to Distributism." *Distributist Review*, January 11, 2021. https://distributistreview.com/archive/an-introduction-to-distributism.

Mises, Ludwig von. *Human Action: A Treatise on Economics*. Auburn, Ala.: Ludwig von Mises Institute, 2008. First published in 1949.

Mitchell, Matthew D., and Peter J. Boettke. *Applied Mainline Economics: Bridging the Gap between Theory and Policy*. Arlington, Va.: Mercatus Center, 2017.

Mokyr, Joel. *The Enlightened Economy: Britain and the Industrial Revolution*. London: Penguin, 2011.

Morris, Kevin L. "Fascism and British Catholic Writers 1924–1939: Part I." *New Blackfriars* 80, no. 935 (1999): 32–45.

Munger, Michael C. "Euvoluntary or Not, Exchange Is Just." *Social Philosophy & Policy* 28, no. 2 (July 2011): 192–211.

Nash, George. *The Conservative Intellectual Movement in America since 1945*. Wilmington, Del.: ISI Books, 2006. First published in 1976.

Newman, John Henry. *The Idea of a University*. San Francisco: Ignatius Press, 2010.

Nisbet, Robert. *The Quest for Community*. Wilmington, Del.: ISI Books, 2010. First published in 1953.

Nobel Foundation. "Elinor Ostrom." https://www.nobelprize.org/prizes/economic-sciences/2009/ostrom/facts/.

Norcross, Eileen, and Paul Dragos Aligica. "Catholic Social Thought and New Institutional Economics: An Assessment of Their Affinities and Areas of Potential Convergence." *American Journal of Economics and Sociology* 79, no. 4 (2020): 1241.

North, Douglass C. *Institutions, Institutional Change, and Economic Performance*. Cambridge: Cambridge University Press, 1990.

———. *Understanding the Process of Economic Change*. Cambridge: Cambridge University Press, 1999.

North, Douglass C., John Joseph Wallis, and Barry R. Weingast. *Violence and Social Orders: A Conceptual Framework for Interpreting Recorded Human History*. Cambridge: Cambridge University Press, 2009. https://doi.org/10.1017/CBO9780511575839.

Ogilvie, Sheilagh. *The European Guilds: An Economic Analysis*. Princeton, N.J.: Princeton University Press, 2019.

Ostrom, Elinor. "Beyond Markets and States: Polycentric Governance of Complex Economic Systems." *American Economic Review* 100, no. 3 (2010): 641–72.

Ostrom, Vincent. *The Meaning of Democracy and the Vulnerability of Democracies: A Response to Tocqueville's Challenge*. Ann Arbor: University of Michigan Press, 1997. https://doi.org/10.3998/mpub.15021.

Ostrom, Vincent, Charles Tiebout, and Robert Warren. "The Organization of Government in Metropolitan Areas: A Theoretical Inquiry." *American Political Science Review* 55, no. 4 (1961): 831–42.

Pakaluk, Catherine Ruth. "Whither Humane Economics? In Defense of Wonder and Admiration in Natural Science." *Public Discourse*, March 27, 2019. https://www.thepublicdiscourse.com/2019/03/50583/.

Pearce, Joseph. "What Is Distributism?" *Imaginative Conservative*, June 12, 2014. https://theimaginativeconservative.org/2014/06/what-is-distributism.html.

Peltzman, Sam. "Mortality Inequality." *Journal of Economic Perspectives* 23, no. 4 (2009): 175–90.

Piano, Ennio E. "State Capacity and Public Choice: A Critical Survey." *Public Choice* 178, no. 1–2 (2019): 289–309.

Pigou, Arthur Cecil. *The Economics of Welfare*. London: Macmillan, 1920.

Pipes, Richard. *Property and Freedom*. New York: Alfred Knopf, 1999.

Pius XI. *Quadragesimo Anno*. 1931. http://w2.vatican.va/content/pius-xi/en/encyclicals/documents/hf_p-xi_enc_19310515_quadragesimo-anno.html.

Pontifical Council for Justice and Peace. "Compendium of the Social Doctrine of the Church." 2004. https://www.vatican.va/roman_curia/pontifical_councils/justpeace/index.htm.

Quinn, Dermot. Introduction. In Wilhelm Röpke, *A Humane Economy: The Social Framework of the Free Market*. Wilmington, Del.: ISI Books, 1998. First published in 1960.

Robinson, Joan. *The Economics of Imperfect Competition*. London: Macmillan, 1933.

Röpke, Wilhelm. *The Social Crisis of Our Time*. Rutgers, N.J.: Transaction Publishers, 1992. First published in 1942.

———. *A Humane Economy: The Social Framework of the Free Market*. Wilmington, Del.: ISI Books, 1998. First published in 1960.

———. Röpke, Wilhelm. *The Economics of the Free Society*. Translated by Patrick M. Boarman. Chicago: Henry Regnery, 1963. First published in 1961.

Rubio, Marco. "Catholic Social Doctrine and the Dignity of Work." Speech at The Catholic University of America, November 2019. https://www.rubio.senate.gov/public/_cache/files/6d09ae19-8df3-4755-b301-795154a68c59/C58480B07D02452574C5DB8D603803EF.final—-cua-speech-11.5.19.pdf.

Sachs, Jeffrey. *The End of Poverty: Economic Possibilities for Our Time*. New York: Penguin House, 2006.

Sachs, Jeffrey, John McArthur, Guido Schmidt-Traub, Margaret Kruk, Chandrika Bahadur, Michael Faye, and Gordon McCord. "Ending Africa's Poverty Trap." *Brookings Papers on Economic Activity* 2004, no. 1 (2004): 117–240. https://doi.org/10.1353/eca.2004.0018.

Salter, Alexander W. "Rights to the Realm: Reconsidering Western Political Development." *American Political Science Review* 109, no. 4 (November 2015): 725–34.

———. "Book Review: Aquinas and the Market: Toward a Humane Economy by Mary Hirschfeld." *Christian Libertarian Review* 3 (2020): R6–R16. https://christianlibertarianreview.com/wp-content/uploads/2020/07/CLR-3-review-by-salter-.pdf.

———. "'Common Good' Conservatism's Catholic Roots." *Wall Street Journal*, May 20, 2021.

Salter, Alexander W., and Andrew T. Young. "Medieval Representative Assemblies: Collective Action and Antecedents of Limit Government." *Constitutional Political Economy* 29, no. 2 (2018): 171–92.

———. "Polycentric Sovereignty: The Medieval Constitution, Governance Quality, and the Wealth of Nations." *Social Science Quarterly* 100, no. 4 (June 2019): 1241–53.

Simons, Henry. *The Simons' Syllabus*. Edited by Gordon Tullock. Fairfax, Va.: Center for the Study of Public Choice, 1983.

Smith, Adam. *An Inquiry into the Nature and Causes of the Wealth of Nations*. Edited by Edwin Cannan. London: Methuen, 1904.

Stasavage, David. "Representation and Consent: Why They Arose in Europe and Not Elsewhere." *Annual Review of Political Science* 19, no. 1 (2016): 145–62.

Stigler, George. "The Theory of Economic Regulation." *Bell Journal of Economics and Management Science* 2, no. 1 (1971): 3–21.

Stiglitz, Joseph E., and Andrew Weiss. "Credit Rationing in Markets with Imperfect Information." *American Economic Review* 71, no. 3 (1981): 393–410.

Troesken, Werner. "Exclusive Dealing and the Whiskey Trust, 1890–1895." *Journal of Economic History* 58, no. 3 (1998): 755–78.

Vanberg, Viktor J. "The Freiburg School: Walter Eucken and Ordoliberalism." Freiburger Diskussionspapiere zur Ordnungsökonomik, No. 04/11. Institut für Allgemeine Wirtschaftsforschung, Abteilung für Wirtschaftspolitik, AlbertLudwigs-Universität Freiburg, Freiburg, 2004.

Vermeulle, Adrian. "Beyond Originalism." *The Atlantic*, March 31, 2020. https://www.theatlantic.com/ideas/archive/2020/03/common-good-constitutionalism/609037/.

Weaver, Richard. *Ideas Have Consequences*. Chicago: University of Chicago Press, 1948.

———. *Visions of Order: The Cultural Crisis of Our Time*. Wilmington, Del.: ISI Books, 1995. First published in 1964.

Wicksteed, Philip Henry. *The Common Sense of Political Economy*. London, New York: Macmillan, 1910.

Williamson, Jeffrey. *Coping with City Growth during the British Industrial Revolution*. Cambridge: Cambridge University Press, 1990. https://doi.org/10.1017/CBO9780511664892.

Williamson, Oliver. *Markets and Hierarchies: Analysis and Antitrust Implications*. New York: Free Press, 1983.

Young, Andrew T. "How the City Air Made Us Free: The Self-Governing Medieval City and the Bourgeoisie Revaluation." *Journal of Private Enterprise* 32, no. 4 (2017): 31–47.

Index